2750.ml

# Governing an African City

# Governing an African City

*A STUDY OF NAIROBI*

Herbert H. Werlin

AFRICANA PUBLISHING CO. NEW YORK AND LONDON
*A division of Holmes & Meier Publishers, Inc.*

Library of Congress Cataloging in Publication Data

Werlin, Herbert H      1932-
    Governing an African city.

    A revision of the author's thesis, University of
California at Berkeley.
    Includes bibliographical references.
    1.  Nairobi--Politics and government.  2.  Nairobi--
Economic conditions.  3.  Nairobi--Social conditions.
I.  Title.
JS7648.9.N3W46  1974      320.9'676'2504      73-84989
ISBN 0-8419-0139-2

Published in the United States of America 1974 by
Africana Publishing Company, a Division of
Holmes & Meier Publishers, Inc.
101 Fifth Avenue, New York, N.Y. 10003


*Great Britain:*
Holmes & Meier Publishers, Ltd.
Hillview House
1, Hallswelle Parade
Finchley Road, London N.W. 11 ODL

PRINTED IN THE UNITED STATES OF AMERICA

# CONTENTS

# PREFACE

Eight years ago I wrote that "in the voluminous literature on local government, there is no systematically conceived theory of local government."[1] Indeed, as Robert T. Daland points out, the first serious effort in American studies to go beyond "seriatim descriptions of discreet situations" for the purpose of analyzing municipal reform campaigns was not made until 1963.[2] Since then, much progress has been made in comparative local government, particularly comparative urban studies, as indicated by Stanley D. Brunn's very useful bibliography.[3]

Hopefully, this book will make a contribution to the theory of urban systems or micropolitics. While much of the recent literature on this subject has been concerned either with the inputs into the political system (the actions of individuals and groups that determine governmental policies) or the outputs (the distribution of benefits derived from official decision-making), this book focuses on the transformation of inputs into outputs (in other words, public administration). I have here tried to determine the requisites for, as well as the meaning of, good administration, including the conditions under which decentralization will be successful. While I am doubtful that any of us working in the social sciences can increase our predictive ability, I do hope that the theory here presented —

that of "elasticity of control"— will increase our descriptive ability.

My study of Nairobi began almost ten years ago as a Ph.D. dissertation for the University of California at Berkeley, largely encouraged by Professor Carl G. Rosberg. This dissertation (*The Nairobi City Council: The Problems of Cooperation in African Local Politics*) was based on a twelve-month stay in Kenya in 1963-64. The revision here presented was facilitated by three additional trips to Kenya in the summers of 1966, 1967, and 1972, two of which were made possible by grants from the State University of New York Research Foundation. Part of it was written while an Adlai Stevenson Fellow with the United Nations Institute for Training and Research. The General Research Board of the University of Maryland paid for much of the typing.

A book of this sort cannot be written without the help of a great many people. Over the years, I have taken advantage of many of those associated with the Nairobi City Council. Since what I have written may be embarrassing to some of them, I hesitate to mention their names. While I relied very heavily upon interviews in doing my research (based on my memory of what was said rather than tape-recordings), I have tried to avoid attributing statements to particular individuals. However, I do want to express my thanks to those who were kind enough to comment on the drafts of chapters that periodically appeared: John Bucher, Philip Clark, Wolfram Eberhard, Abe Goldman, Edgar Edwards, Victor Jones, Jonathan Kariara, Bob Marshall, Merton Reichler, Carl Rosberg, Emil Sady, Aaron Segal, Parmeet Singh, Isadore Somen, Fred Temple, and Annmarie Walsh, among others. Konrad Kressley, my former research assistant, prepared an initial index for the book. Since parts of this book have appeared as articles (in *Africa Today, Comparative Studies in Society and History, The Philippine Journal of Public Administration,* and the *Journal of Comparative Administration*), I have benefited from the work of editors and those commenting on the articles. I must also mention the great help of the librarians at the *East African Standard* and the members of the Nairobi Urban Studies Group. Above all, I relied upon my wife for editorial assistance during the later stages of this book. While I did not realize the extent of her editorial skills when I married her (nor did she), I have certainly come to appreciate them. I cannot, however, share with others the blame for the weaknesses of this book.

This book is dedicated to the memory of my father, Professor Joseph S. Werlin, who died during my first trip to Africa, unable to finish the book he was working on. May this ease the pain of the lingering frustration.

*College Park, Maryland*
*April 5, 1973*

## NOTES

1. *Proceedings of the Third Graduate Academy of the University of California* (Los Angeles: UCLA Graduate Student Association, 1966), p. 241.
2. "Comparative Perspectives of Urban Systems," in Robert T. Daland, ed., *Comparative Urban Research* (Beverly Hills, Calif.: Sage, 1969), p. 30.
3. *Urbanization in Developing Countries: An International Bibliography* (East Lansing: Michigan State University Latin American Studies Center, 1971).

# 1  ELASTICITY OF CONTROL: A FRAMEWORK FOR ANALYSIS

*Introduction*

It is axiomatic that urbanization is essential for the development of a country. It is, first of all, required for economic progress. Only through urbanization is it possible to gain the concentration of population, the specialization of labor, and the purchasing power necessary for industrialization. Similarly, urbanization facilitates the utilization of financial resources and educated personnel necessary for schools, libraries, theatres, music halls, etc. Educational and cultural activities, in turn, provide the basis for integrating the population and stimulating those in the rural areas to make an effort to improve their lives. Finally, urbanization is necessary for mobilizing the population, communicating with the component groups, and meeting the political demands that are presented.

Urbanization, however, may be as dangerous as it is essential for the development of African countries. There is a tendency for the African urban areas, stimulated by progress in education, transportation, and communication, to grow more rapidly than employment opportunities. Governments lack the capital and the educated manpower to industrialize rapidly enough to absorb the urban migrants. At the same time, the urban authorities are unable to cope with the housing, educational, health, welfare, and recreational needs of the population. The unmet needs of the urban population can then cause or exacerbate dysfunctional social reactions: crime, family instability, and racial or ethnic conflict. Such an unhappy urban population may eventually create more political pressures than the governments can cope with, leading to a cycle of governmental repression and breakdown.

Whether urbanization becomes more of a liability than an asset to a developing country will, of course, depend upon many factors. The particular problems that facilitate or hamper the government of Nairobi will be the concern of the following chapters. However, the problems of the Nairobi City Council are most understandable in the context of the general problems of African urban government. In the absence of a comparative approach, observations tend to become distorted. Consequently, what will be suggested in this chapter are certain generalizations which will hopefully facilitate the analysis of municipal government in Nairobi.

Nairobi is an example of what Aiden Southall calls a "type B" town — one characterized by rapid development, the domination of foreigners, careful control of African urban settlement, and the development of a pattern of segregation and stratification along racial lines.[1] This contrasts with the "type A" towns that prevail in West Africa, characterized by long histories, slow development with little industry, urban settlement along tribal or traditional lines, and the persistence of subsistence farming in the towns as a way of life. Actually, there are so many variations among African cities (depending upon demographic, economic, and administrative factors) that none can be considered as typical.[2] But while Nairobi has more in common with an American or European city of comparable population (about 500,000) than it has with such traditional towns as Kano or Timbuctoo, it shares many of the problems common to all African cities.

## The Urban Malaise

For those of us living in what one author refers to as the "sick cities" of America (overwhelmed by air pollution, noise, traffic, crime, racial tension, slum conditions, etc.), the problems of urban administration are certainly obvious.[3] Yet, the urban crisis in Africa (and, indeed, the rest of the Third World) is in many respects more serious than it is or ever was in the United States or Western Europe. While the problems of African cities may be similar to those of European or American cities, African governments are less able to deal with them. Consequently, developments in the major urban centers of Africa, particularly in the capital cities, often have a devastating impact upon the national governments. The overthrow of the Keita regime in 1968, for example, stemmed most directly from the malaise of the Malian civil servants in Bamako.[4]

Almost everywhere in Africa the urban population is growing far more rapidly than the population as a whole (between 5 and 7 per cent a year compared with an annual population rise of 2 to 3 per cent). Since the urban population of Africa is relatively small, with approximately 15 per cent of Africans living in cities of 20,000 or more inhabitants (a smaller percentage than in 17th Century England), this rapid urban growth would seem to be desirable.[5] What is worrisome, however, is the concentration of much of the urban population in the capitals where there is insufficient industrial capacity to cope with it. Abidjan, for example, has expanded from a town of 10,000 in 1929 to over 400,000 by 1970.[6]

A. L. Mabogunje has pointed out that the ratio of population to resources is higher in Africa than it was at the time of the equally rapid urban growth in Europe.[7] Cities, rather than providing the basis for sustained economic growth, may therefore be serious impediments to development. This accounts for the phenomenon of the "parasitic city"— one which drains the resources and manpower of the country for the benefit largely of foreigners.[8] Such cities tend to stimulate the importation of luxuries rather than domestic production.

This rapid growth of urban population is a result of a quest not simply for economic gain, but also for such amenities as electric lights, piped water, modern sanitation, and educational, health, and recreational facilities. Unfortunately, the great expectations that urban migrants have of life in the cities all too frequently remain frustrated by the conditions actually encountered. Included, in the vivid words of a recent United Nations report are: "narrow, squalid streets and alleys, streets that are sewers, streets that are refuse-bins, teeming streets or no streets at all; crowded, dilapidated, antiquated buildings, hovels made of sheet-metal, old tin cans, or wooden boards that have been salvaged from the rubbish dump; no green spaces, no community facilities; and, on top of all else, the spatial segregation which is the mark of colonial town planning — the settlers or the new ruling class in the good neighbourhoods and the low density areas, and the natives (those who were and still are poor) elsewhere."[9]

Yet, the lure of the cities, stimulated by expanded primary education and improved communication and transportation facilities, remains too great to easily discourage people, especially the youth anxious to escape the confines of traditional rural life. The resulting population pressure can be overwhelming because, as Guy Hunter points out: "Conditions which no government can long tolerate arise very quickly when poor country folk flood into towns — over-crowding, total lack of sanitation, neglect of children, gross under-nourishment, and frequently a breakdown of moral and cultural discipline under the pressures of poverty, competition, and the absence of the sanctions of village life."[10] In certain countries, such as Tanzania, an effort has been made to deport the unemployed from certain of the more densely populated urban areas. But even where this is politically feasible and enforceable, it may be impractical because of the lack of employment opportunities in the rural areas.

"No-where in Africa," noted the report of the 1956 East African Town Planning Conference at Kampala, "has the problem been solved of enabling the mass of Africans who live in urban areas to live in healthy and socially desirable conditions."[11] More recent surveys of African urban life are similarly disheartening. In one African capital city, cited in a 1967 World Health Organization report, where the estimated population had expanded from 125,000 to 200,000 since 1960, 70 per cent of its homes were improvised, and very few had either indoor piped running water or water-borne sanitation facilities: "There is no organized public waste collection service, and community clean-ups are not usually carried out until conditions have become unhealthy to a high degree."[12] Urban public health is also worsened by the shortage of medical facilities and physicians (1 to 21,000 compared to 1 to 740 persons in the United States).[13]

It has been pointed out in regard to Africa that "even those who are unskilled in towns make a desperate attempt to achieve what they consider to be a 'civilized' or 'European' way of life."[14] In many countries, particularly those just emerging from colonialism, there is the insistence upon welfare benefits which the wealthiest countries have difficulty in affording: free and compulsory primary education, public scholarships for higher education, free medical service, old age and unemployment insurance, low-cost public housing, modern sanitation facilities, efficient and cheap public transportation, etc. In an effort to meet the demands of the politically vocal urban population and to fulfill the possibly unrealistic promises of politicians, there is a tendency to spend excessively in the urban areas to the neglect of the rural areas. This may have the effect of accelerating the urban drift and, with it, urban difficulties. Rapid urban growth then would be an indication of economic deterioration rather than of economic progress.[15]

Of all the problems confronting urban areas in underdeveloped countries, the lack of decent housing is usually the most apparent. In many metropolitan areas, one-quarter to one-half of the population are found in slums and shanties, and the situation is generally worsening.[16] The shortage of inexpensive, well-constructed houses in Africa is so great that most urban households (consisting of three to six persons) occupy a single room.[17] Consequently, African urbanites are forced to move to peri-urban areas where the houses tend to be poorly constructed, inadequately furnished, and lacking sanitation facilities, water supplies, paved streets, electricity, fuel, transportation, and other services.

Because private building (even of a substandard sort) is seldom sufficient for the needs of African cities, the national governments or local authorities are expected to undertake large housing programs. Unfortunately, there may be relatively few people who can afford to pay an economic rent for the housing built, especially in areas of great unemployment and low wage rates such as prevail in

Africa. Governments must therefore bear an increasingly heavy financial burden in dealing with housing problems — a burden that may prevent them from dealing with other needs such as education, health, and transportation. However, it has been estimated that few of these African governments are able to meet more than one-fifth of their minimum housing requirements.[18]

The lack of decent housing in the urban areas is associated with many other problems: disease, crime, family instability, demoralization, etc. Education becomes difficult without the necessary privacy and social stability to encourage the learning process. Lack of housing may mean that men are reluctant to establish families in the urban areas. This is indicated by the fact that in many African cities males outnumber females to the extent of two or three to one. Consequently, the men are forced to divide their time between the rural and the urban areas, thereby possibly neglecting their families and farms in the rural areas and fostering prostitution and juvenile delinquency in the urban areas. The migrant labor system may also discourage Africans from staying at a job long enough to acquire the skills which would warrant anything above a minimum wage.

According to a Nigerian commission of inquiry into wages held in 1964, the existing wage scales needed to be doubled to enable an unskilled laborer with a wife and child to maintain the essentials of existence.[19] The indication from this and other studies is that most African urban dwellers suffer from extreme poverty.

While the prevailing wages in urban Africa may be inadequate, they may nevertheless be too high in relationship to national productivity and rural income. Under pressure from governments and unions, wages, together with fringe benefits, have gone up in most of the large cities, encouraging both an ever increasing influx from the rural areas and the introduction of capital-intensive machinery by employers. This means that an increase in national income is not associated with an equivalent increase in employment. "In recent years, it is estimated that in some African countries, total employment has increased at only about one-third or less of the rate of the increase in national income."[20] The situation is likely to get worse, according to W. Arthur Lewis, because "the underdeveloped countries lag so far behind in technology that the opportunities for introducing labor-saving methods are immense, and it could well happen that the new employment created in the factories, in modern forms of transportation and in modern services could be more than offset by the employment destroyed in handicrafts, traditional forms of transportation and old-fashioned types of personal service."[21]

The poverty of Africans in the urban areas is, of course, the result of a variety of inter-related factors. To begin with, only a small percentage of the African working population (less than 5 per cent in most parts of Africa) is engaged in regular wage-earning employment. Of this wage-earning group, from one-third to one-half work in some aspect of the public sector, while only a small fraction are employed in large-scale manufacturing. Most urban Africans, either by themselves or in some small and uneasy partnership, eke out a living in service occupations, commerce and trading, and craft industries. Most African wage-earners fall into the lowest-paid categories with an income of less than $25 a month.[22] And they are kept from rising much above this not only by the lack of employment opportunity, but also by their lack of education, skills, and attitudes conducive to high productivity. This would be particularly true for the illiterates who constitute more than 80 per cent of the population of most African countries. Moreover, poverty creates a vicious cycle. Those who are poor are also likely to be undernourished or ill, poorly housed, uneducated or uninformed, and exploited by others. This gives rise to a deep sense of frustration on the part of these urban dwellers — a feeling that they cannot by their own efforts raise themselves above the squalid conditions in which they live.

The poverty of urban Africans is obviously a concomitance of the low per capita income (less than $150) prevailing in most African countries. But it is not so much the poverty as the barriers to economic development that must be taken into account. The immense size of Africa (more than four times that of the United States), the lack of navigable rivers and good natural harbors, the presence of vast deserts and rain forests, and the prevalence of human and animal diseases associated with the tsetse fly and other pests are among the geographical aspects which have historically retarded progress in Africa. According to W. A. Hance, over 90 per cent of the African continent suffers from climatic disability (particularly, lack of rainfall).[23] This retards not only agricultural production but human activity generally. These geographical conditions account for the poor sites where many African cities are situated.[24]

While Africa as a whole is sparsely populated (the density of population being about one-third that of the United States), there are areas that are very overpopulated.[25] A combination of high birth rates with a reduction in infant mortality rates has resulted in a rapid increase in population and, within this population, a high proportion of young people (nearly 50 per cent under the age of sixteen as against about 25 per cent in England). The presence of such a large percentage of dependents is obviously burdensome on any economy, necessitating heavy expenditure for sustenance, health, education, and eventually jobs.

In Africa, farming is largely carried out on small, scattered plots, inefficiently laid out and cultivated, with most of the produce consumed on the farms, where perhaps 90 per cent of the population live and work.[26] Consequently, food production is low in Africa — one-eighth of a ton per person in agriculture as against 2½ tons per farmer in America. Unless an effective program of agrarian uplift is implemented, healthy urban growth is practically impossible.

Most African countries, being dependent upon the sale of one or two agricultural products or minerals in the world market, are exposed to often sharp fluctuations in world market prices. Overall, the terms of trade have gone against African countries in the last decade by 10 to 20 per cent, indicating that the demand for what Africa has to sell does not keep pace with the cost of what she needs to buy.[27] "This is largely the result of the new technology," according to Andrew Shonfield, "which helps the industrial countries to get along with less raw material for any given volume of output."[28] Consequently, the already large gap between the incomes of African countries and those of developed countries is likely to increase not only absolutely but also relatively. And it is the urban Africans who are likely to become most aware of this gap. But how they cope will depend upon solving the problems of urban administration, to which we next turn.

## The Failure of Decentralization

In the United States, most of the older treatises on local government tended to idealize decentralization in the form of "states' rights," "local government," or the autonomy of certain respected professional groups and bureaucratic units. "The traditional Jeffersonian theory asserts for localities a right to self-determination as an expression of the sovereignty of the individual, derived from the doctrine of the sovereignty of the people, the individual's presumed condition in the state of nature, and a theory of natural rights."[29] Such Lockean arguments tended to be reinforced by pragmatic considerations. Strong local government was thought to be an important means of limiting or counterbalancing the power of the central government. It was thus part of the check-and-balance system set up by the American Constitution. Moreover, in a country as large as the United States, it was felt to be desirable for decision-making to be done by those most familiar with the local situation — i.e., by the local people. The central government was thought to be too remote or uninformed as well as too inefficient to handle local affairs. Above all, local government was felt to be necessary for the invigoration of popular participation. In the absence of strong local government, the public could become too apathetic or passive for a meaningful democracy.

This idealization of decentralization has been associated in the United States with a narrow legalistic framework. Within this framework, importance was given to questions concerning the sovereignty of local authorities. Were the towns simply creations of the state legislatures, or vice-versa? Did the states precede the localities, or did their powers initially derive from those delegated by the localities? It was on the basis of their answers to these questions that judges attempted to determine the extent to which American local government could act independently of the state legislatures.

Within this legalistic framework, political power has tended to be viewed as quantitative and finite. Consequently, every increment of power gained by the central government was seen as lost by regional or local governments. In this regard, grants-in-aid have frequently been blamed for seriously diminishing the authority of

American state and local governments to implement their programs. At the same time, it is clear that grants-in-aid have enabled state and local governments to do far more than they could otherwise. "The result is considerable perplexity," James W. Fesler notes, "as to whether federal grants-in-aid programs are centralist or decentralist in their total effect."[30]

In the United States, the increasing failure of state and local governments in recent years to handle the problems they face has given rise to a realization that decentralization is not necessarily desirable. Writers on the subject have come to argue that the powers of the various units of government should be related to effectiveness rather than to a legal or moral conception of rights.[31] In other words, considerations of administrative competence should be given precedence over considerations of legal prerogatives.

Many scholars have also criticized the presumed relationship between local government and democracy. "In some countries," Georges Langrod points out, "local government, with its structural anachronisms, the high degree of its internal fractionalization, the preponderance in practice of appointed officers over elected and temporary councilors can be a brake on the processes of democratisation."[32] Hugh Whalan suggests that the theory supporting local government contains a circular argument.[33] While local government is supposed to develop naturally because of the social attributes of the small community, we are increasingly told that local government must be strengthened in order to promote the very conditions which supposedly render its existence natural and necessary. However useful local government may prove to be, there is no *a priori* principle which could determine the proper division of functions between national and local governments.

Under the circumstances prevailing in most underdeveloped countries, it is understandable that enthusiasm for local government is often lacking, despite the advantages that are ascribed to it. In the Philippines, for example, the prevailing opinion, notes Lloyd M. Short, is that any increase in local autonomy would redound to the benefit of corrupt local bosses.[34] It is felt here that the central government is more reliable and impartial than the local governments. Indeed, the practical difficulties involved in introducing a satisfactory system of local government are so great that the governments of most of the developing countries have largely ceased to try. Generalizing on the basis of his study of urban administration in these countries, Harold F. Alderfer writes:

> In these nations, the present position of municipal and local government in urban areas is minor and secondary in importance. The national government has controlled it down to the minutest detail, has reduced its natural sources of revenue. . . . Moreover, there is little or no popular participation in the process of urban government — councils are either nonexistent as policy-making bodies, or else their decisions may be ignored and disapproved at the will of the executive or higher level of government.[35]

Many African countries have made a determined effort to establish some form of representative municipal government, under which municipal administrators, even when they are appointed or approved by the central government, are responsible to popularly elected councils. The hope was that the public, led possibly by respected and responsible functional associations or interest groups, would be encouraged both to initiate useful community projects and to criticize harmful or corrupt activities. For various reasons, however, representative municipal government, particularly in the capitals, has had to be partly or entirely abandoned in a sizeable number of African countries.

Municipal elections are by no means easy to carry out where the population is largely illiterate and politically uninformed or inexperienced. It must be kept in mind how complicated and expensive the running of elections is: the choosing of candidates, the printing of ballots, the setting-up of election rolls, the establishment of polling places, the protection of the voters against intimidation, and finally, the counting of ballots. The qualified and respected administrators that are required for this purpose are by no means easy to find, and the public as a whole may be unwilling or unable to cooperate. Thus, even the handling of relatively noncontroversial municipal elections is frequently so inept as to make suspect the whole enterprise. Where the competition for votes between politicians at periodic elections is nonexistent or meaningless, local politics obviously must take a different form from the way it is understood in most Western countries.

Because opposition parties tend to reflect existing regional, communal, or ideological differences, they are often accused of fostering disunity, retrogression, and "neo-colonialism" or subversion of one sort or another. Consequently, they are discouraged, even when not completely disallowed. Members of opposition parties are often victimized or denied any representation at all in committees and other decision-making activities. "The power of the majority party pervades every aspect of a council's life and work, even to the extent of compelling the council's employees to join the party under threat of dismissal."[36]

Yet, the implications of the one-party system for municipal government remain unexplored. Without competitive parties, how is political pressure brought to bear upon those in power? How are elections made meaningful and public support ascertained? How does the absence of political parties affect the roles that politicians and administrators perform? Above all, how can governmental decisions be legitimized and orderly change brought about without appropriate outlets for political strife? In other words, does not the stifling of politics, however justified, bring about more problems than it solves?

Without minimizing the importance of these questions, it should be emphasized that political parties are not necessarily the most important agencies for the expression and reconciliation of public opinion at the local level. Considering the operation of local government in the United States, one is struck by the relatively small role played by competitive party politics. Indeed, non-partisan elections are here quite common. But even where political parties are active, there are a wide variety of well-organized groups in addition to and associated with them. Upon these private interest groups rests much of the responsibility for the initiation, administration, and perhaps dissipation of policies. In any case, urban officials in this country do not act in a vacuum; they are constantly guided, prodded, and threatened by competing associations.

In Africa, on the other hand, few people are experienced in voluntary work along highly organized and functional lines. Intense participation in this sort of activity is limited to a small number even in such a relatively sophisticated city as Accra.[37] Those African interest groups that exist generally lack the resources (wealth, competent personnel, and communication facilities) to make a constructive political impact. In Kampala-Mengo, for example, the groups are described by Southall as "quite small, rather informal and somewhat ephemeral."[38] This is not to say that they are altogether unimportant or ineffective. The effort of many governments to control them would belie this. However, because associations in Africa tend to be primordial (with a membership restricted in regard to race, religion, tribe, language, or geographical location) rather than functional (based upon limited or specialized objectives having to do with acquired occupation, avocation, economic status, or opinion), their effectiveness as agencies of change is somewhat limited.

Even the best organized urban associations in Africa, which are usually the trade unions, are relatively unsuccessful in socializing Africans to urban styles of life.[39] Typically these groups are "reactive" in that they "more frequently protest specific government actions that affect them than generate pressures for general improvement of urban facilities."[40] These groups, as a result of frustration, may resort to mass action and civil disobedience in the conviction that the political-administrative establishment will not respond to a process of orderly persuasion. But should such civil disobedience succeed, it stimulates still further civil disobedience, leading to the enactment of repressive measures.

Representative government in the urban areas of Africa is also made difficult by the lack of potential civic leaders (people with ample leisure, wealth, ability, prestige, and genuine public spirit)— the sort who play such an important role both in official and advisory capacities in the local government of the more developed countries. And those who might be useful to a municipal government may be discouraged by the money, time, and political skill or enthusiasm that it takes. Such is the case in Ibadan (one of the largest and most important of African cities) where, writes George Jenkins: "At present, only the three lawyers on the Council are professionally trained and, while most of the rest are lilterate, few possess any technical qualifications which would give them any special insight into the problems of health, town planning and water supply, which the city faces."[41]

The meagre education and experience of most municipal council members in African countries makes their relationship with their administrative staff uneasy. Even in Western countries, the communication gap between scientifically oriented experts and the ordinary politicians with training in law and business is wide enough to be troublesome. But this is somewhat overcome by a largely unwritten code of conduct that has been gradually worked out. Under it, the professional qualifications of administrators are respected by the politicians. Administrators are supposedly hired and promoted on the basis of their competence as revealed through examinations or the record of their experience, and they are retained as long as their work is satisfactory. For their part, the administrators are expected to carry out the policies for which the politicians claim an electoral mandate.

In African countries, however, a code of conduct harmonizing relations between administrators and politicians seldom exists. The tendency of politicians to meddle unduly in administration is sometimes a result of their enthusiasm for progress, coupled with their lack of faith in the civil service.[42] It also stems from pressure for concessions from relatives, ethnic associates, or patrons — pressure that is intensified by the general failure to understand or appreciate the requirements of an efficient bureaucracy. This is true even in a country such as Tanzania where the government has explicitly set limits on what politicians are entitled to do in regard to administration. In the case of Ibadan, according to A. L. Mabogunje, "with a Council most of whose members are uneducated and most of whom see in Council work a means of earning their living, a background to inefficiency in the administration of the city is clearly set."[43]

The strained relationship between urban administrators and politicians so common in Africa does not result entirely or necessarily from the ignorance or malice of the council members. It may also be due to the inexperience, incompetence, or tactlessness of the administrators. After all, most African local authorities have great difficulty in attracting and retaining qualified personnel. And few of them hire or promote on the basis of a rational merit system. Under the circumstances, there tends to be a dearth of administrators who can exercise the authority that is required to coordinate administrative activities and to guide the decision-making of the council members. This means that the men who formally hold positions of power in the cities of Africa frequently lack the prestige associated with their titles.

The common distrust of administrators in African municipal governments prevents them from exercising the initiative and flexibility so necessary for bureaucratic efficiency. It also undermines the proper relationship of personnel within the administrative structure. This would be especially true where Africanization policies have excessively hastened the promotion of some of the personnel who happened to have entered the system at the right time. When those at the top hold their positions merely on the basis of a year or two in seniority, they are likely to feel inadequate in their posts and threatened by those ranked below them who may be far better qualified.[44]

The work of administrators is made difficult to the extent that the council members lack the unity and ability to decide upon policies. The existing conflicts are certain to reflect the racial or ethnic tension prevalent in the community together with divergent ambitions, temperaments, viewpoints, and expectations regarding deference and perquisites. These conflicts will emerge even under the umbrella of a one-party system; and they tend to be more severe than those in the more developed countries because of the extreme competition for jobs, inadequate procedures for resolving disputes, and weak institutions for ameliorating discontent.

For reasons that have been mentioned, local politicians in Africa seldom have sufficient prestige to reconcile conflicting groups and to give guidance to decision-making. This would be obviously so in those communities where, as the Hannas found, "the overall image of local government is very negative, with local councillors the objects of severe denigration."[45] The administrators themselves may therefore be forced into disputes that make their positions vulnerable to political attack. Moreover, insofar as the administrators cannot anticipate the reaction of their political superiors, their ability to act with confidence, speed, and flexibility is very much reduced. The possibility of a vicious cycle can be suggested in which the failure of politicians to give adequate guidance to administrators contributes to the failure of administrators to facilitate the decision-making of the politicians.

To the extent that relations between politicians and administrators within a particular municipal government are strained, relations between the local authority and higher levels of government (regional or national) are apt to be adversely affected. Distrust between units of government may be apparent and even intensified where the local administrators are appointed by the central government either directly or through the workings of the national party. In any case, the more incompetent, corrupt, or politically irresponsible a municipal government is reputed to be, the less likely it is to be delegated the authority that it normally seeks.

Most urban authorities in Africa desperately need financial assistance. First of all, the population is generally impoverished and frequently transient (without settled employment and residence). Secondly, local businesses are often small, barely profitable, and poorly run. Much of the commerce may be carried on by unlicensed street hawkers or market women on a relatively unorganized or haphazard basis. Thirdly, property values and ownership are likely to be uncertain. These factors make income, property, and sales taxes very difficult to collect even when there are the requisite personnel and authority to do so.

African municipalities, however, are impoverished not simply by the lack of resources. Their financial affairs suffer from confusion and corruption brought about by the inadequacy of procedures for assessment and collection, of regulations or legal requirements, and of enforcement practices. This situation, in turn, severely impedes the borrowing power of these towns, their budget-making capacity, and their relations with higher levels of government.

Most African leaders would agree with the conclusion of the

1961 Cambridge Conference on Local Government in Africa that "poor local governments, like poor people, are likely to get poorer if left to their own resources; they need help if they are to overcome their disabilities and realize their potentialities for useful service."[46] Decentralization seems to be anathema to the regimes most anxious for rapid development. In Tanzania, for example, "centralizers" argue that political development could be achieved much more rapidly by shifting executive functions away from district councils into the hands of agents of the central government.[47] Decentralization is especially resisted where social and political differences cluster along regional lines. For this reason, General Mobutu, soon after seizing power in the Congo, reduced the number of Congolese provinces from 21 to 8 and then appointed the provincial governors personally rather than allowing them to be selected by the provincial assemblies. Because centralization is associated with the struggle for national unity, it is common for those taking control to abolish the federal constitutional structures left by the colonial regimes. Thus, Nkrumah in 1959 rendered the elected regional assemblies advisory rather than executive and at the same time abolished their role in ratifying constitutional change.[48] These steps, together with measures taken to select friendly chiefs and regional and district commissioners, effectively eroded the degree of decentralization provided for in the 1957 constitution.

## The Failure of Centralization

Those who are responsible for the administration of underdeveloped countries tend to see solutions to existing difficulties in terms of increasing or decreasing central control. Indeed, many countries have gone through rapidly alternating phases of centralization and decentralization in an effort to cope with administrative problems in much the same way as did the Soviet Union under Khrushchev in trying to raise agricultural production.[49] In West Africa, as independence approached, the British district-officer system tended to be abolished or weakened because of its colonial implications.[50] Instead, what was attempted was a rather indiscriminate adoption of the British local-government system with little central control. Soon, however, it became apparent that the local communities were unable to carry on in this way. Most suffered from appalling governmental inefficiency, corruption, disorder, and insolvency. By 1960, reports Ronald Wraith, the trend towards a more representative system of local government, that had emerged ten years previously, was being reversed: "What we see happening is a reversion to provincial (or in Ghana regional) authorities, with the important difference that the head of the province is a nominee of the party in power and not a civil servant."[51] This resumption of central control, however, merely recreated the old problems of implementing useful programs quickly and carefully, while avoiding public apathy or hostility.

It is frequently the case in Africa that central or regional governments suffer from the same weaknesses as do municipal governments: lack of qualified staff, conflict between administrators and politicians, inter-racial or inter-ethnic animosity, etc. Consequently, the higher tier of government may fail to exercise the guidance and encouragement expected of it and the supervision essential to good government. Instead, it may needlessly interfere with or delay the carrying out of programs in the urban areas. This, of course, may bring about a contentious rather than a cooperative relationship between the various units of government.

It obviously does no good for a municipal government to turn for help to a higher tier of government that is inefficient or irresponsible. In Ibadan, for example, an estimated 25-30 per cent of the taxable citizenry, including some of the most important civil servants and political figures, were not inscribed on the tax rolls in the 1950's.[52] The regional government then undertook with more success the collection of taxes in Ibadan, but it refused to return more than about a third of the money collected, thereby leaving the city as badly off as before.

To maintain a satisfactory relationship between governmental units, a well-developed communication system between the various authorities is essential. Such a communication system tends to be difficult in Africa because of geographical, social, and technical impediments. Moreover, African local authorities and the associated professional groups are seldom well-organized, with authoritative representatives readily available for discussions with the various ministries. Indeed, communication within the central governments may be so inadequate that the minister of local government (or other ministries) may be uncertain of official policies or lack the confidence to negotiate in a meaningful way. In Tanzania, for example, the problem has been "less that of Ministers acting on important issues without referring them to the Cabinet than the tendency of Ministers to submit too many matters to the Cabinet because they were afraid to act without the backing of their colleagues."[53] This means that local authorities may be forced to reconcile vague and even conflicting policies.

The relationship between governmental units is not necessarily made any easier by the existence of a single-party system. A single-party system, however, may decrease the significance of the formal organization of municipal government (including the legal prerogatives of mayors, committees, and staff members) inasmuch as the central government dictates through the dominant party the choice and activities of the local power-elite. In any case, much depends upon the performance of the local agents. Indeed, the competence and autonomy of local government may be greater in a country where administration is carried out by local agents of the central government than in one where the administrators are chosen by locally elected councillors.[54]

In Africa, the local agents of the government tend to be less than satisfactory. Though regional and district commissioners are frequently appointed to supervise the work of local government, they often fail to undertake the initiative expected of them because of their general feeling of insecurity or diffidence. In regard to Tanzania, Henry Bienen notes the lack of experience of commissioners in all aspects of their work but particularly in high-level economic decision-making: "Their movement from one place to another has not allowed them to become familiar with local conditions; and they operate in a situation where information is hard to come by."[55] A similar situation prevails in other African countries. Consequently, the substitution of field units for representative local or metropolitan governments in these countries does not necessarily facilitate the governmental process.

Because of the frequent unreliability of governmental field agents in the underdeveloped areas, decentralization is likely to take various unauthorized forms. In other words, the regimes of these areas, however autocratic they seem to be, often find themselves unable to exercise authority. Typical might be Burma where it is said that the government controls about two-thirds of the country by day, only half by night.[56] While underdeveloped countries generally are distinguished by their incapacity to enforce their proclaimed policies, those with large areas or geographical impediments are obviously more handicapped. In the Congo, for example, it was reported in 1969 that in many localities, even along the railroad line, there was practically no evidence of public administration at all.[57] In Nigeria, under the Belewa regime, each region operated almost as a separate entity, with scarcely any national planning or economic coordination. De facto decentralization is similarly evident in Brazil, India, and Indonesia.

## Elasticity of Control

It is apparent in much of the Third World that neither centralization nor decentralization provide a satisfactory way of coping with the problems of urban administration. This means that we need to search for a new approach. Unfortunately, the academic literature so far seems not to be very helpful. According to Professor Warren Ilchman, the articles and books having to do with public administration in developing countries yield only untested and contradictory propositions. "Most of what the intellectual has to say is useless to the statesman," he writes: "The latter's decisions, if not positively harmed, would be only negligibly improved by the fruit of the scholar's research."[58]

In order to be more helpful to those concerned with municipal government in emerging nations, we must begin by improving our capacity to describe existing conditions. Fesler has recently complained about the way in which "centralization" and "decentralization" are used as descriptive or analytical terms: "Our language dichotomises 'centralization' and 'decentralization,' a peculiarity that easily converts to a polarization and antithesis that poorly serve political science. We appear to have neither a term that embraces the full continuum between the two poles, nor a term that embraces the middle range where centralizing and decentralizing tendencies are substantially in balance."[59] His criticism applies to much of the literature on federalism, local government, and public administration.

In countries that are considered to be politically modernized, a description of the existing administrative systems as either "centralized" or "decentralized" would be quite misleading. Indeed, one can argue that the governments of the United States and Great Britain, though one is labeled a "federal system" and the other is not, are far more similar to each other than either is to any of the types of government prevalent in the Third World. The cooperative nature of American federalism has long been realized. "Any governmental activity," to quote Morton Grodzins, "is almost certain to involve the influence, if not the formal administration, of all three planes of government."[60] While the influence of the central government is much more apparent in the United Kingdom, the authority of the various local governments has not been diminished.

Although the existing jurisdictional or legal rigidities certainly complicate the American system of government, they must be seen within the context of the American pattern of politics, particularly the procedural consensus necessary for conflict resolution. For example, the relationship between New York City and New York State can become quite contentious, so much so that some leading city dwellers have wanted to secede from the state. Yet, according to Wallace S. Sayre and Herbert Kaufman: "Much of the influence of the state is brought to bear not by coercion but by cooperation and agreement among officials of the two units of government intent upon doing the best jobs they can and working in harmony with one another both formally and informally, more often than in conflict."[61] Similarly, in Britain, as Ronald Wraith points out: "The fact that most local authorities behave responsibly means that controls are kept to a minimum and consultation to a maximum, and hence there can grow up a partnership between ministries and local authorities comparable to that between councillors and officials."[62] An adequate understanding of this sort of relationship between and within governmental units necessitates a revised terminology.

When demand is responsive to changing price, economists speak of "elasticity of demand." Likewise, when political control is responsive to variations of need, we can speak of "elasticity of control." But where there is excessive or inadequate control in relationship to requirements, we must consider that control to be inelastic.

Political elasticity has to do with the variables of capability, need, and control much as economic elasticity has to do with the variables of supply, demand, and price, though they cannot be quantified as in economics. In economics, elasticity depends on the freedom of the system (i.e., the existence of a free-enterprise system in which there is an absence of monopolistic competition); in politics, on the legitimacy of the system. Insofar as control lacks legitimacy (i.e., social acceptability), it will be inelastic because it then depends upon nothing more than force or patronage (rewards for loyalty rather than competence). As such, it tends to be counter-productive.

Elasticity of control exists when leaders feel willing and able to delegate specific responsibility to subordinate officials or governmental units without relinquishing their supervisory accountability. The capability of the entire political system thereby expands because (a) the capacity of subordinate officials and units is encouraged and enhanced; (b) the potential output of superiors also increases insofar as they are left free to undertake additional activities; and (c) the possibilities of constructive criticism and open confrontation of issues are introduced, as subordinates come to be respected. Under conditions of legitimacy, in other words, the need for control is lessened as subordinates become more trusted (without affecting the potential for control), thereby strengthening the government's capability to increase the nation's standard of living.

In developed nations, such as the United States and Great Britain, the full authority of the central governments is usually held in abeyance, only to be released when absolutely necessary. Normally, however, the degree of control that is employed is sufficient to uphold governmental policies or goals, while leaving subordinate units relatively free to handle the responsibilities delegated to them. Consequently, in these countries, the relationship between governmental units is characterized by elasticity of control. This suggests a cooperative relationship in which political power takes more of a persuasive than a coercive form, and one which is mutually gratifying rather than disruptive. Under these circumstances, interference of a disciplinary or compulsory sort is potentially possible but actually rare, while varying forms and degrees of supervision and guidance are common.

In underdeveloped countries, the situation is relatively "inelastic." The exercise of political power does not readily increase or decrease in reaction to need. It does not flow as a gently fluctuating stream of influential suggestions. This inelasticity results from a general lack of cooperation, so that control tends to be authoritarian or ineffectual, or a sporadic alternation between the two poles. Instead of the normally easy and spontaneous working relations found in the Western democracies in which leaders can usually get what they want by various forms of subtle persuasion or incentives, there exists in underdeveloped countries the frequent necessity to use intimidating or corruptive forms of power that are likely to be dysfunctional to the working of the political system as a whole.

Elasticity of control requires devices by which supervision can be exercised, advice given, and, if necessary, guidance enforced. The most important instrumentalities in the United States for directing the actions of the states are the grant-in-aid programs administered by the federal agencies and the Congressional or administrative programs as interpreted by the courts. For this purpose, there are a large number of federal field agents who are kept in tow by, among other ways, the reports that are periodically required, the investigations that are constantly carried out, and the budgetary and personnel changes that are made. This system of controls operates so that relations among the levels of government become, in the words of Herbert Kaufman, "like a tangled web of rubber bands — intricate, elastic, capable of accommodating all sorts of pressures yet retaining their shape, under the tension of many forces and counter-forces, and very taut much of the time."[64] Similarly, elasticity of control in

Great Britain involves the use of special advisory personnel, a system of auditing and inspection coupled with grants-in-aid, the regular law courts together with administrative tribunals, statutes giving grants of power or prescribing qualifications and tenure of certain officials, the power to approve loans, bylaws, fees and tolls, etc.[65] In France, the *grandes corps,* particularly the *Conseil d'etat,* are responsible for maintaining the existing internal controls.[66]

What makes these devices reasonably effective are the sets of rules, practices, and standards that are commonly shared. The duties of officials are understood and their qualifications appreciated. Moreover, the political leaders and institutions are respected by the administrators and the population as a whole. Under these circumstances, delegation of authority is acceptable because, as Henry Maddick points out: "The degree to which the government is prepared to decentralize will turn upon its confidence in the unity of the country and in the ability of those in the field whose judgment will have to be relied upon."[67]

For reasons that have earlier been explained, the devices facilitating elasticity of control hardly work in underdeveloped areas. A system of law courts may formally exist, but the laws themselves are seldom respected or understood. Many of the laws are simply carried over from the colonial regime, without much relevancy for the countries trying to use them. In the absence of proper staff research, legal draftsmanship, legislative or public criticism, and administrative coordination, the new laws or rules tend to be carelessly formulated. Moreover, there is apt to be a dearth of independent and competent judges and lawyers. Likewise, experienced and trustworthy auditors and inspectors are not likely to be available; and those who are employed are generally hampered by inadequate guidelines. Rules obviously cannot be enforced where they are poorly formulated or understood, or where adequate personnel and supervisory programs are lacking.

Where rules are unfairly or improperly enforced, they simply become formalities to be disregarded whenever possible. This would be so where the public is convinced that public funds are misappropriated. In a Mexican municipality, Leonard Cardenas notes, it is common for a citizen to say, "Why should I pay taxes when they will only be stolen by the authorites"; or "I wouldn't mind paying my share of taxes as long as 'they' show something for it."[68] Likewise, where local participation is discouraged and local interests are ignored, the local population, particularly the elite, are unlikely to cooperate with the central government. Cooperation is further impeded where there is great social insecurity and anxiety or an appearance of regional or ethnic discrimination.

Elasticity of control pertains not merely to local-central governmental relations, but also to general relations among officials in a political system. The success of a political leader or an administrative head can be measured by his ability to formally or informally delegate authority to subordinates without losing his authority. The willingness of American leaders to encourage the participation of subordinates and to give them responsibility has long been recognized. According to an observer of President Johnson and Secretary of Defense McNamara, their practice was to push decisions down as far as possible, giving the men under them as much responsibility as they could, making them come to conclusions and send up options.[69] Only in this way can large-scale organizations become more flexible and eliminate some of their bureaucratic vicious circles.[70]

Elasticity of control is based upon the idea that, as a country modernizes politically, the forms by which authority is exercised become progressively less coercive and more persuasive.[71] As the basis for consensus widens with the political development of a nation, more reasonable ways for inducing compliance can be utilized. This becomes possible to the extent that politics shifts from the severe and often violent conflicts necessary for political unification to the ordinarily more placid type of struggle for the distribution of the national product. Thus, in the United States today, political power is frequently viewed as the ability to persuade others that cooperation is in their own self-interest. According to Richard E. Neustadt, it consists of vantage points within a bargaining relationship, and is derived from the ability to help or hinder others in pursuit of their various goals, or, what is more important, from the "appearance" of having such an ability.[72] This concept of power would be more indicative of what Robert A. Dahl calls "reliable influence" ("influence in which the probability of compliance is very high") than of "coercive influence" ("influence based on the threat or expectation of extremely severe penalties or great losses, particularly physical punishment, torture, imprisonment, and death").[73] Political power is usually regarded as at its weakest when it is based upon "coercive influence" of this nature because to have constantly to enforce obedience is obviously the most troublesome and expensive way to gain compliance.[74]

Elasticity of control, however, requires more than "vantage points in a bargaining relationship." Ultimately, elasticity of control depends upon the development of a normative basis of support — a loyalty to the goals of a particular political system based upon an acceptance of its values rather than merely its utilitarian potential.[75] Where there is this normative basis of political integration, officials can expect compliance with regulations insofar as the public views them as legitimate. In other words, elasticity of control becomes possible to the degree that political power is both legally sanctioned ("authorized") and socially sanctioned ("legitimate").

Because of the illegitimacy of legislation and administration in most underdeveloped countries, the exercise of power rests upon a fragile base of nonnormative integration. The elites of emerging nations are predisposed to believe that coercion is necessary for reform and then are surprised at its futility. They fail to realize, according to J. M. Lee, that they are weak "not so much because their security forces are weak, but because they lack the power to convince others that their own definitions of what is political can be generally accepted."[76]

Where resources are limited, it may not even be possible to gain support through the distribution of jobs and other perquisites. The major impediment to economic development in Tanzania, Henry Bienen suggests, is that the government cannot give its local leaders the goods and services which would enable them to reward or punish on a wide scale.[77] In any case, the reliance on patronage may increase the difficulty of inducing public cooperation and social harmony because of the inevitable accusations of ethnic or regional bias that this reliance gives rise to. Moreover, insofar as patronage is an inappropriate reward (i.e., one unrelated to merit), it does not encourage an improved standard of performance. This is evident in the Brazilian situation, described by Lordello de Mello, in which public employment is utilized, not for the performance of public services, but to perpetuate the existence of a parasitic social element.[78]

"In modern societies," writes Gerald Caiden, "change is institutionalized. It appears natural and automatic. The main effort is devoted to preventing obstruction."[79] The inability or unwillingness of governments or organizations to facilitate innovation is an indication of their weakness. Those that are weak tend to consider reform as a threat to their survival. However, the capacity to survive depends upon the ability to absorb change with minimum disruption.

Elasticity of control facilitates innovation. In the United States, for example, where there is a complex relationship among many diverse units of government, Michel Crozier notes that the system encourages numerous kinds of initiatives, making it possible to tap a variety of human resources which might otherwise become indifferent or hostile.[80] In contrast, one of the reasons for Nkrumah's downfall, according to Henry Bretton, was his stifling of innovation. Even minor decisions had to await his approval. "As a result, the learning and correcting capacity of the government and administration of Ghana was submerged in a welter of irrational, contradictory, erratic, highly emotional perspectives concerning events at home and abroad: The learning capacity of Ghana was reduced to the learning capacity of Kwame Nkrumah."[81]

Where there is elasticity of control, conflict becomes not only permissible but also functional. Criticism from subordinates or the general public is then considered as "loyal opposition" and allowed to affect the operation of the political or institutional structure. On the other hand, where there is inelasticity of control, conflict is likely to be repressed and tends therefore to take violent or revolutionary forms.

It is a well-known fact that only well-established governments can openly tolerate political opposition. Likewise, "cooperation" and "conflict" within a political system can only be reconciled under conditions in which the state is fairly stable and the exercise of authority is socially acceptable.[82] The ability of a political system to tolerate political conflict depends on the self-restraint of the political participants and their mutual respect. Where, as in the Mali Federation described by W. J. Foltz, there is no way of resolving or limiting conflict, the necessary mutual respect among leaders cannot develop.[83] In this atmosphere, the possibilities of compromise are obscured by manifestations of fear.

Elasticity of control, it must be added, is a relative term. There are degrees of inelasticity in all countries, resulting from the social and political problems of these countries. In the United States, the uneasy relationship between the states and the cities partly stems from the racial tension in this country which has resulted in the rise of ghettoes and accounts for the failure of many federal programs having to do with education, housing, and welfare. With regard to France, Crozier blames the nation's determination to uphold its paternalistic arrangements of status and privilege for its bureaucratic overcentralization and inflexibility.[84] In France, however, the extent of bureaucratic rigidities is not nearly as great as in the Soviet Union. Yet, the Soviet Union has also developed a certain degree of elasticity of control, possibly necessitated by the need to free from aspects of party control the growing elite of scientists, engineers, and technicians.[85]

Organizational effectiveness, it is here contended, requires that both leaders and subordinates have a certain sphere of maneuverability or flexibility. In Toronto, according to Harold Kaplan, the strategy of the chairman of the metropolitan government was to protect the technical discretion of the administrators while minimizing their political role.[86] E. D. Simon, a former Lord-Mayor of Manchester, writing as long ago as 1926 about the management of the Manchester City Council's Electricity Committee, noted that the relationship between City Council members and staff provided the professional staff the leeway that they needed for their work and, equally important, their pride:

> The whole of the management is under a chief engineer, who holds a position almost exactly equivalent to that of managing director of a limited company. He works under the direction of a chairman and a deputy chairman, both competent businessmen, who have

held their present positions for fourteen or fifteen years. They know and trust the engineer, and work excellently with him.[87]

Because of its primary concern with productivity — relating administrative practices directly to the output of an organization — the literature of business administration may offer clearer evidence of the utility of elasticity of control than that of public administration. Paul R. Lawrence and Jay W. Lorsch have carefully compared similar firms, showing how the more productive organizations (particularly those concerned with complicated or changing technologies or markets) facilitate greater participation by lower levels of management in decision-making and allow greater scope for conflict and differences in orientations and in behavior patterns.[88] This is possible insofar as the top executives and those responsible for integrating the diverse sections of the organization are respected for their competence, knowledge, and experience. This enables them to openly confront differences (rather than avoiding or suppressing them) without intimidating or antagonizing subordinates.

On the other hand, where a managing director has nothing more than political qualifications, as was the case with the Ghanaian State Furniture and Joinery Corporation under the Nkrumah regime, he can neither exercise leadership nor maintain morale. Because the branch managers did not respect him, they refused to carry out his instructions and to give him the technical information that he needed. In the words of the Tsegah Commission report, the whole corporation was reduced to a "leaderless army:" "Every employee of the Corporation took advantage of the situation and did what he or she liked. The Management failed to control the workers with the consequence that production dropped miserably."[89]

Elasticity of control would suggest a modification of the "ideal-type" bureaucracy posited by Max Weber — one characterized by a rigid hierarchy of positions, each with carefully prescribed qualifications, responsibilities, and privileges. Weber's analysis has long been criticized from many points of view.[90] This model of bureaucracy which he associates with industrialization is likely to stifle creativity and innovation, to impede the flow of communication, to diminish the cooperation of subordinates, and to impair the fulfillment of goals. Yet, the virtues of Weber's ideal type of bureaucracy must also be acknowledged. Political modernization is indeed dependent on the development of a stable, predictable, disciplined, professional, and impersonal system of administration.

In truth, there is a need for both centralization and decentralization, for the concentration of responsibility and for delegation of authority, for strict adherence to rules and for administrative adjustment of rules. These are interdependent requirements for successful administration. Samuel H. Beer notes that no single British minister has final, overriding authority over any other: "Similarly, the relation of command and obedience is foreign to the habits and spirit of the Civil Service, particularly members of the Administrative Class. No more than ministers do departments — not even the Treasury — order one another about."[91] But this situation depends on the legitimacy of those in authority to reach decisions that will be implemented by subordinates and on their supervisory capacity to maintain control. With regard to the political system as a whole, William Kornhauser, in *The Politics of Mass Society,* argues that both elites and non-elites need to be protected from excessive subversion. This necessitates a pluralistic society in which "a wide variety of independent, limited-function organizations permit democratic control but also insulate both elite and non-elite from undue interference in the life of the other."[92]

Under elasticity of control, "boundary maintenance" (the limitations on the exercise of power by the holder of a particular position) is a result not of a lack of political resources, but rather of an atmosphere of trust and respect together with an underlying sense of discipline and self-restraint derived from the internalization of Weberian norms. "Direct coercion is still in reserve as a last resort," Crozier points out in reference to modern progressive organizations, "but it is very rarely used, and people apparently no longer have to see it operate often to retain it in their calculations."[93] In other words, a coercive capacity is not inconsistent with the use of influence rather than force to gain compliance. While the influence of leaders is certainly enhanced by their decision-making authority, this depends ultimately upon the respect with which they are regarded.

## Conclusion

We began this chapter by painting a rather grim picture of urban life in Africa. The purpose was to indicate the difficulties encountered by African urban administrators. Yet, despite all the problems mentioned, the city can occasionally be an exciting, happy place for even the very impoverished residents, with music and dancing, bars and clubs, sports and festivities to divert the mind from the more troublesome conditions of life. Many an African, like Chief Obafemi Awolowo, has found "a sea of zinc roofs stretching as far as the eye can see" (his impression of Abeokuta as a child) staggering to the imagination and invigorating to tired legs.[94]

Nairobi, to a greater or lesser extent, shares all the aspects of the urban malaise. It is, however, a city of great charm, beauty, and importance. The Nairobi City Council remains anxious to preserve these qualities. The proposition that emerges from this chapter is that its success will require the achievement of "elasticity of control." Consequently, there must be an effort increasingly to delegate authority throughout the bureaucracy while enhancing the capacity of top administrators and leaders to supervise and correct what goes on. In any case, decentralization cannot properly take place without centralization, based upon the necessary cooperative relationship arising out of mutual trust and the sharing of goals.

For reasons that will be discussed, the conditions for elasticity of control did not exist in Kenya during the years immediately after independence (i.e., after 1963). However, the basis for improvement gradually began to emerge, despite the existing impediments to progress. What has here been suggested is a framework for analyzing the existing situation, the remaining problems, and the possibilities for reform. In the chapters that follow, the utility of the elasticity-of-control concept will hopefully be made apparent.

## NOTES

1. "Introductory Summary," in Aiden Southall, ed., *Social Change in Modern Africa* (London: Oxford U. Press, 1961), *passim.*

2. Cf. A. L. Epstein, "Urbanization and Social Change in Africa," *Current Anthropology,* October, 1967, pp. 276-84.

3. Cf. Mitchell Gordon, *Sick Cities: Psychology and Pathology of American Urban Life* (Baltimore: Penguin Books, 1963).

4. Cf. William I. Jones, "Economics of the Coup," *Africa Report,* March-April, 1969, p. 53.

5. Cf. Guy Hunter, *The Best of Both Worlds?: A Challenge on Developmental Policies in Africa* (London: Oxford U. Press, 1967), pp. 64-65.

6. Cf. William J. Hanna and Judith L. Hanna, *Urban Dynamics in Black Africa* (Chicago: Aldine-Atherton, 1971), p. 24. This book contains a very useful summary of the literature on urban Africa.

7. Cited, George Jenkins, "Africa as it Urbanizes: An Overview of Current Research," *Urban Affairs Quarterly,* Vol. 2, No. 3 (March, 1967), p. 512.

8. Cf. William J. Barber, "Urbanisation and Economic Growth: The Cases of Two White Settler Territories," in Horace Miner, ed., *The City in Modern Africa* (New York: Praeger, 1967), p. 108.

9. Committee on Housing, Building and Planning, *Progress Report of the Secretary-General on the Activities of the Centre for Housing, Building and Planning,* E/C.6/59, August 28, 1967, p. 1.

10. *The New Societies of Tropical Africa* (London: Oxford U. Press, 1962), p. 68.

11. (Entebbe, Uganda: Government Printer, 1956), p. 7.

12. Charles W. Senn and Thomas Ferguson, "Urbanization and Public Health," *Who Chronicle,* Vol. 21, No. 10 (October, 1967), pp. 64-65.

13. Cf. Jenkins, *op. cit.,* p. 69.

14. "Two Views of European Influence on African Behaviour," in A. A. Dubb, ed., *The Multitribal Society* (Lusaka: Rhodes-Livingstone Institute, 1962), p. 39.

15. Barber, *op. cit.,* p. 122.

16. Committee on Housing, Building and Planning, *op. cit.,* pp. 1-2.

17. Cf. United Nations Bureau of Social Affairs, *Urban Growth and Social Development in Africa* (Pittsburgh: U. of Pittsburgh, 1966 — Working Paper No. 5, Agenda Item No. 1 and 3), pp. 24-25; P. C. Lloyd, *Africa in Social Change* (Baltimore: Penguin Books, 1967), pp. 122-23.

18. Cf. Committee on Housing, Building and Planning, *op. cit.,* p. 1.

19. P. C. Lloyd, *op. cit.,* p. 122.

20. United Nations Bureau of Social Affairs, *op. cit.,* p. 29.

21. Quoted, Hunter, *The Best of Both Worlds?, op. cit.,* pp. 31-32.

22. Cf. Lloyd, *op. cit.,* p. 122.

23. Cited, Andrew Kamarck, *The Economics of African Development* (New York: Praeger, 1967), p. 91.

24. Church, *op. cit.,* pp. 512-13.

25. Cf. Kamarck, *op. cit.,* pp. 24-25; Lloyd, *op. cit,* pp. 86-87. The density of population in Africa is estimated to be 20-25 persons per square mile.

26. Cf. Kamarck, *op. cit.,* pp. 97-98.

27. *Ibid.,* pp. 18-19.

28. *The Attack on World Poverty* (New York: Vintage Books, 1962), pp. 18-19.

29. Anwar Syed, *The Political Theory of American Local Government* (New York: Random House, 1966), p. 5. Syed's entire book is here relevant.

30. "Approaches to the Understanding of Decentralization," *The Journal of Politics,* Vol. 27, No. 3 (August, 1965), p. 556.

31. Seyd, *op. cit..* pp. 142-143.

32. "Local Government and Democracy," *Public Administration,* Vol. XXXI, Spring, 1953, p. 13.

33. "Ideology, Democracy, and the Foundation of Local Self-Government," *The Canadian Journal of Economics and Political Science,* Vol. XXVI, No. 3 (August, 1960), pp. 377-394.

34. *The Relationship of Local and National Government in the Philippines* (Manila: Institute of Public Administration, University of the Philippines, 1955), p. 63.

35. *Local Government in the Developing Countries* (New York: McGraw-Hill, 1964), p. 175.

36. Ronald Wraith, *Local Government in West Africa* (London: George Allen and Unwin, Ltd., 1964), pp. 60-61.

37. Cf. Jenkins, *op. cit.*, p. 73.
38. "Kampala-Mengo," in Miner, *op. cit.*, p. 320.
39. Cf. Lloyd, *op. cit.*. p. 203.
40. Annmarie Hauck Walsh, *Administrative Aspects of Urbanization: A Comparative Survey* (New York: Institute of Public Administration, 1967), p. 28.
41. "Government and Politics in Ibadan," in P. C. Lloyd, A. L. Mabogunje, and B. Awe, *The City of Ibadan* (Cambridge: Cambridge University Press, 1967), p. 230.
42. Cf. United Nations Technical Assistance Programme, *Decentralization for National and Local Development* (New York: U.N.—ST/TAO/M/19—1962), p. 156.
43. "The Problems of a Metropolis," in Lloyd, Mabogunje, and Awe, *op. cit.*, p. 269.
44. Cf. Lloyd, *op. cit.*, pp. 149-50.
45. "The Political Structure of Urban-Centered African Communities," in Miner, *op. cit.*, p. 175.
46. Quoted, United Nations Technical Assistance Programme, *Decentralization for National and Local Development*, *op. cit.*, p. 66.
47. Cf. William Tordoff, *Government and Politics in Tanzania* (Nairobi: East African Publishing House, 1967), p. 128.
48. Cf. Henry Bretton, *The Rise and Fall of Kwame Nkrumah* (New York: Praeger, 1966), pp. 46-47.
49. Cf. Zbigniew Brzezinski and Samuel P. Huntington, *Political Power: USA/USSR* (New York: The Viking Press, 1963), ch. 7.
50. Cf. Wraith, *op. cit.*, ch. 8.
51. *Ibid.*, p. 106.
52. Cf. Jenkins, in Lloyd, Mabogunje, and Awe, *op. cit.*, pp. 232-33.
53. Tordoff, *op. cit.*, p. 74.
54. Walsh, *op. cit.*, p. 207.
55. *Op. cit.*, p. 332.
56. Robert Karr McCabe, "When China Spits, We Swim," *The New York Times Magazine,* February 27, 1968, p. 48.
57. Malcolm A. McConnell, "After Years of Violence the Congo is Afloat But Who Knows Where It's Headed?," *The New York Times Magazine,* September 21, 1969, p. 78.
58. "The Unproductive Study of Productivity: Public Administration in Developing Countries," *Comparative Political Studies,* Vol. I, No. 2 (July, 1968), p. 228.

59. "Approaches to the Understanding of Decentralization," *The Journal of Politics,* Vol. 27, No. 3 (August, 1965), p. 537.

60. "The American System as a Single Mechanism," in Duane Lockard, ed., *Governing the States and Localities* (London: MacMillan, 1969), p. 10.

61. *Governing New York City* (New York: Norton & Co., 1965), p. 584.

62. *Op. cit.,* p. 98.

63. Cf. two articles by the author: 'Elasticity of Control: An Analysis of Decentralization," *Journal of Comparative Administration,* Vol. 2, No. 2 (August 1970), pp. 185-209; "The Nairobi City Council: A Study in Comparative Local Government," *Comparative Studies in Society and History,* Vol. VIII, No. 2 (January, 1966), pp. 183-186.

64. *Politics and Policies in State and Local Governments* (Englewood Cliffs, New Jersey: Prentice-Hall, 1963), p. 32.

65. Cf. Herman Finer, *English Local Government* (London: Methuen, 1933), pp. 280 ff.

66. Cf. Alfred Diamant, "A Case Study of Administrative Autonomy: Controls and Tensions in French Administration," *Political Studies,* Vol. VI, No. 2 (1958), pp. 147-166.

67. *Democracy, Decentralization, and Development* (London: Asia Publishing House, 1963), p. 40.

68. "Contemporary Problems of Local Government in Mexico," *The Western Political Quarterly,* Vol. XVIII, No. 4 (December, 1965), p. 863.

69. Cf. Tom Wicker, "The Awesome Twosome," *The New York Times Magazine,* January 30, 1966, p. 64.

70. Cf. Michel Crozier, *The Bureaucratic Phenomenon* (Chicago: U. of Chicago Press, 1964), p. 299.

71. Cf. Reinhard Bendix, *Nation-Building and Citizenship* (N.Y.: Doubleday Anchor, 1969), pp. 1-35.

72. *Presidential Power* (New York: Wiley & Sons, 1960), *passim.*

73. *Modern Political Analysis* (Englewood Cliffs, New Jersey: Prentice-Hall, 1963), p. 50.

74. Cf. Charles E. Merriam, *Political Power* (New York: Collier Books, 1964), p. 50.

75. Cf. Harold Kaplan, *Urban Political Systems: A Functional Anal-*

*ysis of Metro Toronto* (New York and London: Columbia U. Press, 1967), pp. 25-26.

76. *African Armies and Civil Order* (New York: Praeger, 1969), p. 162.

77. *Tanzania: Party Transformation and Economic Development* (Princeton: Princeton U. Press, 1967), p. 412.

78. "Decentralization for Development — I," *Journal of Local Government Overseas,* Vol. II, No. 1 (January, 1963), p. 24.

79. *Administrative Reform* (Chicago: Aldine Publishing Co., 1969), p. 54.

80. *Op. cit.,* p. 236.

81. *Op. cit.,* p. 142.

82. Cf. Lewis A. Coser, *The Functions of Social Conflict* (Glencoe, Ill.: The Free Press, 1956), *passim.*

83. *From French West Africa to the Mali Federation* (New Haven and London: Yale U. Press, 1965), p. 187.

84. *Op. cit.,* pp. 282-286.

85. Cf. Peter Grose, "The Communist Party is the Rear Guard of Russia," *The New York Times Magazine,* March 27, 1966, p. 131.

86. *Op. cit.,* pp. 60-61.

87. *A City Council From Within* (London: Longman's Green & Co., 1926), p. 8.

88. *Organization and Environment* (Homewood, Ill.: Irwin, 1969), *passim.*

89. S. A. X. Tsegah, Chairman, *Report of the Committee of Enquiry Into the State Furniture and Joinery Corporation* (Accra-Tema: State Publishing Corp., 1967), p. 5. Also see two articles by Herbert H. Werlin: "The Roots of Corruption, the Ghanaian Enquiry," *The Journal of Modern African Studies,* Vol. 10, No. 2 (July, 1972), pp. 247-266; "The Consequences of Corruption: The Ghanaian Experience," *Political Science Quarterly,* Vol. LXXXVIII, No. 1 (March, 1973), pp. 71-85.

90. Cf. Crozier, *op. cit.,* pp. 175-208.

91. *British Politics in the Collectivist Age* (N.Y.: Knopf, 1965), p. 201.

92. (Glencoe, Ill.: The Free Press, 1959), p. 101.

93. *Op. cit.,* p. 185.

94. *Awo* (Cambridge: Cambridge University Press, 1960), p. 36.

# 2 NAIROBI AS A SETTLER CAPITAL

## Introduction

Nairobi was established for the economic and administrative convenience of Europeans and has remained "the most European of the East African cities," despite the fact that Europeans have never formed much more than 10 per cent of its population.[1] Unlike other capitals in East and West Africa, there was no large cluster of African population near the site upon which Nairobi came to be situated. There were a number of African groups who did use this land, but neither of the major tribes in this area (the Masai and the Kikuyu) had developed villages or a system of settled agriculture. While they did put up a considerable amount of resistance at various times, they lacked sufficiently well-organized and large-scale political systems to prevent European encroachment.

Nairobi was established some 300 miles from the Indian Ocean as a railroad depot, a convenient stopping place en route to Uganda, another 300 miles to the northwest. The purpose of the railroad was to facilitate access to the highly regarded political kingdom of Buganda, with which missionaries had maintained contact for a number of years. It was as a part of Uganda that the colonization of Kenya was formally sanctioned by the Anglo-German agreement of July, 1890, and, more effectively, by the proclamation of a British Protectorate in June, 1895.[2] In 1899 Nairobi became the head-quarters of the Uganda Railroad (in place of Mombasa) and of the Administration of Ukamba Province, which was shifted from Machakos.[3]

"The site of the township," according to an early European resident, "was a favourite spot for animals, and during the wet season large herds of game were attracted by the fertile land and grazed along with the cattle."[4] The town's early days, however, were difficult, with several severe plague attacks and the persistence of malaria, brought on by poor soil drainage, lack of water (despite the proximity of the river from which the city derives its Masai name), and improper sanitation arrangements. At that time it was obviously a frontier town, with few amenities of any sort. Elspeth Huxley describes it well in her book, *The Flame Trees of Thika,* as "a single street of Indian *dukas,* made of corrugated iron, and Government offices on wooden piles of the same harsh material, which used to creak and crack, like a man pulling his finger-joints in the hot sun."[5]

By 1907 Nairobi was reluctantly accepted as the official capital of Kenya. Its position became firmly established during the First World War when it was used as a military base in the Tanganyikan campaign against the Germans. Afterwards, following the development of the railroad and the influx of settlers into the Rift Valley, Nairobi continued to grow from approximately 15,000 in 1919, when it was allowed a municipal council with corporate rights, to 266,794 according to the 1962 Census.

As some of the town's earlier difficulties were overcome, its virtues came to be more appreciated: its wonderfully even and moderate climate, tempered by an altitude of 5,300 feet, and its gently irregular and open terrain, capable of housing an expanding population. To have shifted the capital further north would have brought it to the rugged land of the Kikuyu Escarpment, and in other directions, to arid and climatically unpleasant country.

## The Nature of the "Settler Regime"

Because of its central geographical location, the history of Nairobi can only be understood in the context of the history of Kenya. This is the history not simply of a typical "colonial regime," one administered by foreign agents on behalf of the mother country, but rather of a "settler regime," which was dominated by a European elite determined for many years to establish a "white man's country."[6] The objective of establishing an independent country governed by settlers was challenged by the 1923 White Paper, enunciating the "paramountcy of native interests," and by the more specific 1930 *Memorandum on Native Policy in East Africa.* Even so, the expectation that Kenya would continue to be controlled by Europeans under the patronage of a sympathetic Colonial Office persisted until the Lancaster House Conference of 1960. Consequently, the characteristic feature of Kenya politics was a rigid hierarchy based upon race. This situation had great significance for the development of Nairobi.

If a racial hierarchy was the dominant feature of Kenya politics during the colonial period, "land" was the issue around which it revolved. The building of the railroad to Uganda for administrative purposes at the end of the Nineteenth Century gave rise to a need to justify economically such an expensive undertaking. Since much of the land through which the railroad passed seemed at the time to be sparsely populated, relatively fertile, and climatically attractive, the decision was soon made to invite European settlement.[7] This decision was initially presented in 1901 as a Parliamentary Paper by Sir Harry Johnston, the then Special Commissioner for Uganda.

The idea for the "white highlands" took its first concrete form in the 1903 public speech of Sir Charles Eliot, the then newly appointed commissioner for the East African Protectorate, guaranteeing practically exclusive rights to Europeans to the land between Machakos road station and Fort Ternan.[8] It was assumed that Africans had neither the mental capacity nor the numerical strength to work this land profitably, and it was rationalized that the growing number of Asians in the country would prefer the warmer climates near the Coast and near Lake Victoria. Consequently, Eliot, with the enthusiastic support of Lord Delamere and a small group of like-minded adventurers, soon began to seek settlers from England and South Africa. However, the full implications for such an undertaking only gradually came to be realized.

First of all, to reserve land exclusively for European ownership contradicted the traditional British policy of equal rights and opportunities for all — a policy that might at times have been overlooked for practical reasons but was never completely repudiated.[9] This meant that the European settlers could never be altogether certain of the sanctity of the "white highlands" (no matter how much avowed by successive governors), so long as they remained ultimately under the jurisdiction of the British government. Likewise, their political demands could not be accepted without reservation. As early as 1907, Winston Churchill, then the Under-Secretary of State, wrote that it would be "an ill day for the native races" should their fortunes be "removed from the impartial and august administration of the Crown and abandoned to the fierce self-interest of a small white population."[10]

Since independence from colonial rule was hardly conceivable in the initial period of settlement, the settlers sought in various ways to gain a formidable political position within the colonial framework. By 1906, the 600 resident settlers had succeeded in obtaining a Legislative Council, prompting Churchill to exclaim in Nairobi the following year that "never before in Colonial experience has a Council been granted where the number of settlers is so few."[11] The settlers soon afterwards began to demand elected representation based on a franchise restricted to those of European origin ("whole blooded descent from European ancestors"), arguing: "that at this stage of the Protectorate's development when the coloured races outnumber the white it is not desirable that the franchise should be extended to Asiatics or Natives."[12] In 1919 the settlers gained elected representation, justified by the expansion of European population during World War I and following the decision to give farms to British veterans.[13]

Between the two World Wars the constitutional arrangement was such that the Europeans elected from the rural constituencies in the Highlands dominated the proceedings of the Legislative Council.[14] This required the Government to subject all important measures to the criticism of the elected members before submitting them to the Legislative Council for passage. Similarly, the settlers were permitted to be very influential in all stages of administration. The functioning of the administrative arrangement under Sir Edward Grigg (Governor from 1925 to 1930) has been described by Norman Leys: "Sir Edward provided the different departments with boards or committees, dealing with education, roads and so forth, composed of settlers, which, though like the Legislature, had only advisory functions, found that their advice was generally decisive."[15]

A high level of organization and unity intensified the power of the settlers who were led by the Colonists' Association which, according to W. McGregor Ross, "had begun at an early date to exhibit some of the propensities of a political machine."[16] The fact that some of the settlers came from the influential and ruling class of England increased their social ties with the administrators coming from the same class.[17] This closeness flourished in the informal "country club" atmosphere that emerged in Kenya. Increasing identity of viewpoint occurred in the 1930's when civil servants were allowed for the first time to acquire land in the country.

## The Evolution of European Settler Control in Nairobi

The settlers eventually gained an even greater degree of political control in Nairobi than in Kenya as a whole. Thereafter, settler efforts were directed to an expansion of their powers in the government of Nairobi by minimizing interference from the Central Government and the Colonial Office.[18] By 1949 they had gained for the Municipal Council a privilege unique to a colonial urban community of borrowing directly on the London Money Market.[19] The next year this achievement was capped by Nairobi's becoming a city by Royal Charter, an honor which aroused the fears of many Africans that Nairobi was destined to remain a European city.

A government for Nairobi first came into being in 1900 with the establishment of a township committee under a regulation based on an 1897 Order-in-Council. The committee then consisted of four leading residents (two Europeans and two Asians) together with the Sub-Commissioner of Ukamba. "Following the enactment in 1903 of the East African Townships Ordinance, Nairobi was, on

September 9 of that year, declared a township and defined as 'the area comprised within a circle having a radius of 1-1/2 miles with the Sub-Commissioner's Office as centre.' "[20]

Until the end of World War I, Government officials held the chairmanship together with a majority of the township committee. In 1916, however, a system of informal elections was set up, enabling the European residents of Nairobi to increase their political influence. Those who were elected (the so-called "unofficial European members") succeeded in getting a municipal council for Nairobi in 1919. But some of their influence was lost under a 1924 constitutional arrangement which equalized the representation on the Council of the European and Asian populations of Nairobi. Because the European and Asian representatives tended to vote as separate blocs, the Government officials on the Council continued to hold the balance of power.

The complete domination of the European settlers in Nairobi had to await the Feetham Commission Report of 1927. The position of this Commission, under the leadership of the Town-clerk of Johannesburg, was that ". . . it is essential that the European community should, under the present circumstances, be entrusted with the larger share of responsibility for the municipal government of Nairobi, and that the proportion of European representation on the Council should be in conformity with the obligations of this trust."[21] Consequently, the Feetham Commission recommended that three European members, as against one Asian member, be added to the Council, thus making it nine elected Europeans to six Asians. This was to be facilitated by the incorporation of the suburban areas and the establishment of a ward system because "the Ward System usually has the effect of encouraging voters to organize themselves into local groups for the purpose of urging their views on their ward representatives, and of thus providing each councillor with one or more groups of voters with whom he feels it his duty to keep in touch."[22]

The Asian community was understandably upset by the Feetham Commission Report (which meant one European elected member for every 401 persons, as against one Indian representative to 1,611).

This resentment was expressed from 1929 to 1931 in a boycott of the Council and a refusal to pay municipal taxes. Indeed, this was the apex of a long and bitter struggle in Nairobi between Europeans and Asians.

As early as 1908, the Asians, then having but two representatives in a Council of thirteen, complained to the Governor: ". . . we humbly submit that the Indian community numbering half of the whole alien people of the town is not adequately represented on the township committee."[23] In the absence of the desired equality of representation on the municipal body based on communal representation, the Indian leader A. M. Jeevanjee advocated in 1920 "a common electoral roll including the Arabs and the natives" with a "common qualification." He argued that this would force candidates to seek the goodwill of all sectors of the population.[24]

However, the religious divisions within the Asian population (especially between Hindus and Muslims) weakened the political influence of Asians generally and contributed to their subordinate political position in Nairobi, despite the three-to-one edge they maintained over the Europeans in population. The victory of the European settlers, ordained by the Feetham Commission Report, put an end for many years to any possibility of a common roll, the lack of which resulted, according to Mary Parker, "in apathy over elections and an attempt in the few cases where sufficient candidates are forthcoming for elections to take place on racial issues."[25]

European control over the Municipal Council was further enhanced in 1946 with the establishment of an "aldermanic bench," which added seven Council members, five of them Europeans. The official justification for this was to relieve the pressure on overworked councillors in the transaction of public business and to reward councillors and other citizens for outstanding service, thereby saving them the inconvenience of standing for election.[26] Another reason, according to Mary Parker, was "to make it possible to maintain European numerical superiority without laying too heavy a burden upon European members."[27]

## The Degradation of Africans

Unlike the colonial policy in certain other parts of British Africa, no sustained effort was made to create a prosperous, well-contented African rural population. The 1915 Crown Land Ordinance declared the African reserves to be Crown land, thereby denying Africans, particularly the Kikuyu, the security that they sought. "This ordinance," writes Margery Dilley, "was interpreted to provide no legal right to land for natives, either individually or tribally."[28] Despite the 1928 Native Lands Trust Bill which, together with the Passfield Pledge of 1929, were intended to curtail encroachment by Europeans upon the Reserves, Africans continued to be fearful about their land because of the dominance of Europeans on the Central Board which was set up to enforce these measures.

African farmers were also handicapped in other ways. Transportation facilities, agricultural services of various sorts, and marketing arrangements were all developed and administered in such a way as to benefit Europeans to the neglect or disadvantage of Africans.[29] Significantly enough, several of the early proposals to help African agriculture were discouraged by the settlers for fear of competition and the diminishing of their labor supply. Most notorious of all was the persistent refusal to allow Africans to grow cash crops, particularly coffee, in certain areas where they could be competitive. Moreover, the shortage of land became increasingly serious for a few tribes. By the 1950's, in contrast to the Highlands with a proportion of 1 European to 4 square miles, the population densities (based on the 1948 Census) in Kiambu was 421 and in Fort Hall, 412 per square mile.[30]

For all these reasons, Africans in Kenya remained poor. Whereas neighboring Uganda Africans had a *per capita* income of $32 a year in 1951, in Kenya it was less than $9. This was an amount scarcely more than what it had been thirty years before, despite great prosperity in the Colony after World War II.[31] The real value of African income, it is estimated, rose by about 1 per cent annually between 1922 and 1952 while their population during this period rose by nearly 3 per cent per annum. Though more than 95 per cent of Kenya's population were Africans, only 6 per cent of Kenya's net geographical produce in 1952 came from African commercial activity. Since African farming in Kenya remained largely a subsistence enterprise, Africans had to turn to wage-labor, from which about two-thirds of African earnings were derived (as against less than 15 per cent of Uganda African income). This process was stimulated by a number of governmental measures, including taxation, which had the effect of inducing an estimated 50 per cent of the able-bodied men in the country from the agricultural tribes to be employed in European agriculture.[32] This indicates the extent to which Africans came to be looked upon largely as a labor force for planters and farmers — one that was to be as cheap as possible.

The economic exploitation of Africans was accompanied by various other types of racial discrimination and neglect. The extent to which race played a part in the life of East Africa is summarized by J. E. Goldthorpe, writing in 1948: "Under the law, a person's racial status — that is, the racial category into which he is officially assigned — affects such fundamental matters as his civic rights and obligations, for instance, whether he has to obey a chief's orders and whether he is subject to collective punishment; the tax he pays; where and how he may hold land; his political representation, generally speaking, the way he is tried for an offence, and the way he is treated in prison; and the way in which civil disputes in which he is involved are heard, and before which court."[33] In 1956 the Government of Kenya announced that there were more than 100 Kenyan ordinances differentiating between people because of race.[34]

The educational disadvantage suffered by Africans during Kenya's colonial period was as great as their economic disadvantage. The government placed almost the entire burden of educating African children upon the Christian missions. As late as 1931, Norman Leys noted that less than one per cent of African children were in Government schools.[35] The inadequacy of this education is indicated by the fact that in 1945 only sixteen Africans passed the school certificate (necessary for the successful completion of secondary school) and as late as 1951, only eighty-seven did so. In 1955 more than 14 times as much was spent on a European child's education and $3\frac{1}{2}$ times as much on an Asian child's education as on that of an African child.[36]

Lack of education, together with the different wage scales which were applied to Europeans, Asians, and Africans, accounts for the employment in the public service in 1947 of only nine Africans drawing salaries of 300 shillings a month (about $40) and over.[37] The paucity of well-educated Africans gave the Kenya Government a convenient excuse for failing to appoint, after half a century of European rule in Kenya, a single African to a major post in the civil service.[38]

The initial rationalization for the exploitation of Africans was the innate inferiority of Africans generally and, particularly, those encountered in the Kenya Highlands. Since Africans were considered to be practically useless, it was felt necessary to bring more than 30,000 laborers from India to build the Uganda railroad. "Most of the tribes were still untouched by civilization," wrote Dr. E. Boedecker in his memoirs of the early history of Nairobi, "and their lack of physique and constitutional stamina, coupled with their lack of intelligence, were real handicaps for the performance of the intricate and hard work required in the preliminary stages of construction."[39] This viewpoint was crudely as well as vigorously espoused by the settler leader Ewart S. Grogan. "I will ignore Biblical platitudes as to the quality of men," he wrote in 1900, and takes as a hypothesis that the African is "fundamentally inferior in mental development and ethical possibilities to white men."[40]

A more subtle justification for the prevailing policy towards Africans was the often expressed opinion that Africans, while not innately inferior, were generations behind the Europeans in their mental and moral development. They must, therefore, be treated as children because, to quote a 1909 memorandum on native policy:

> In dealing with African savage tribes we are dealing with a people who are practically at the genesis of things . . . and we cannot expect to lift them in a few years from this present state to that of a highly civilized European. . . . The evolution of races must necessarily take centuries to accomplish satisfactorily.[41]

Thus, the role of the European was to be a firm and gentle teacher, recognizing, in the words of J. F. Lipscomb (one of the leading, if more moderate, exponents of settler thought) that "time and discipline are needed in order that the African may gain the strength of character that will perpetuate his better instincts as the dominant side of his character."[42] According to Lipscomb, the person best fitted for this task is the long-resident settler because: "if that European is himself a white African who has been properly educated in the basic tenets of Western civilization, he should be able to do his work better and with more sympathetic understanding than the man whose home is not in Africa. . . ."[43]

In line with this way of thinking, emphasis was placed on the need for the African to have direct contact with Europeans through a labor contract to hasten the processes of civilization. "A good sound system of compulsory labor," suggested Ewart Grogan, would "do more to raise the nigger in five years than all the millions that have been sunk in missionary efforts for the last fifty."[44] The same sort of argument, noted Norman Leys, was used by the settlers regarding the heavy taxation that Africans had to pay in the belief "that the benefits and advantages Africans derive from white settlement are worth to them far more than the sums, always alluded to as 12s per family, that they have to pay in taxation."[45]

## Impediments to African Urbanization

An understanding of the development of Kenya leads to an understanding of that of Nairobi — a basically non-African city built for the needs of the White Highlands and in conformity with the predilections of the European settler elite. Two facts are especially relevant to seeing Nairobi in an historical perspective. First of all, it is essential to remember the newness of urban life for most East Africans. Prior to the arrival of the Europeans, the people of East Africa did not live in towns or villages, but rather in individual homesteads consisting of small clusters of huts made of temporary material. Nothing more was required by the prevailing economy of pastoral or subsistence agriculture, employing unsophisticated techniques or shifting cultivation. "It is, therefore, broadly true that, in inland East Africa, towns are things of no more than the present century, and that the great majority of the African population is quite unfamiliar with town life."[46]

What retarded African urbanization in Kenya, however, was not so much African unwillingness as discouragement by Europeans. "The dominant vision of African development in British eyes," notes Guy Hunter, "was of an agricultural society, based on the village, technically improved, wisely guided by more educated chiefs, and later by democratic counsellors. This would least disturb the cultural pattern of Africa which they found."[47]

This viewpoint stemmed partly from the British philosophical teachings of Edmund Burke and Herbert Spencer, that traditional culture was an "organic" structure of mutually dependent parts which would be seriously disrupted by the innovations associated with urbanization.[48] The resulting cultural void would provoke violence and decadence. Those who shared this outlook tended to distrust the Westernized, educated African. According to Lord Lugard, who developed the prevailing British colonial policy of indirect rule, such an African was a socially "displaced person" and, thereby, somewhat degenerate.[49]

This widespread distrust of the urbanized African can be seen in the statement of the Chief Native Commissioner in Kenya at the time of the Feetham Commission Report (1927) in support of the contention "that the ingress of natives in towns and their residence therein should be strictly controlled:

> It is unfortunately the case in any Colony with a native population that among those to whom a town naturally offers attractions are idle, vicious, or criminal natives, who seek to avoid tribal control or indeed any control at all. Such undesirables do not come to town to work but rather to live "on their wits," which generally means either begging or stealing, and they become not only a menace to public security but a definite incubus upon the honest working natives from whom they beg lodging and food, relying on tribal custom to preclude a refusal.[50]

Likewise, detribalization was to be discouraged and avoided in the fear that Africans who broke away from traditional forms of control would be encouraged to challenge the existing European forms of control.[51]

Because Africans were regarded as merely temporary residents in the towns, leaving their families in rural areas to which they would periodically return and eventually retire, very little public accommodation was provided until the end of World War II. As late as 1955, the *East African Royal Commission Report* could declare: "They are still, however, regarded socially and financially as liabilities for whose housing and welfare the urban authorities are responsible."[52]

It was often argued that extensive public housing elaborate enough for African family life would encourage an excessive influx into Nairobi, resulting not only in additional crime and disease but also in an undesirable economic burden on the city. For this reason, the earliest public housing for Africans consisted of dormitories suitable only for single men. Nairobi's policy of providing accommodation for labor largely on a bachelor basis was explained in 1955 by the City's Medical Officer of Health, A. T. G. Thomas: "It was considered that, owing to the migratory habits of labour, cost of family housing, and for other reasons, it was not desirable to encourage permanent African family settlement."[53]

Even those such as Mayor Udall (the leader of the Council, 1942-44), who recognized the need to improve housing conditions for Asians and Africans, insisted that the Central Government pay for it:

> If it is the opinion of Government that accommodation must be found for all Africans and Asians who wish to live here, I consider that it is the duty of Government to provide the funds for an undertaking of such magnitude in the shape of housing, and if the housing is to be on a subeconomic basis, Government should bear any loss that might be incurred. . . . To ask ratepayers to bear the loss of such an enterprise as the housing of all the poorer immigrant classes is asking too much, considering Council's present economic problems.[54]

It was frequently pointed out in this regard that so long as African wages remained abysmally low on the average, good family housing in the urban areas could never be an economic proposition.[55]

When it was finally deemed necesary to furnish lodging for African employees in Nairobi, together with the required social, health, and recreational facilities, the costs were partly recovered from the sale of beer and other items to the poorly paid Africans, with the revenue held as a "Native Trust Fund."[56] This practice was justified on the grounds that the Africans were not ratepayers and, therefore, had no claim on the rate revenues. Such an argument led the Commissioner for Local Government, Land and Settlement to protest in 1935 that the interests, particularly in health, of the various communities were interwoven and that: "The Native Trust Fund can properly be used to supplement and accelerate improvement of health services amongst the Africans, but it cannot rightly be regarded as a milch cow on which the initiation of much-needed services is to depend."[57] Yet, the Commissioner's outcry did not prevent Nairobi's City Treasurer from continuing to segregate Africans for taxation purposes and to require them to pay separately from the other races for the services they received.[58]

The upshot of this thinking was, with certain exceptions, an appalling neglect of the needs of the Africans in Nairobi until the shock of the Mau Mau troubles in the 1950's. According to the 1941 "Report on the Housing of Africans in Nairobi," by the Senior Medical Officer of Health and the Municipal Native Affairs Officer: "Until 1930 the only distinct native housing as such in Nairobi open to the general population was Pangani village, where the lodging housekeeper was indistinguishable from the brothel manager."[59] This report went on to estimate that (as of 1941) 6,000 Africans, which was about 40 per cent of those seeking housing in the city, had no accommodation. This situation led it to conclude "that lack of native housing is a major evil in Nairobi today, and that further delay over the provision of housing may result in demoralization and the undermining of the Nairobi native community which will take many years to redress."[60] The overcrowding that resulted was indicated by a 1941 survey of African housing in Nairobi which showed that houses with a permitted occupancy of 171 were illicitly sheltering 481 persons.[61] Unfortunately, further delay did occur creating an estimated shortage of 20,000 "bed-spaces" by 1953.[62]

Employers in Kenya were legally required to provide housing for their African employees or additional income to cover rent. But, as a 1946 Government report pointed out, most business premises and residential flats did not provide adequate housing accommodation for African staff, thus shifting the burden on to the Municipality.[63] To put too much pressure on employers to construct houses for Africans, it was felt, would discourage these employers from establishing businesses in Kenya. On the other hand, the existing shortage of housing, according to the 1948 "Annual Report of the African Affairs Officer," was holding up the development of industry in Nairobi. It was asserted that for this reason a firm of clothing manufacturers could not keep skilled African labor for more than nine months despite good wages. Legitimately employed Africans were sleeping under verandahs, in the streets, in various and often dangerous shacks on vacant swampy land, or in overcrowded rooms in the African locations.

In addition to inadequate housing, Africans in Nairobi at the end of World War II had to endure a lack of medical and educational facilities. The inadequacy of medical services and public conveniences was causing a fearsome rise in the rate of tuberculosis and other diseases. There were only six schools altogether for Africans in 1946 in Nairobi with 1,770 pupils, which was less than half of those of school-age. The majority of these students were in the most rudimentary classes. In 1952 only thirty-four passed the Kenya African Preliminary Examination in Nairobi, of which only nine went on to secondary school. It was argued that education for African children would reduce juvenile crime, but, according to Mary Parker: ". . . the conflict between the European desire to reduce crime on the one hand, and dislike of expenditure on the other prevented any great improvements until certain suggestions of the Municipal African Affairs Office, who was seeking a way out of the impasses, were brought forward in 1949."[64] Reasons of parsimony kept the City Council from taking on educational responsibilities until 1963.

## Racial Segregation

The living conditions for Africans in Nairobi at the end of World War II are vividly described by the American educated Kenyan

R. Mugo Gatheru in his autobiography, *Child of Two Worlds:*

> In the African locations there were poor lights in the streets. Library facilities and social halls were ill-equipped. Public lavatories were very, very dirty. Some of them did not have running water. Instead, they had hard tins like dustbins in which people "eased" themselves. There was an inescapable offensive smell when these bins were full of faeces, and especially when the municipal workers who removed them were late (as they always were). One public lavatory was used by over a thousand people.
>
> In the African houses there were no lights, water supplies, or gas for cooking. The Africans used paraffin or kerosene oil lamps, charcoal fires for cooking, and water drawn in tins or emptied oil drums.
>
> In each African location there was a water tap where long queues of people lined up with their tins and drums. If you wanted to cook a quick meal, it was impossible unless you had some spare water in the house.
>
> Like public lavatories, one water centre served about one thousand people and was open only three times a day. You could see three or four columns of queues around one centre. Some people had to line up with their tins and drums about fifteen minutes to six in the morning. The last hour of closing the centre was seven in the evening. The water was supplied by one pipe.[65]

In contrast to the African sections of Nairobi, those of the Europeans tended to be luxurious. Even before World War I, this great contrast between the houses of the poor and the rich was noted by a visitor: "The palatial residences of the railway officers, with tiled roofs and graceful structures lining the lovely flower-spangled and tree-crowned hills, have awakened a sense of injustice in the hearts of men that no plausible speech can eradicate. . . ."[66]

It was the idea of a "garden city" that appealed to the early European residents, with suburbs far removed from the commercial center of the town. "When the residential area of Parklands was first opened up, most of the people here were people who had been accustomed at home to living in rather confined conditions, and it appealed to them that at least four or five acres around a house would be desirable. . . ."[67] However, as the Feetham Commission goes on to note, these people did not realize how expensive it would be to service such a spread-out urban environment. In some parts of Nairobi in 1948, there existed more than an acre per person, as against 100 people per acre in most European cities.[68]

In fear of disease, crime, and a rise in the cost of land (a fear, of course, intensified by prejudice), racial segregation was very early insisted upon by the politically dominant European settlers. Indeed, as Aiden Southall points out, it was "inevitable at this stage, undoubtedly taken for granted and desired by all. It was only the quality of facilities that was in dispute."[69] The Government very openly prevented non-Europeans from buying certain plots in Nairobi, as indicated by the 1908 advertisement quoted by Mary Parker: "The auctioneers have been requested to give notice at the auction that although it is open for any person to bid for any of the town or residential plots in Nairobi, Parklands, or on the Ngong Road, Asiatics or Natives will not be allowed to reside on those in the New Post Office Road, Parklands, or on the Ngong Road."[70] The resulting pattern of town-development was sanctioned by the Simpson Report of 1913: "In the interests of each community and of the healthiness of the locality and country, it is absolutely essential that in every town and trade centre there should be well-defined and separate quarters for Europeans, Asiatics, and Africans. . . ."[71]

Though the 1923 White Paper prohibited separation of the races in the townships by means of legislative enactments, the same effect was gained through restrictive covenants (written particularly to exclude Asians) and policies followed to preserve the White Highlands. In 1926, the land set aside for use by Europeans (comprising 10 per cent of Nairobi's population) encompassed 2,700 acres of the total municipal area of 6,400 acres, leaving the far more numerous Asians (30 per cent of the Town's population) with only 300 acres for residential purposes.[72]

The Bazaar, where the Asians lived and worked, was a continual source of the plague during the early years of Nairobi's history. Eastleigh, which was laid-out in 1913 to relieve overcrowding in the Bazaar, had to be abandoned during the depression of the 1920s because it lacked roads into town in wet weather and lacked a proper water supply in dry weather.[73] In 1951, according to an Asian councillor, Eastleigh, with a larger population than any other area, still had no roads, no drainage, and no lights.[74] Almost exactly the same complaint was made in the Legislative Council nearly ten years later: "In summer, dust reigns, and when the rain comes in that slum area the young children go knee deep in the water and eventually they get pneumonia and so on and so forth."[75] To this, the Minister for Local Government and Lands (Mr. Havelock) replied: "Some of the other races have not got the money to pay, it is not their fault, but the fact of the matter is that the Europeans pay for these services and therefore they get them when the estate is first developed."[76]

The policy of requiring Africans (except for the domestic servants who comprised about one-sixth of the African urban population) to live in segregated areas was implemented through a variety of by-laws, including those which prohibited Africans from leaving these areas at night and those which pledged the local authorities to erect housing in the African locations.[77] The argument for this was authoritatively set forth in the 1933 Carter Commission Report:

> Having regard to the widely different standards of living observed by natives in Nairobi as compared with other races, we are convinced that considerations of health as well as of social amenities demand separate areas. We are, therefore, satisfied that special residential areas for natives are needed in which they should be required to reside unless exempted.[78]

Over the years, historical and economic circumstances combined with legal requirements to reinforce racial segregation. Schools and hospitals were built for Africans in such a way as to discourage them from living far from their locations. Services were provided in the locations "which would avoid the necessity for the African to frequent other parts of the town. Isolation and control were the prime motives."[79] In 1955, to justify the City Council's policy of not housing the families of African employees in non-African residential areas, the Minister for Local Government, Health and Housing noted the expense of caring for Africans outside of their own areas: "There are difficulties, and there will be difficulties, of providing for amenities, for nursery schools and so on for the families of Africans who live in areas where the majority of the population is not African."[80]

Segregation of housing was accompanied by a general "color bar" — a denial of access to hotels, restaurants, and other private establishments. This was especially resented by the educated African. "The colour bar," to quote Guy Hunter, "only becomes painful or important when there are real possibilities of contact. While the white man is a god, he can and should be aloof; but when an African can speak his language, drive his car, wear his clothes, and worship his god, it is different."[81] How this struck Gatheru, the Kenyan African already quoted, is quite revealing in this regard:

> In the city there were beautiful restaurants, hotels, and bars, but for use by the Europeans only. The Asians had their own, too, but, on the whole, Africans were not welcome there, although, outwardly, the Asians sympathized with the lot of the Africans. Africans were not allowed to buy hard liquor or European beer. In fact, there was only one drinking place for Africans in all Nairobi. It was situated in one of the African locations and, however far away he lived, any African wanting a drink had to travel there for the privilege of buying the local Nairobi Corporation brew made especially for Africans.
>
> The Africans, therefore, were always complaining about their life in the city. I found myself deeply involved and asked myself the cause of this universal misery, and why something could not be done to satisfy the grievances of my people. Why were the Africans always treated in such a humiliating and degrading fashion and always accorded the last place in what was, after all, their own country? I asked many people and, depending on the race of the person to whom I was talking, I learnt the various stock explanations.
>
> For example, many young Indians, perhaps because they felt their own position in society to be insecure, suggested that ignorance and lack of education among the Africans was the root of the problem. The Europeans would agree with the Indians but would add, somewhat mysteriously: "Rome was not built in a day," which was no great comfort to the Indians. Others, of course, offered colour or racial prejudice as the cause. I listened to all these

theories. They sounded interesting but I found them all unsatisfactory: if the problem was so easily expounded, why was it so difficult to resolve?[82]

## Governmental Paternalism

Poor living conditions and segregation were not the only causes of discontent among Africans in Nairobi. As the 1955 *East African Royal Commission Report* noted: "It is the isolation and frustration of African town-dwellers, who feel that they cannot by their own efforts raise themselves above the squalid conditions in which they live and that they are denied the rights and advantages which members of the other races enjoy, which are the major causes of the crime, immorality and drunkenness which are rife in many East African towns."[83] Africans in Nairobi constantly came up against various forms of European paternalism, some of which greatly discouraged potentially constructive aspects of African urban enterprise.

At various times the Municipality operated canteens, beershops, dairies, and meat shops and provided free meals for public employees. The justification for this was, in Mary Parker's words, that: "He (the African) does not know how to protect himself against exploitation by his fellows, so we must protect him."[84] This paternalism also, according to Mary Parker, coincided with a desire to keep down disease and the cost of living and to ensure an efficient labor force. Understandably, however, it was resented by Africans who felt a community of interests with the economically threatened African traders, of which there were an estimated 2,000 in 1941.[85] In 1947, the revenue of the City's beershops and canteens was reduced by 50 per cent as a result of a boycott, including threats of violence against the Superintendent of the Locations and the African Municipal Councillor who attempted to intervene.[86] By 1950 the public canteen for Africans had to be abandoned. Yet, to quote Guy Hunter:

As, at any given time, the existing towns were necessary, government policy too often issued as a half-hearted attempt to prevent them from growing and to discipline them — a continuous minor harrying of the urban African by permits and passes, hygienic regulations, licensing, ineffective efforts to control room densities, and, as a concession to positive action, the establishment of "community centres" for communities which did not exist. If one of the happier pictures of colonial Africa is that of the District Officer and local chief proudly surveying a cotton crop or a new village well, the most gloomy is that of the police of East Africa harrying the vegetable sellers, usually women, on a periodic round-up of unauthorized markets in an urban estate.[87]

This paternalism was especially humiliating for the educated African. According to Gatheru, before an African was given a pass to go to a film in Nairobi, he was advised as follows:

It is desirable to go to the cinema house properly dressed and clean, and when you see something funny on the screen, don't laugh loudly with your mouth open as most of the "natives" do. Finally, don't turn your head about observing other customers or go about touching other people with your shoulders. . . .[88]

A very big problem for Africans throughout Kenya, but particularly in the urban areas, was the lack of a social security or pension program. Sir Michael Blundell noted in 1963 that ten years earlier the question of old age security had been raised to no avail with the Government of Kenya.[89] More important, the security that might have come with the right of Africans to own property in the town did not exist. "There is a need for a system of land tenure," stressed the *East African Royal Commission Report*, "which gives Africans who live inside and outside the towns full security to develop their holdings. This is essential if Africans are to settle down as members of the whole urban community."[90]

Occasionally land was set aside for Africans to build their own houses, but seldom was there financial assistance or encouragement for the building of a substantial section of good African-owned housing. One reason for this, at least in the early post-World War I period, was to encourage Africans to occupy the unpopular dormitories that had been constructed in the 1920's in Pumwani, where the Administration hoped to centralize the African population.[91] So it was that Pangani, the earliest authorized area in Nairobi where Africans could put up their own dwellings (an admittedly unhealthy, unsightly place but where Africans felt somewhat "at home") was eventually eradicated. An African-built estate was permitted in Pumwani, but it was quite limited in area and care-lessly laid-out "so that rather than setting a standard in housing and family life, it became notorious for high rents, over-crowding, bad sanitation, prostitution, violence and crime."[92] In addition, "shanty towns" persistently arose in and near Nairobi, but these were always viewed with misgiving by the Government and were removed and redeveloped to the extent that resources were available.[93]

Where programs for African-built housing were put into effect, their attractiveness was limited by restrictions as to type of con-struction and to sub-letting or subdivision. Thus, one such project in Nairobi in 1950, requiring £400 of capital (about $1,000), cost too much for all but a handful of Africans. The standards required of African dwellings were based on the usual regulations of a Brit-ish community, with little relevance to Africa. But trained as they were in British local government, the officers of the Nairobi City Council adopted what the *East African Royal Commission Report* called "a procrustean attitude . . . to the social needs of Africans as far as housing is concerned."[94] What might have succeeded was the sort of carefully planned site-service scheme advocated in 1950 by E. A. Vasey, one of the most far-sighted liberals in Kenya, but it was never really tried during the colonial period.[95]

The failure of earlier tenant-purchase proposals for Africans caused the rejection of later ones and reinforced the contention of Nairobi City Councillors, expressed as late as 1955, that Africans were not yet permanent residents of the city.[96] This attitude reflect-ed the paternalism of the Government as pointed out by the *East African Royal Commission Report*: "As they are not permanent residents with a stake in the towns which the ownership of property would give them, Africans have been regarded as 'wards' of the urban authorities rather than as citizens, and they have had little say in the conduct of urban affairs."[97] Consequently, Nairobi ap-peared to most Africans more as a hostile manifestation of colon-ialism than as a city.[98]

## The Control of Africans in Nairobi

The management of the African locations was divided between Kenya's Central Government and the Local Authority. Until 1949,

the officer in Nairobi directly responsible for African affairs had
been co-opted from the Kenya Administration.[99] That year the
Municipal Council set up an African Affairs Department, headed
by a Native Affairs Officer appointed directly by the Council. Following the outbreak of the Emergency in 1952, the Central Government largely resumed control of Africans in Nairobi through a
network of District Officers and Chiefs throughout the City.[100] The
subsequent division of responsibility for the administration of Africans living in Nairobi was described in a memorandum submitted
to the East African Royal Commission in this way:

> The responsibility of the Central Government can best be sum-
> marized by saying that the Central Government is responsible for
> the administration of the Ordinances, Proclamations, Rules and
> Regulations of the Colony of Kenya. The Local Authority is re-
> sponsible for public health, housing, medical treatment (other
> than that required in a hospital), public works, the development
> of the housing estates, recreation, community development and
> social services.[101]

In 1958 the African Affairs Department was changed to the
Department of Social Services and Housing, in line with the policy
of "multi-racialism" then being advanced. Oddly enough, this change
was resented by at least one African Legislative Council member
who complained that Africans in Nairobi did not know whether to
go to the police, the District Commissioner, or the City Council with
their problems. It would be better, he contended, if each location
were placed under the charge of one official, "helped by the office-
boy and one or two askaris."[102]

Of all the measures carried out by the Government, probably the
most resented by Africans was the "pass system." The pass system
was designed to control the influx of Africans into Nairobi, but it
had the effect of intensifying the insecurity of those residing there.
Two by-laws were particularly disliked by Africans: 208, prohibiting Africans from being outside the locations in which they resided
between 10 p.m. and 5 a.m. without a valid pass, and 212, forbidding Africans from remaining in the Municipality for more than
thirty-six hours, excluding Sundays and public holidays, without

employment, unless they had the required visitors' or residents' permit.[103] The argument for these by-laws is contained in the *Feetham Commission Report* (1927): "A municipal body which is responsible for providing locations and housing for natives within its area must be protected from having its obligations made unduly onerous owing to the presence in its area of natives who have no legitimate reason for remaining there."[104]

Since a surplus of labor benefited employers in Nairobi, the pass system was not really enforced until 1950 when the Voluntary Unemployed Persons' Ordinance was enacted, under which unemployed men could live in Nairobi only seven days.[105] Nevertheless, despite strong police action in Nairobi in the two or three years prior to the Emergency, the number of homeless transient Africans in Nairobi was estimated to have been 10,000 by the Member for Law and Order in 1952 because "as fast as they returned them as vagrants to the Reserves the faster they flocked back in again."[106] During the Emergency, however, especially during the years 1953 to 1957, Africans in Nairobi, particularly the Kikuyu/Embu/Meru tribesmen, were strictly controlled. To stay in Nairobi, they generally had to show that they had paid their poll tax. If they were found in the city looking for a job without evidence of having paid this tax, they were liable to arrest and imprisonment. Of course, those without jobs could not pay the tax. It was, in the words of Gatheru, "a confusingly vicious cycle."[107]

## Conclusion

Despite the difficulties which they encountered in Nairobi, the number of African inhabitants significantly grew over the years. By 1952 Nairobi's African population was believed to be about 95,000, which was at least twice what it had been ten years earlier.[108] Africans then consisted of about 60 per cent of the entire population. However, lack of housing and security for Africans in Nairobi retarded their urbanization and thus hindered the educational process that usually accompanies urbanization.

It is estimated that over 60 per cent of the Africans in Nairobi were merely temporary residents before the Mau Mau rebellion.[109]

The 1954 *Report of the Committee on African Wages* (the Carpenter Report) pointed out that only 20 per cent of African employees had a record of service in their jobs of more than two years. Consequently, few employees stayed long enough in a job to become skilled and, thereby, to earn above the prescribed minimum wage. This wage, the Carpenter Report emphasized, was insufficient for a single man, and much more so, for a family: "We have to face up to the fact that, for the great majority of the urban African labour force, married life is at present only obtainable at the sacrifice of health and decency."[110]

"There are very few Africans in Nairobi at the moment who have more than one meal per day, very few indeed," argued Eliud Mathu in the Legislative Council in December, 1948, in opposing the Native Poll Tax (Municipalities) Bill, which was intended to discourage the influx of Africans by making taxes for them higher in the urban than the rural areas.[111] Although the minimum wage in Nairobi rose from 38 shillings a month in 1947 to 56/50 shillings (about $8.00) in 1952, this increase was practically negated by the rising cost of living.[112] An important contributing factor here was that *posho* or maize meal, the basis of the African diet, went up nearly 800 per cent in price between 1939 and 1953 because of the alleged "scandalous" price-fixing policies of the Maize Control Board.[113]

The difficulty of life in Nairobi for most African workers caused them to keep their wives and children in the rural areas. In 1958 the male-female ratio in Nairobi was reported to be three-to-one (and before 1945, nine-to-one).[114] This intensified the migrant-labor system which, in the words of Nairobi's Medical Officer of Health in 1955: ". . . tended to foster instability among the labourers, to encourage the development of shanty dwellings, to give rise to prostitution and generally to produce the conditions which had reached their worst at the beginning of the emergency."[115] The implications of this situation are clearly revealed in the *East African Royal Commission Report:*

> Under the existing system the organic growth of towns is impossible. Whereas urban growth in the United Kingdom and else-

where has been on the whole a spontaneous process whereby the administrative area of the town has been enlarged after a new area has become urbanized, in East Africa it has been a process of rolling back the African population in the interests of urban communities which have been until now predominately non-African. This, more than any other single factor, has retarded the growth of a settled urban population able to regard the towns with pride as places to which they belong. Instead, they look upon them with jealousy as non-African centres from which they are excluded.[116]

The European settlers, for all their mistakes, had gradually transformed Nairobi into one of the most beautiful cities of the world. It was a city with wide avenues, lined with flowery bushes and waving palm trees, with lovely parks and gardens, and with smart shops and handsome multistoried buildings. It would be wrong to say that Africans on the whole did not appreciate the beauty of Nairobi, but it remained for them an alien place — a part of Europe (and to some extent, Asia) but not of Africa. With the receding of colonialism, Africans finally had the opportunity to possess Nairobi not only politically but also economically, socially, and culturally, thereby inculcating a certain liveliness — a real vitality and character — which it never had as a "settler capital."

## NOTES

1. A. W. Southall, "The Growth of Urban Society," in Stanley Diamond and Fred G. Burke, *The Transformation of East Africa* (New York and London: Basic Books, 1966), p. 467.
2. Cf. George Bennett, *Kenya: A Political History* (London: Oxford U. Press, 1963), ch. I.
3. Carl G. Rosberg, Jr. and John Nottingham, *The Myth of Mau Mau* (New York: Praeger, 1966), p. 23.
4. Dr. E. Boedecker, *The Early History of Nairobi Township* (Kabete: Original Manuscript, 1936), p. 1.
5. Elspeth Huxley, *The Flame Trees of Thika / Memories of An African Childhood* (Harmondsworth, Middlesex: Penguin Books Ltd., 1959), p. 238.

6. *British Policy in Kenya Colony* (New York: Thomas Nelson & Sons, 1937), p. 275.

7. Cf. M. P. K. Sorrenson, *Land Reform in the Kikuyu Country* (Nairobi: Oxford U. Press, 1967), pp. 16-17. The apparent paucity of Africans in the Kenya Highlands at this time may have resulted from an accidental combination of inter-tribal warfare, disease, drought, and locusts.

8. Dilley, *op. cit.*, p. 13. Also important in this regard was the 1908 "Elgin Pledge," prohibiting the sale of land in the uplands to Asians.

9. Cf. Norman Leys, *A Last Chance in Kenya* (London: Hogarth Press, 1931), p. 10.

10. Quoted, Richard K. P. Pankhurst, *Kenya: The History of Two Nations* (London: Independent Publishing Co., 1964?), p. 43. In contrast to the settlers in Southern Rhodesia, who gained internal self-government in 1923, those in Kenya were relatively few in number at this time. Moreover, there were far fewer Asians to contend with in Southern Rhodesia. Thus, a common roll that was theoretically non-racial could be used for elections there without threatening European control.

11. Quoted, Bennett, *op. cit.*, p. 22.

12. Quoted, Dilley, *op. cit.*, p. 49.

13. Bennett, *op. cit.*, pp. 39-40.

14. Cf. Elspeth Huxley, *Whiteman's Country: Lord Delamere and the Making of Kenya,* Vol. II (London: Macmillan & Co., 1935), p. 88.

15. Leys, *op. cit.*, p. 11.

16. *Kenya from Within* (London: George Allen & Unwin, 1927), p. 311.

17. Dilley, *op. cit.*, pp. 176-77; Rosberg and Nottingham, *op. cit.*, p. 323.

18. Cf. Mary Parker, *Political and Social Aspects of the Development of Municipal Government in Kenya with Special Reference to Nairobi* (London: Colonial Office, 1948?), pp. 210-254. This is the best source of information for the history of Nairobi prior to World War II.

19. Cf. Richard Woodley, "City in the Sun, Niarobi from 1950 to Today," *Kenya Weekly News,* December 13, 1963, pp. 23-25.

20. Justice Feetham, Chairman, *Report of the Local Government*

*Commission,* 1927, Vol. I, *Nairobi and Its Environs, Mombasa and Its Environs* (London: Colonial Office, 1927), p. 6.

21. *Ibid.,* p. 53.
22. *Ibid.,* pp. 54-55.
23. Quoted, Parker, *op. cit.,* p. 213.
24. *Ibid.,* p. 218.
25. *Ibid.,* pp. 232-33.
26. Commissioner for Local Government, *Report for the Year 1946,* pp. 3-4.
27. *Op. cit.,* p. 239.
28. *Op. cit.,* p. 252. The entire chapter (pp. 248-274) is here relevant.
29. Cf. Leys, *op. cit.,* pp. 93-96; Dilley, *op. cit.,* pp. 182-83.
30. Cf. D. H. Rawcliffe, *The Struggle for Kenya* (London: Victor Gollancz, Ltd., 1954), p. 167; J. E. Goldthorpe, *Outlines of East African Society* (Kampala, Uganda: Makerere College, the University College of East Africa, 1958), pp. 248-277.
31. Rosberg and Nottingham, *op. cit.,* pp. 203-7.
32. *Ibid.,* p. 22. The authors suggest that this figure of "50%" given by Norman Leys might be too high.
33. *Op. cit.,* pp. 262-67.
34. *East African Standard,* March 3, 1956. (Hereafter referred to by the initials E.A.S.)
35. *Op. cit.,* p. 106.
36. Cf. H. S. Potter, *Some Aspects of the Development of Kenya Government Services for the Benefit of Africans from 1946 Onwards* (Nairobi: Government Printer, 1953), p. 2; Goldthorpe, *op. cit.,* p. 263.
37. F. D. Corfield, *The Origin and Growth of Mau Mau; An Historical Survey* (Colony and Protectorate of Kenya: Sessional Paper No. 5, 1959/1960), p. 25.
38. Rupert Emerson, *From Empire to Nation* (Boston: Beacon Press, 1960), p. 49.
39. *Op. cit.,* p. 3.
40. Quoted, Pankhurst, *op. cit.,* pp. 19-20.
41. By Ainsworth and Hobley, quoted, Sorrenson, *op. cit.,* p. 27.
42. *White Africans* (London: Faber & Faber, 1955), p. 43.
43. *Ibid.,* pp. 41-42.
44. Quoted, Pankhurst, *op. cit.,* pp. 19-20.
45. *Op. cit.,* pp. 30-31.

46. Goldthorpe, *op. cit.,* p. 162.
47. *The New Societies of Tropical Africa* (London: Oxford U. Press, 1962), p. 25.
48. Cf. Lucy Mair, *New Nations* (London: Weidenfeld & Nicholson, 1963), pp. 194-227.
49. Sir F. D. (later Lord) Lugard, *The Dual Mandate in Tropical Africa,* 3rd ed. (Edinburgh & London: Blackwood, 1926), pp. 79-80.
50. *Op. cit.,* pp. 157-58.
51. Rosberg and Nottingham, *op. cit.,* p. 143.
52. Cmd. 9475 (London: Her Majesty's Stationery Office, 1955), p. p. 201.
53. E.A.S., January 24-25, 1955.
54. Speech to the Nairobi Municipal Council. Quoted, E.A.S., July 28, 1943.
55. Cf. G. C. W. Ogilvie, *The Housing of Africans in the Urban Areas of Kenya* (Nairobi: The Kenya Information Office, 1946), pp. 13-14.
56. Cf. Parker, *op. cit.,* p. 76.
57. *Report,* p. 23.
58. Cf. W. Bestwick and A. H. Brazier, *Report on the Control and Management of the Nairobi City Council's African Housing Rental Estates* (Nairobi: City Hall, April 11, 1958), p. 102.
59. Submitted to the Native Affairs Committee of the Municipal Council of Nairobi on April 30, 1941.
60. Quoted, A. T. G. Thomas, "Some of the Practical Problems About African Housing," E.A.S., January 24-25, 1955.
61. Ogilvie, *op. cit.,* p. 17.
62. F. W. Carpenter, chairman, *Report of the Committee on African Wages* (Nairobi: Government Printer, 1954), p. 95.
63. Ogilvie, *op. cit.,* pp. 13-14.
64. *Op. cit.,* p. 123.
65. (London: Routledge & Kegan Paul Ltd., 1964), pp. 73-74.
66. Quoted, James Smart, *A Jubilee History of Nairobi* (Nairobi: East African Standard, 1950), p. 21.
67. Feetham Commission Report, *op. cit.,* p. 9.
68. Cf. L. W. Thornton White, L. Silberman, P. R. Anderson, *Nairobi: Master Plan for a Colonial Capital* (London: Her Majesty's Stationery Office, 1948), p. 65.

69. *Op. cit.,* p. 486.
70. *Op. cit.,* p. 68.
71. Quoted, Smart, *op. cit.,* pp. 32-33.
72. Parker, *op. cit.,* p. 239.
73. Feetham Commission Report, *op. cit.,* pp. 24-25.
74. E.A.S., September 24, 1951.
75. Leg. Co., *Debates,* June 1, 1960, cc. 1133-34.
76. *Ibid.,* c. 1183.
77. Cf. 1941 "Report of the Senior Medical Officer of Health and the Municipal Native Affairs Officer," p. 5.
78. *Report of the Kenya Land Commission* (Nairobi: Government Printer, 1933), p. 165.
79. Parker, *op. cit.,* p. 110.
80. Leg. Co., *Debates,* April 14, 1955, c. 140.
81. *Op. cit.,* p. 37.
82. *Op. cit.,* p. 75.
83. *Op. cit.,* p. 209.
84. *Op. cit.,* p. 61.
85. *Ibid.,* p. 64. Figure for number of traders given on p. 19.
86. Superintendent of Locations, *Annual Report on African Affairs in Nairobi,* 1947, p. 4.
87. *Op. cit.,* pp. 25-26.
88. *Op. cit.,* p. 72.
89. *So Rough a Wind* (London: Weidenfeld & Nicholson, 1964), p. 207.
90. *Op. cit.,* p. 248.
91. Parker, *op. cit.,* p. 85.
92. Southall, *op. cit.,* p. 475.
93. *East African Royal Commission Report, op. cit.,* pp. 212-13.
94. *Ibid.,* p. 230.
95. *Report on African Housing in Townships and Trading Centres* (Nairobi: Colony and Protectorate of Kenya, April, 1950), p. 23.
96. E.A.S., September 17, 1955.
97. *Op. cit.,* p. 247.
98. Southall, *op. cit.,* p. 475.
99. Cf. *The Sunday Post,* December 8, 1963, p. 41.
100. John Nottingham, "The Development of Local Government in Kenya," p. 16. (An unpublished article.) The chiefs here referred to were not "chiefs" in the traditional sense but, rather, Africans

who seemed to have a certain amount of prestige among their people together with enough ability, education, or experience to be useful to the government.

101. *Report, op. cit.,* p. 234.
102. E.A.S., May 28, 1959.
103. Cf. S. and M. Aaronovitch, *Crisis in Kenya* (London: Lawrence & Wishart, 1946), p. 120.
104. *Op. cit.,* p. 153.
105. *Annual Report on African Affairs in Nairobi,* 1950, p. 2.
106. Rosberg and Nottingham, *op. cit.,* p. 239.
107. *Op. cit.,* p. 76.
108. Rosberg and Nottingham, *op. cit.,* p. 69.
109. R. E. Wraith, *East African Citizen* (London: Oxford U. Press, 1959), p. 108.
110. *Op. cit.,* p. 14.
111. *Debates,* December 20, 1948, c. 508.
112. Sorrenson, *op. cit.,* p. 85.
113. Cf. Rawcliffe, *op. cit.,* p. 102.
114. Cf. City Council of Nairobi, *Annual Report of the Social Services and Housing Committee,* 1958, p. 22; Parker, *op. cit.,* p. 98.
115. E.A.S., January 24-25, 1955.
116. *Op. cit.,* p. 222.

# 3 THE POLITICAL TRANSITION
# OF NAIROBI

## Introduction

Much of the plight of Africans in Nairobi prior to the independence of Kenya stemmed from their limited influence upon public policy. It was not until 1944 that an African was appointed to the Legislative Council (three others being nominated by Government in 1948); and no African was appointed to the Executive Council until 1951 or elected to the Legislature until 1957. The Nairobi City Council was even slower than the Central Government to give Africans adequate representation.

Because the institutional structure of the Nairobi City Council was determined by the Kenya Legislative Council, Africans had to gain power at the national level before they could do so in Nairobi. Consequently, it is necessary to understand political developments in Kenya as a whole in order to understand occurrences in Nairobi. We will therefore interrelate the political history of Kenya with that of Nairobi, focusing on the national scene before looking at developments in Nairobi itself.

## The Progress of Race-relations in Kenya

Very early, the Asians challenged the control exercised by the European settlers and the racial discrimination that went with it.

They were therefore considered by Europeans, until at least the end of the Second World War, as the chief threat to their domination.

The Asians, mostly from the Indian states of Bombay (or what is now Gujarat) and Punjab, had for a long time traded along the East African coast, but their penetration inland came with the building of the railroad at the beginning of the twentieth century. They functioned initially as "coolies" and later as merchants.[1] Thereafter, their population rapidly increased, attracted as they were by the favorable economic opportunities and geographical conditions of East Africa. By 1911 there were 11,886 Asians in Kenya, as against 3,167 European settlers; and this approximate three-to-one ratio of Asians to Europeans more or less persisted.

As the political power of the European settlers expanded, the rivalry between the two races intensified. The Asians were especially opposed to the 1919 arrangement, under which the European settlers were allowed two seats on the Executive Council and eleven elected representatives on the Legislative Council, compared to a mere two nominated members for the Asians. They were also resentful of the "white highlands," the increasing pattern of urban segregation, and the threat to restrict Asian immigration.

The arguments used against sharing political power with Africans could not so readily be used with regard to Asians. Since the aggregate wealth of the Asians, based on their increasingly important commercial position, surpassed by 1919 that of the Europeans, the contention often used by the European settlers that taxation and political power should go together ("no taxation without representation") could easily be redirected against them.[2] Likewise, the educational advantage possessed by Europeans was not large enough to support their case. It is significant in this regard that in 1919 a proposed amendment to the voting laws, suggesting that certain selected Indians of approved university standing should be added to the voting rolls, was contemptuously rejected.[3] A common roll based partly on education, as contained in the Wood-Winterton proposals of 1922, was vehemently opposed by the Government of Kenya in support of the European contention that the acceptance of the principle of election on a common roll, regardless of safeguards, would inevitably lead to Indian domination.[4]

Lacking rational arguments for denying to Asians the civil rights they demanded for themselves, the settlers vented their fears in other ways. As early as 1906 an anti-Indian propaganda campaign was initiated, led by a small group of settlers from South Africa, arguing that Indian competition would force up land prices and lead to "Asiatic domination."[5] This animosity towards the Asians frequently took the paternalistic guise presented in the 1919 final report of the Economic Commission, composed of Lord Delamere, Major Grogan, and a number of other militant settlers. Among the accusations herein contained were: "Physically the Indian is not a wholesome influence because of his incurable repugnance to sanitation and hygiene. In this respect the African is more civilized than the Indian, being naturally clean in his ways; but he is prone to follow the example of those around him." Moreover, the "moral depravity of the Indian is equally damaging to the African, who in his natural state is at least innocent of the worst vices of the East. The Indian is the inciter to crime as well as vice, since it is the opportunity offered by the everready Indian receivers which makes thieving easy." Therefore, concluded the Report: "It is our firm conviction that the justification of our occupation of this country lies in our ability to adapt the native to our civilization. If we further complicate this task by continuing to expose the African to the antagonistic influence of the Asiatic, as distinct from European, philosophy, we shall be guilty of a breach of trust."[6]

"There never had been heard, inside or outside Kenya," notes R. K. P. Pankhurst regarding this period, "so much outspoken advocacy of the welfare of the 'native' as when the Indians were being attacked!"[7] This argument that Asians were potentially a threat to the progress of Africans was put forward most forcefully by the Bishop of Uganda in 1923:

> While the Indians have created trade facilities, they have also brought into their (the Africans') midst a very undesirable class, whose influence has been bad, and who have made money at their expense. The African today naturally asks: Why should this alien race hold the monopoly of trade in our country, and trade as we ourselves can be trained to carry on? The presence of the Indian,

while not a good influence [*sic*], has retarded the development of the African, which contrasts with that of his near neighbors in Uganda, who have learned to carry on their own trade.[8]

The need to protect the interests of the Africans, here so benignly acknowledged by the European settlers, was eagerly seized upon by the British government in 1923. This is the basis for the famous "paramountcy of native interests" decision in the White Paper by the Duke of Devonshire:

> Primarily, Kenya is an African territory, and his Majesty's Government think it necessary definitely to record their considered opinion that the interests of the African natives must be paramount, and that if and when those interests and the interests of the immigrant races should conflict, the former should prevail. Obviously the interests of the other communities, European, Indian, or Arab must severely be safeguarded. . . . But in the administration of Kenya His Majesty's Government regard themselves as exercising a trust on behalf of the African population, and they are unable to delegate or share this trust, the object of which may be defined as the protection and advancement of the native races.[9]

The full implications of the 1923 White Paper were not realized by the European settlers as a whole for several years. Of more immediate significance to them was the fact that for the time being the political ambitions of the Asian community had been rebuffed. As time went on, however, the threatening nature of the "paramountcy of native interests" decision was recognized, and the settlers began to search for an alternative formula to soothe the fears of the British government while safeguarding their interests. This is the origin of the "dual policy," which was invented to secure the Europeans against the Africans just as the doctrine of "paramountcy" had supposedly secured them against the Indians.[10]

The "dual policy," as set forth in the White Paper of 1927, first of all, recognized the permanence of European settlement as well as the numerical dominance of the African population, as emphasized by the 1923 White Paper. Secondly, it suggested that the welfare of Africans was not the exclusive responsibility of British agents but rather the joint responsibility of settler and Imperial representatives.[11] The idea of the "paramountcy of native interests" was not, however, completely forgotten, at least in theory, and it was brought up again, to the intense annoyance of the settlers, by the 1929 report of the Hilton Young Commission and, the next year, by the Labor Government's *Memorandum on Native Policy in East Africa* (also known as the Passfield Report).

The key words of the 1930 *Memorandum* were incorporated into its opening statement; the members of His Majesty's Government "fully accept the principle that the relation of His Majesty's Government to the native populations of East Africa is one of trusteeship which cannot be devolved, and from which they cannot be relieved. The ultimate responsibility for the exercise of this trusteeship must accordingly rest with them alone."[12] It went on to emphasize:

> that the creation and preservation of a field for the full development of native life is a first charge on any territory, and that the Government having created this field in the establishment of an organized governmental administration of the modern type has the duty to devote its energies to assisting the natives to make the best possible use of the opportunities open to them.[13]

Despite the reassurance of the Passfield Report that its stress on "paramountcy of native interests" was not in any way incompatible with the prosperity of the immigrant communities, there was a bitter outcry against the Report on the part of the European settlers. This stress on "native interests" might be an acceptable policy when directed against Asians, but not when used against Europeans.[14] Yet, for the mass of the African population, these arguments over the meaning of the various Government proclamations were almost totally devoid of significance, lacking any apparent impact on the policies actually carried out. This was also true of the policy of "racial partnership" (or "multi-racialism," as it was called in Kenya), so widely proclaimed during the 1950's.

The settler leader most closely associated in Kenya after 1954 with the idea of multi-racialism was Michael Blundell (now Sir Michael). In his autobiography, *So Rough a Wind,* Blundell discusses the concept of multi-racialism which he had slowly and painfully evolved in an effort to end the Emergency through a program that would elicit the support of the entire country:

> I was fortified in this belief by my liking for my colleagues of other races in the Legislative Council and my dislike of such stupidities as the colour bar and the arrogance which dictated that only Europeans were capable of bringing civilized progress to Africa. It seemed to me that anyone, whatever his colour, who had accepted the ideas and standards which we were trying to plant in Africa should be accepted as an equal in the task. I was supported in these beliefs by a number of my colleagues; out of our ideas grew the concept of a Kenya nation which would gradually dismantle the old racial barriers and compartments, and be supported by men of all races with the same civilized standards.[15]

Whatever its theoretical merits, multi-racialism as a policy was destined to be frustrated by a number of factors, chief of which was the refusal of the overwhelming majority of the European settlers to surrender the idea of Kenya as a "white man's country." Consequently, it was a matter of too little and too late. By 1958 African nationalism, with its appealing cry of "one man, one vote," had become an overwhelming force, burying not only any idea of special privileges for Europeans but also Blundell's vague hope of "multi-racialism."

### Emerging African Nationalism

While the political domination of the settlers ultimately gave way to African nationalism, European rule was so exercised as to retard and hamper the development of a sense of common purpose and loyalty among Kenyan Africans. Government policy in a number of ways discouraged intertribal contact and cooperation. The failure to facilitate the urbanization of Africans and the development of a prosperous African rural population, able to work together within a market economy, must be reiterated here. The number of Kenyan Africans living in towns of over 2,000 has always remained below 10 per cent of the nearly nine million in the country (as of the 1962 census); and many of them have never stayed in a town for any considerable length of time. This is true despite the fact that by 1946, African wage labor was no longer predominately agricultural.[16]

The slowness of Africans to become urbanized made it very difficult for them to organize a nationalist movement that would arouse the masses in every section of the country. Thus, until 1960, African political activity in most parts of Kenya can be considered, first of all, largely tribal in character and, secondly, directed more to rural than to urban conditions. This was true of such organizations as the Kikuyu Central Association, the Kikuyu Provincial Association, and the Kavirondo Taxpayers' Welfare Association which arose during the 1920's and 1930's. What efforts there were to form a nationalist movement (one that went beyond mere protest against Government policy to the creation of a viable state) were largely frustrated.

Furthermore, the Government, by dividing and maintaining the land on a tribal basis through a system of tribal reserves, reinforced the tribal orientation of the Africans. This was the purpose and effect of the 1933 Carter Land Commission report, explain Rosberg and Nottingham: "to institutionalize the tribally and racially organized land system that had gradually developed in Kenya since the turn of the century."[17]

It was the view of Governor Mitchell, as stated in 1951, that "the major problem in Kenya and East Africa generally is social and agrarian and not nationalistic."[18] His refusal to recognize the emergence of African nationalism stemmed from his opinion that it was an "emotional movement" without rational policies, led by "educated" men "with the sort of education our children have by the time that they are 12 years of age."[19] The most that he was prepared to allow was the participation of Africans in public affairs through election to the Local Native Councils. This was the proposal made to Jomo Kenyatta, upon his return from London in 1947, but it was rejected. "Even if the L.N.C.'s had increased in importance since then," George Bennett points out, "no really effective national leader could accept to be buried thus."[20]

When the Kenya African Union (founded in 1944 as the Kenya African Study Union to replace the Kikuyu Central Association that had been banned in 1940) threatened to become a nationally oriented party, it was continually harrassed by the Government until finally in June, 1953, it was proscribed. The original stimulus for the KAU was the introduction in 1944 of an African in the Legislative Council. The system created for nominating Africans to the Legislative Council included a hierarchy of nominative committees, composed of Africans from the various Local Native Councils. While having some merit, the system did "operate (as it was intended to do) to discourage the emergence of any African electoral organization, so that there was a sharp distinction between the process of choosing African members of the Legislative Council and the beginnings of African party organizations."[21]

From 1952 to 1956 political activity was largely confined to trade unions and tribal welfare associations. It was the hope of the Government, through its Emergency powers, to control the pattern and pace of African political activity.[22] Until June 1955, African political organizations and independent newspapers were prohibited, and, until 1960, African political organizations formed on a colony-wide basis were disallowed. Summarizing the impact of this refusal to allow national parties from 1953 to 1960, Mboya concluded: "We have never been able to escape completely from the district consciousness which developed during this period. No other country under British rule has started off with such difficulties in forming a national movement as we faced after the Emergency."[23]

In the absence of a national party, political unity was dependent upon the cooperation of the African Elected Members. Though an appearance of unity was sometimes maintained, it was often undermined by conflicting personality, ambition, outlook, and tribal background.[24] The election of Africans to the Legislative Council in March 1957, under the restricted franchise introduced by the Coutts Constitution, accelerated formation of a number of district associations. Though most of these district associations were politically insignificant, they were, according to Mboya, considered "a threat to national unity, because we could see district loyalties building up and reflecting tribal loyalties (since district and tribal boundaries were often the same)."[25]

## The Intensified Challenge to Colonialism

The difficulties of forming a nationalist movement in Kenya were complicated by the extraordinary heterogeneity of the African population, being divided according to cultural or linguistic categories (Bantu, Nilotic, Hamitic, and Nilo-Hamitic) as well as by tribe (Kikuyu, Luo, Kamba, Luyia, to name only the larger ones), with considerable diversity of language, organizational systems, historical experience, and ways of life among them.[26] Even when groups appear to be similar in origin, traditional social and political structure, or language (such as the Kikuyu and the Kamba), they may see themselves as being quite distinct.[27]

For a long time there has been keen competition for the relatively scarce fertile land existing in the country. This was intensified not only by the coming of Europeans but also by the fact that, while most of the land of Kenya is claimed by the Hamitic and Nilo-Hamitic peoples, most of the inhabitants (over 70 per cent) are Bantu. These Bantu emerged as densely populated clusters in the midst of their nomadic neighbors — a situation that has not been conducive to either easy inter-tribal communication or peaceful coexistence. Moreover, the Coastal Swahili (a mixture of Bantu and Arabic) culture never penetrated far enough inland to give Kenya the degree of underlying unity existing in Tanganyika.[28] Therefore, a large portion of the population cannot speak Swahili, the language of the multi-tribal urban areas, much less English, the language of the educated. In addition, most of the tribes have traditionally been very disunited, lacking a chieftaincy or any centralized system of authority. Since the social structure of the Kenya tribes has been largely restricted to the clan level, cooperation on a tribal basis has been almost as difficult to achieve as on a multi-tribal basis.

Kenya, like most African countries, has been affected by the fact that the urbanization, industrialization, Westernization process has taken place in such a way as to create different levels or rates of development. Therefore, here as elsewhere, those in the sparsely populated rural areas and those not yet much influenced by the market economy and the Western system of education feared domination by the groups that were likely to gain control with the transfer of power. To be more specific, the fear in Kenya was of the Kikuyu and, to a lesser extent, the Luo.

There are a number of reasons why the Kikuyu were earlier and more intensively aroused for political action than the other tribes of Kenya. First of all, they constitute the largest tribe in the country, having a population in excess of 1.6 million (based on the 1962 Census), which is about 20 per cent of the total African population. Secondly, their organization, including an age-grade system, possibly facilitated a greater degree of unity than that possessed by the other tribes of the country.[29] A much more obvious explanation, however, has to do with the extent and nature of interaction with the European settlers.

Beginning with the British East Africa Company in the 1890's, the contact of the Kikuyu with the Europeans was persistent, painful, and disruptive. The capital city, Nairobi, was on the edge of the Kikuyu tribal reserve. Thus, soon after the First World War, the Kikuyu became the largest African element in Nairobi, overtaking the Swahili people from the Coast. By 1948 the Kikuyu constituted 42 per cent of Nairobi's African population. Prior to the Emergency, most of the 200,000 Africans who worked and lived in the White Highlands were Kikuyu. Many adult Kikuyu males did military service during both World Wars, and these veterans played a large role in the political agitation that followed.

While many Kenyan tribes lost an undetermined amount of land to European settlement, the most disturbing proved to be the 109 fertile square miles lost by the Kikuyu population, as estimated by the 1933 Kenya Land Commission Report. The most valuable part of the alienated land (23 square miles) was in Kiambu, where the Kikuyu population was even in 1902 estimated to have been 150 to the square mile.[30] As the population expanded, this land was increasingly coveted, particularly by Kikuyu who were working or squatting during the 1940's within the boundaries of the Highlands. No other cause agitated the urban as well as the rural Kikuyus so much as the return of the "stolen lands."[31] All other grievances were subordinated to that of land hunger, intensified as it was not only by growing population pressures in the rural areas, but also by the existing insecurity in the urban areas.

Another possibility is that the Kikuyu were more upset than other tribes by the impact of Western civilization upon their social organization and way of life.[32] Particularly resented was the opposition of the missionaries (largely directed by the Church of Scotland) to female circumcision and polygamy. When the Kikuyu who supported these practices were denied access to the churches, or, more important, to the schools maintained by these churches, they began to form their own churches and schools. These later played an important part in the uprising of the 1950's. In this and other ways, many Kikuyu sought to offset the erosion of their indigenous culture by the current forces of social change.

Because the Kikuyu were more politically conscious than the other tribes of Kenya, they tended to dominate the African political organizations that arose prior to the Emergency of the 1950's. Jomo Kenyatta, who took over the leadership of the then newly formed Kenya African Union soon after his return to Kenya from Britain in 1947, sought to create a national movement, paralleling the efforts of his friend Nkrumah in the Gold Coast. Although he visited throughout the country, particularly Nyanza, and tried to keep non-Kikuyu prominent in the KAU, he was not completely successful. The discouragement of the Government was only part of the problem. More important, Kenyatta and the other leaders of the KAU simply could not divorce themselves from the rural interests then uppermost in the minds of the Kikuyu people. The other tribes (except for the ethnically related Embu and Meru) were neither prepared nor aroused enough to follow their lead, though they were inevitably stirred by what was being done.[33]

During the period of intense agitation between 1950 and 1952, mostly Kikuyu appeared to be involved in the violence that came to be associated with the so-called "Mau Mau" movement. In the process, a certain amount of intimidation of non-Kikuyu Africans took place, doubtlessly provoked by the use of mostly Kamba, Kipsigi, and Kalenjin tribesmen as soldiers and policemen. In Nairobi, Asians and moderate African leaders were also attacked, culminating in the assassination of Chief Waruhiu and Tom Mbotela in 1952. The serious weakness of the Mau Mau movement was revealed; based on an "oath of secrecy," it appealed to the Kikuyu but could not be used to build a mass trans-tribal party.

The period of the Emergency restrictions, from 1952 to 1960, caused almost traumatic anguish and upheaval for the Africans of Kenya. Especially hard pressed were the Kikuyu, Embu, and Meru in Nairobi, half of whom were removed from the city, with Kamba and Nyanza peoples largely replacing them.[34] The Kikuyu/Embu/Meru who were allowed to remain were placed in separate locations and strictly controlled by means of a curfew and passbook system. Africans generally were restricted in their movements, but none so long or so systematically as the Kikuyu.

Under the circumstances, political leadership in Nairobi (and, thereby, Kenya as a whole) passed to non-Kikuyu, the most prominent being a Luo, Tom Mboya, who, like Kenyatta, began his career as an employee of the Nairobi City Council. His success as a trade union leader in Kenya was unprecedented, partly because of the existing labor shortage in Nairobi, which was cleverly used for political objectives. In 1957 he entered the Legislative Council as the African Member for Nairobi, defeating Clement Arwings-Kodhek who, after the lifting of the prohibition on African political activity (see page 75), had formed the Kenya African District Congress (changed to the Nairobi African District Congress when its earlier name was refused registration for having too "national" a connotation).

The 1957 election (based on the Coutts Constitution) was of great importance in the development of African nationalism, even though the extremely complicated franchise allowed only about 10 per cent of those of voting age to register and though political meetings were relatively unpublicized and limited to about 600 (the number that could get into the designated halls).[35] It meant, according to Michael Blundell, that: "All the African members who had entered Legislative Council by nomination through the old electoral college system were swept away, and in their place stood men who were conscious of representing their people for the first time. . . . The wall protecting us from the sea was breached, and the waters of African nationalism were pouring in around us."[36]

After this election, Mboya formed the Nairobi People's Convention Party (the PCP), which adopted a "cell-type" organization to survive efforts of the government to outlaw it. "We introduced to Kenya the idea of women's and youth wings," writes Mboya, "and it was one of the most effective and disciplined youth wings Kenya has known."[37] It was this organization that Mboya used both to spread his influence beyond Nairobi (particularly through the periodical *Uhuru*) and to agitate for constitutional change. Those who disregarded the instructions of the PCP, such as the Nairobi City Councillor Musa Amalemba, in agreeing to cooperate with Europeans and Asians under the 1957 Lennex-Boyd Constitution, were discredited.

Though the PCP was never allowed to become a national party and though it eventually merged with the Kenya African National Union, it was most useful in providing an urban-based, trans-tribal foundation for African nationalism in Kenya. The explanation for the Party's success, according to Mboya's biographer, Alan Rake, was its emphasis upon urban issues. "Unlike many other Kenya parties based on tribal and rural loyalties, the PCP was a party of urban workers, drawn from all tribes and held together by a good organization and by loyalty to Tom Mboya's brilliant leadership."[38]

In 1958, with the easing of restrictions on the movement of Kikuyu, Embu, and Meru peoples, many who had been detained or expelled from Nairobi returned. They were naturally resentful of the fact that, during their absence, jobs or positions of leadership that they had held (or might have held) had been taken by non-Kikuyu or "loyalists." Some of this latent hostility was utilized by a group of the more ambitious Kikuyu "intellectuals" and their associates to challenge Mboya's political leadership. Mboya also was faced with the opposition of the leaders of the still largely rural-oriented tribes (in particular, the Nilo-Hamitic peoples).

Towards the end of March 1960 (after the Lancaster House Conference and considerable factional maneuvering among the African leaders), Mboya joined a number of his rivals, including Ngala, Kiano, Odinga, and Arwings-Kodhek, to form the Kenya African National Union (KANU). In opposition to this move (castigated as a Kikuyu-Luo alliance), the Kenya African Democratic Union (KADU) was formed, bringing together a number of previously established tribal or regional groupings (the Kalenjin Political Alliance, the Masai United Front, the Somali National Association, the Kenya African People's Party, and the Coast African People's Union). "Thus urban and rural nationalism had become aligned in two opposed parties to contest the forthcoming elections."[39]

The threat of inter-tribal conflict appeared quite serious during the period leading up to the independence of Kenya. Much of the trouble resulted from the refusal of the Government to release Jomo Kenyatta from detention. It was the hope of KANU to build a nationalist movement with organizational roots reaching the masses throughout the country. But the absence of Kenyatta severely inhibited the formation of such an organization.[40] Consequently, KANU declined to form a government, even though it had won over two-thirds of the popular vote in the 1961 elections and held a nineteen-to-fifteen edge in Legislative Council membership. The refusal of the Government to release Kenyatta not only resulted in the formation of a minority government, but also stimulated the divisive forces inherent in Kenya politics.[41]

KANU, frustrated by the denial of governmental power, showed signs of disintegrating.[42] As it did, all the old bugaboos of tribalism, corruption, and mismanagement came to the fore, especially in Nairobi. Rumors were then widespread of the formation by Kikuyu ex-detainees of a Land Freedom Army to take over the White Highlands by force. The Kipsigis and related tribes were reported at this time to be "sharpening their spears" to go on the warpath. It seemed nothing could prevent a violent intertribal struggle for the "spoils of independence." Only Kenyatta, it was thought, could control the situation; but upon his release in August 1961, he seemed unable to exercise the leadership expected of him.

Despite the uneasy political situation prior to independence, the principle of African majority rule embodied in the 1960 Lancaster House Constitution was firmly established at the national level. However, this principle was not established at the local level. This meant, in the case of Nairobi, that after 1960 the political orientation of the City Council began to sharply diverge from that of the Central Government. The hesitancy of the Central Government to reform the City Council's racial composition in accord with the

Lancaster House Constitution caused the Council to be burdened by severe political tension.

To understand the extent of this political tension, we must go back to the beginnings of African political activity in Nairobi, showing the relationship of local political developments to those at the national level. In the case of Nairobi, the existing political activity had special national significance because of the importance of the city not only as the seat of government, but also as the economic and cultural center of the country. The attempt of Africans to gain greater political power in Nairobi, therefore, helped them to increase their political power in Kenya as a whole. On the other hand, as already indicated, African political control of Nairobi was tied to developments leading to the independence of Kenya.

### Emerging African Participation in Nairobi Politics

The first important African political group to have an impact on Nairobi was the East African Association in 1920, which was composed largely of office boys and domestic servants. While motivated generally by post-war unrest and economic depression, it was specifically directed against the repressive Nairobi by-laws, associated with the pass-system and the required "kipandes" (the small metal identification-discs that had to be worn).[43] The reaction of the government to the agitation of this organization (which culminated in the so-called "Thuku riots") was to deport its leader in 1922 and then to search for ways to bring the Africans into closer contact with Government.

In 1923 Native Village Councils were formed in Pangani and Pumwani (the two African settlements in Nairobi at that time), and in 1926 the Nairobi African Advisory Council was established to channel communication between Africans and Government and, more specifically, to advise on the expenditure of native trust funds. "I have started something in the nature of a Local Native Council composed of twenty leading representatives of the village," stated the Acting Senior Commissioner in a 1926 memorandum to the Nairobi Council, "who meet from time to time and discuss with the District Commissioner and myself matters connected with the Native Villages of Pangani and Pumwani."[44] Prior to this there had been a very informal "baraza" (or council) of elders, consisting of the senior Swahili people (immigrants from the Coast who were the earliest Africans in this area to adapt to urban life) and tribal leaders to represent the up-country laborers.[45]

Initially the Nairobi African Advisory Council (or "Native Advisory Council," as it was first called) was composed of representatives from tribal and religious groups. In 1946, representatives from various functional or occupational associations and from village committees (those set up in the urban locations) were added.[46] Following the suggestion of the African Affairs Officer, the African Advisory Council was changed in 1955 to the African General Ward Council, with representatives chosen entirely on the basis of place of residence rather than on religious, tribal, or occupational affiliation. Its meetings were held in the chamber of the City Council in accordance with British local government procedure, guided by the City's African Affairs Officer. A further evolutionary stage took place in 1958 when representatives to the General Ward Council were elected from their wards rather than chosen by the thirteen village committees (each consisting of twelve elected members) that had been established.

The transformation of the Advisory Council to Ward Council was done in an effort to attract Africans with a wider affiliation and outlook than the particular tribal or occupational groups which had previously been represented. In other words, it was felt by many European observers that Africans on the Advisory Council were supporting the limited interests of their narrow affiliation (particularly traders) rather than Africans as a whole. Moreover, inter-tribal conflict seemed at times to be encouraged, and the more educated, capable Africans, to be ignored. Also wanted were African representatives who would be more receptive to European influence. This was indicated in the 1954 statement of A. C. Small, the Nairobi District Commissioner at this time, alleging that "the record of the African Advisory Council since the Emergency is a poor one. Too many of its members have been detained under the Emergency regulations; too few of these members have joined the security forces and taken up arms against the enemy."[47]

However, both as Advisory Council and as Ward Council, this

government-sponsored agency to channel and placate African political pressure never really proved successful, though it was useful
as a training device and was at times taken seriously by the City
Council.[48] It was never accorded executive powers of any sort or
any control over expenditure of funds. Some of the positions it took
proved to be unpopular, including a 1947 request that the influx of
Africans into Nairobi be controlled and the unemployed be expelled, a 1948 recommendation that African policemen be housed
in the locations to act as village constables, a 1956 proposal that
the poll tax be increased to provide for social services, and a 1960
complaint regarding the allocation to Africans of additional hawkers' licenses. At times, such as during the 1930's, the African Council fell almost completely into disuse because of the apathy of participants. Other organizations, therefore, such as the Nairobi African
Tenants' Association in 1956, attempted to usurp the authority and
function of this supposedly official organ of African opinion.

The relationship between the Advisory Council and the two Africans chosen to be on the Municipal Council was never made clear.
Occasionally, there was lack of communication and even conflict
between them. Whether the African councillors were to act as
"delegates" or "representatives" continued to be a source of confusion. The African councillors were supposed to act as a link between the Advisory Council and the Municipal Council, but they
seldom did so. There was in actual fact very little communication
between the two bodies, according to Mary Parker, writing in 1948:

> Nowhere did I find a lively interest taken by Municipal Council-
> lors in the activities of the African Advisory Councils. The meet-
> ings of the Advisory Councils are open to all, yet some Councillors
> did not even know this, and the majority of Councillors did not
> know how the Advisory Councils were constituted. Spasmodic at-
> tempts have been made, on official suggestion, to keep Municipal
> Councillors in touch with the workings of the Advisory Councils
> and to get them to show some interest in their activities; but it is
> only when faced with resentment by the Advisory Councils be-
> cause some matter in which they were concerned had not been
> referred to them that Municipal Councillors become alive to the
> activities of these bodies.[49]

While this situation improved somewhat with the coming into being of the General Ward Council, it remained unsatisfactory.

The *raison d'etre* of the Nairobi African Advisory Council (and its successor, the Ward Council) was not only to discuss all matters affecting Africans in the urban areas, but also to exercise influence in the enactment of policy. "What the African wants is not principally greater representation," according to Desmond O'Hagan, a Native Court Officer in Kenya writing in 1949, "but greater recognition of the Advisory Council, a greater readiness to respect its views on matters affecting Africans, a greater sympathy in listening to its complaints and more patience in allowing it to discuss changes of policy proposed by the Municipal Council."[50] Yet, the constant pleas of Africans in Nairobi for better living and working conditions, better health and educational facilities, the removal of discriminatory by-laws, and the promotion of Africans to responsible administrative positions continued to go more or less unheeded. Thus, African leaders increasingly turned to other ways of getting what they wanted because, to quote a 1957 speech by Tom Mboya in the Legislative Council: ". . . the African Ward Council cannot in effect be a substitute for the need of Africans to be represented on the City Council of Nairobi. . . ."[51]

In 1958 it was reported by the Town Clerk of Nairobi that the members of the Ward Council were no longer as moderate as they once had been and were spending their time "railing against Government and City Council."[52] This obviously had little effect. In 1962, when the City Council was reminded that the General Ward Council was not even being consulted on matters affecting Africans as had been promised, one of the European councillors scornfully remarked: "We are the masters, not the servants. If we allow ourselves to be so bound down, we shall end up by receiving instructions."[53] Understandably, therefore, the General Ward Council suffered increasingly from apathy and could not get a quorum at many of its committee meetings. By this time, moreover, it no longer appeared to have the respect of Africans. Mboya argued that "there have been aspects of the functions and responsibility of the ward councils which have tended to isolate and discriminate as far as the

African is concerned, sometimes under the guise of giving him a privileged position, but very often having the result of making it impossible for him to be effectively represented at the place which matters, the City Council itself."[54]

From 1946 to 1953 the number of African councillors in Nairobi remained at two. The frustration felt by these two African councillors is indicated by one of their memorandums quoted by Mary Parker in 1948:

> At the moment being only two against an overwhelming majority of Europeans and Indians, our views have little influence, and more particularly as we do not have the sympathy of the European Councillors and Aldermen, who have by far the greatest influence on Council matters. It is our experience that unless we have increased representation, present representation may be of little effect. For this reason we are convinced that it is essential, in the constitutional developments in urban affairs, to consider most seriously the question of increasing African members on the Town Council. African population is rapidly increasing and with it more problems affecting them. To solve these problems African opinion should not be ignored.[55]

The fact that these African councillors were nominated by the Government, on the basis of the Advisory Council's recommendation, made them vulnerable to the charge of being "stooges." This was especially true during the tense period prior to the Emergency when the two nominated Africans became identified with the increasingly repressive police measures supported by the Council to solve the growing housing shortage. "Their participation in the Council's Jubilee celebration," John Nottingham points out, "was the signal for an attempted assassination and one more symbol, to be ignored, of Kenya's malaise."[56] Later, several of the African Council Members gained positions of importance, but this did not really change the over-all situation.

In 1953 the Government agreed to increase by one the number of African City Councillors because "of the growing burden of work."[57] At the same time, the newly formed Nairobi County Council (a completely European body, composed of representatives of the coffee farmers in the outlying areas) was to have two liaison members on the Nairobi City Council, thus offsetting the slight gain in non-European members on the Council. This meant, as Eliud Mathu (the African member of the Legislative Council) was quick to point out, that Africans, comprising 60 per cent of Nairobi's population, were a minority of only 10 per cent in the City Council.[58] But it was then clear that Africans would have to wait until they had increased their political power nationally to gain more power in the City Council. Their frustration, however (as previously mentioned), was intensified when they failed to gain the extent of political power in the Nairobi City Council as in the Legislative Council.

### Rising Inter-racial Conflict Within the City Council

In 1957, Tom Mboya introduced a motion in the Legislative Council "that this Council appoint a select committee to review the method of appointing African representatives and the adequacy of such representation to local government bodies and to make recommendations thereon. . . ."[59] He made it clear that he was concerned with the urban areas, arguing that, in the case of Nairobi, it was unfair to expect the three African councillors to represent 120,000 Africans living in large residential estates on the outskirts of the city, lacking effective means to articulate their interests.[60] The number of African councillors needed to be at least doubled, Mboya argued, and they needed to be elected. "Members to this legislature," he reminded his colleagues, "are directly elected by the Africans, although under a limited or qualified franchise."[61]

In replying to Mboya's motion, the Minister for Local Government, Health and Housing (Mr. Havelock) emphasized the problem of finding Africans who were willing and able to undertake the onerous services without pay which local government entails. In this regard, he noted that "unfortunately, there have been two or three cases in certain councils of Africans who have been appointed to the local authority who have not attended the required number of meetings and, therefore, have been disqualified."[62] He also brought out the old argument that Africans in Nairobi did not contribute enough to the revenue of the City to warrant additional representation. Out of the total rate revenue in Nairobi of £950,000, only £30,000 was collected from the areas of the city where the Africans live.[63]

However, a little later in 1957, Havelock did agree to review the Constitution of Nairobi. He was concerned that "with the great development of the City within the last few years, there may well be a danger of the Council's becoming remote from the people."[64] This would not mean an end to communal representation, he cautioned, because "on the basis of the way of the British government, the feelings of minorities are always highlighted and always should be."[65] While the principle of election to the City Council was acceptable, the administrative problem of drawing up rolls would take a long time.

The years between 1957 and 1963 were particularly difficult for the City Council, making the need for reform appear more urgent. First of all, the City Council was demoralized by a series of scandals that came into the open towards the end of 1955. These had mainly to do with the poor workmanship that was evident in the African housing schemes undertaken by the City Council. While the City Engineer, the City Architect, the Water Engineer, and the Deputy Mayor were directly implicated in these or related matters, all the chief officers and Council members were also indirectly involved. One of the findings of the Rose Commission which investigated these affairs was that racial caucuses were overused:

> In any multi-racial tribunal it is probably inevitable and in itself not objectionable that the various racial groups should meet separately from time to time to consider what their attitudes should be to certain matters subsequently to be debated in open council. This practice is probably not uncommon in countries where multi-racial tribunals exist, and only becomes questionable, we would suggest, if in the case of a majority community the device is used to excess and with the effect of nullifying subsequent discussions in open council.
>
> We would add that unfortunately the indication would seem to suggest that the caucus device is being used to excess in the affairs of the City Council with the effect stated.[66]

The City Council took cognizance of the Rose Commission Report and attempted to meet the criticism of being too racially oriented by formally abolishing racial caucuses. While this eased racial tension to some extent, what eventually happened, according to Alderman E. S. Wilson, was the replacement of racial caucuses by separate meetings of the various races on an unofficial basis.[67] Similarly, the Nairobi Civic Group, formed in 1960 and apparently supported by twenty-eight out of the thirty-five Council members for the purpose of subordinating sectional interests to overall need, proved to be shortlived and insignificant.[68]

There was a period in 1959 when Havelock, who continued to be the Minister responsible for local government, indicated that the necessary reform of the Nairobi City Council was finally going to take place. At a meeting of the Nairobi Study Circle in July 1959, he announced a plan to counter the growing remoteness of local government from the city's residents and their disinterest in civic affairs. "At the local government level we must be prepared to take risks," he exclaimed. "The only way people can be trained for this work is to give them the responsibility and let them learn from their mistakes."[69]

What this plan involved was the setting up of socially harmonious parish councils within the overall jurisdiction of the City Council. In other words, though these parish councils might be elected on a "one man, one vote" basis, they would in effect conform to the pattern of racially segregated residential areas. Their jurisdiction, it was suggested, could be gradually expanded to include most of the city's services. While the City Council would continue to be controlled by those elected on the basis of race, the parish councils could elect a small proportion of members to the "parent" council in such a way as to bring in a non-racial, common-roll aspect.

One week after the Nairobi Study Circle meeting, at which this plan had been broached, it was sharply criticized at a meeting of the Association of Municipalities of East Africa (consisting mostly of the chief officers of the urban local authorities).[70] They argued that the bill embodying Havelock's proposals would give the Minister too much power to control the appointment, pay, and conditions of service of parish council officers and, more generally, too much power to force or prohibit statutory action on the part of the municipal councils. Moreover, the Association concluded, Havelock's plan would lead to the deterioration of local government in the municipalities.

This criticism was advanced a few days later when the "Municipalities (Amendment and Miscellaneous Provisions) Bill" came up for debate in the Legislative Council. R. S. Alexander, a former mayor of Nairobi, then argued that there were not sufficient people with the necessary qualifications in local government to cope with the requirements of the proposed parish councils.[71] At the same time Mboya, speaking for the African legislators, suggested that the parish councils would intensify racial segregation because of the segregated living pattern. More important, they might be used, as had been the case with the African advisory councils, to give the City an excuse for refusing Africans more representation. "We shall not be content with the introduction of parish councils unless we have an effective voice in the parent body," explained Mboya. "The Government should not seek to use this as an alternative to giving the African community an effective say in the parent body."[72]

The hostile reaction to the parish council idea eventually caused it to be eviscerated.[73] Instead of on a mandatory basis, as previously envisaged, the parish councils were to be set up only in areas and in ways approved by the local authorities. As it turned out, very little more was heard about parish councils during the colonial period. Consequently, the Government had to search for a new way to reform the Nairobi City Council.

In June, 1960, Havelock, once again in his capacity as Minister for Local Government and Lands, sent a circular suggesting the constitutional development of municipal government along the lines of the Lancaster House Conference. This would have included a common roll based on income or the worth of property owned or rented as reflected in the amount of rate paid, together with the usual age and residence requirements.[74] "We have tried to follow the principle," argued Havelock, "that those who have made contributions towards the expenses of the local authority concerned with the area in which they live, should be enfranchised, no matter who they are, what race they are, or anything else."[75]

By the time this proposal came up for debate (July, 1961) the Lancaster House Constitution, on which it was based, was already in the process of being changed. A much more drastic type of reform was necessary because, exclaimed Dr. Kiano: "It is unfortunately the situation in this country that the capital city . . . has a form of local government which I consider so archaic and so racial in its composition that if this reconstruction is to take place, the first place should be in Nairobi."[76] In any case, noted Mboya, the proposed franchise qualifications, while stated in non-racial terms, were really racial in their impact.[77]

In April, 1959, the City Council agreed to the election of four African councillors. The franchise was to be restricted to "rateable owners of rateable property," meaning adult residents occupying houses or business premises requiring an annual rent of at least £60 (about $168) or having an income of not less than £15 a month.[78] The African Councillors immediately objected: "The conclusion that we draw is that the number of Africans who would qualify under these stringent rules would be so small that it would not be better than an electoral college."[79] In response to this criticism, the City Council agreed to revise its rules, thereby expanding the number of qualified African voters from between 5,000 and 10,000 to between 15,000 and 20,000.[80] Elections were thereby carried out, and, afterwards in 1960, four African councillors took their seats in the Council chambers; but they very soon began agitating for more fundamental changes in Nairobi's constitution.

In July, 1960, the four newly elected African councillors staged a "walk-out" at the Council meeting in which the mayor and deputy-mayor were to be formally elected, protesting the failure of the Council to conduct itself "in some sort of likeness with what is happening in the country."[81] This point had been stressed by Mboya a little earlier in the year in accusing the City Council of being oblivious to the social and political changes taking place: "They have become so completely drunk with power that they fail to see that other communities are developing . . . so fast that they must be considered in all matters affecting the area which is administered by this local authority."[82] This theme — that "people are assuming greater responsibility in the Central Government long before they assume it in the local areas and in the local councils" — was to be often repeated in the next few years.

Until 1963, however, the Nairobi City Council adamantly refused to accept the common roll desired by the African Councillors or even one patterned after the Lancaster House Constitution (under which fifty-three out of the sixty-five Legislative Council members were elected under a common roll, with literacy for those under forty years of age or an income of £75 *per annum,* being the main franchise requirements). The argument of Nairobi's leaders was that local government in Britain has traditionally been the responsibility of the ratepayers. In the words of one of the European Legislative members: "Local Government is never a replica of parliament anywhere, save in Russia, and in her satellites, and is not run in the same way, although Parliament rightly has a control over it. Local Government is elected by the ratepayers, not by the *hoi poloi,* in that the ratepayers are the people who cough up the money."[83]

In the Legislative Council debate of July, 1961, Odinga and other African legislators attempted to refute this argument by emphasizing that "we should not very much tie ourselves with what is happening in Great Britain, because what is happening in Britain is the result of an evolution which has taken many years."[84] The final word, however, was left to Havelock (the Minister), who reminded Members of their tendency to "call on the example of local government in the United Kingdom to support their case and then reject it when they think it does not support their case. . . ."[85]

African Councillors reacted to this unwillingness to reform the City Council with a display of contempt for the Council. In December, 1960, one of the African Councillors, G. K. Nyawade, was disqualified for absenting himself from five consecutive Council meetings — an action that he felt to be politically inspired because of his animosity towards the Mayor.[86] Thereupon, he was reelected unopposed. Almost as soon as he returned, he disrupted the Council by attempting to attend a meeting of the staff committee, of which he was not a member. This was considered especially objectionable because of his position as General Secretary of the Kenya Local Government Workers' Union, which was then negotiating with the City Council for better terms of service, for which they later went on strike.[87] Yet, Nyawade was supported by most of the African and Asian members on this matter.

In February 1962, the African Councillors again walked out of the Ordinary Monthly Meeting in protest against the pension scheme devised to encourage the more important European staff members to remain for a period of time after the date when internal self-government would be granted.[88] The next month they called for the dismissal of Nairobi's Town Clerk and City Treasurer, claiming that they were holding up Africanization and causing trouble within the African estates in regard to house rents, water meters, market rents, and other matters.[89] In May, 1962, Councillor Nyawade demanded the removal of all senior European officers and members of the Nairobi City Council, and in July of that year, Councillor P. N. Oloo recommended the disbanding of the Department of Social Services and Housing because of its policies towards Africans.[90]

Often the African Councillors could get the support of the Asian Council Members during this period because of the anxiety generally felt by Asians as independence approached. The racial orientation of the Council encouraged the two "underprivileged" racial minorities on the Council to work together to the embarrassment of the increasingly insecure Europeans. Moreover, the Asians were brought closer to the Africans in the process of defending the Asian Deputy Mayor who was accused of corruption in October, 1961, in his effort to maintain his position in defiance of European public opinion.[91]

The effect of the various altercations that arose prior to independence, however, was not so much to disrupt the administration of Nairobi as to reflect the existing racial unrest and suspicion. "We are losing our battles here because we are in a minority," exclaimed an Asian Alderman in the City Council in 1955. "When we try to say something, we are just voices in the wilderness. We are told we are bringing up a racial issue."[92] Similarly, Asians and Africans considered almost everything the City Council did to be motivated by the interests of the European settler elite.

In 1955, Mayor R. S. Alexander, on the fifth anniversary of Nairobi's formally being designated a "city," said:

> In Nairobi we are the centre of a problem of human relations that is unique in the world. It is the tangled and delicate problems that confront anyone attempting a solution of how a multiplicity of races shall live together. With humility and generosity we are evolving an answer here in Nairobi that will be a model for the whole world.[93]

While it is true that serious efforts were made by the City Council after the Emergency to offset the mistakes of the past, the contention of African leaders more than five years later that the City Council was an obstacle in the way of African progress remains basically correct. Yet, to view the City Council and the settlers as malicious would be unfair. "There were other factors," noted a veteran member of the Council in a 1966 interview: "fear, selfishness, and ignorance. The Emergency was also important. It forced the Europeans to reconsider what they had been doing in Kenya. But we failed to realize the pace of events. We also underestimated the potentiality of the Africans."

By the middle of 1962 only about 20 per cent of the top administrative and executive grades and 6 per cent of the professional and senior technical positions of the Central Government were held by Africans. But the tardiness of Africanization was even more apparent in the municipal government of Nairobi. In the middle of 1960, only 136 Africans, excluding manual workers, were employed in a staff of 1,100.[94] Also, none of the Council's chief officers were Africans prior to Kenya's independence. In theory, as Mboya pointed out, local government should be a training ground for people who seek to take part in the central government. "But our local governments have lagged so much that people have come to the national centre for training to serve the local governments."[95]

The reasons for this delay in Africanization are made clear in the interviews conducted by the author. In the words of one senior European officer:

> Africanization did not begin until 1961 because of the feeling that it was too much trouble. It was simply easier to get people from local authorities in Britain than to train Africans. Then, too, there was the vague feeling that Africans in high positions would

either consciously or, by reason of ineptitude, interfere with the working of the Council.

This assertion is corroborated by a former leading European Council member: "The failure to Africanize was partly due to the non-availability of suitable Africans, partly to the failure of the Central Government to provide leadership, and partly to the Victorian notion of long apprenticeships."

According to most of the European officers interviewed, the Councillors were largely to blame for the failure to Africanize: "The previous Councillors opposed Africanization in every way they could. It was considered bothersome, expensive, and a threat to their own control." But at the same time, few of the officers were enthusiastic about Africanization, and some of them even threatened to hinder the City Council's proposed localization scheme unless certain protection and retention measures were taken for the European staff.[96] "Some of the officers disliked Africans or were uninterested in them," one of the City Council's European officers admitted, adding: "The Councillors did not hire Europeans who seemed to be 'pro-African' and discouraged those who showed such inclination."

## The Political Consequences of Kenya's History

KANU began to gain strength early in 1963. With the arrival of the newly appointed Governor MacDonald in January, the approach of elections was imminent. Thus, it became obvious to all that the party would have to intensify its efforts to present a united front. Joseph Murumbi, a very competent Kenyan of Asian-African parentage, took over Party Headquarters as National Treasurer and quickly improved its efficiency, which had previously left much to be desired. More important, Kenyatta finally began to exercise the leadership expected of him. For example, in February, he let it be known that the proposed Kikuyu United Movement would not be tolerated. "There is no accommodation between a tribalist and a nationalist," he declared: "The two are directly in conflict."[97]

In the course of the 1963 election campaign, KANU was successfully able to pin the label "tribalist" on KADU, the APP, and the various other groups opposing it, much the same way as Nkrumah had done in the Gold Coast nearly a decade earlier. Moreover, throughout the campaign, KADU suffered from lack of funds, defections, and disagreements within the Party or with allies. But even if all KADU's candidates had won, too few were entered to win a majority. Consequently, KANU received more than twice as many popular votes as did KADU as well as a clear majority of all votes cast. In the process, it took 83 of the 124 seats in the House of Representatives that were filled (with 33 going to KADU and 8 to the APP). Even in the Senate (constitutionally, a relatively weak second chamber where the rural areas were greatly over-represented), KANU emerged with a small majority. With the exception of Mombasa, KANU had little to worry about in the urban areas. The attempt to arouse tribal animosity was sharply rejected in Nairobi, where such KADU candidates as Musa Amalemba (a former Minister and City Council member) were decisively defeated.

In the six months after the 1963 elections, KANU was able to consolidate its victory. Every effort was made to have the various tribes, races, and regions properly represented in the Cabinet.[98] This enabled KANU to increase its control of the House of Representatives to something approaching 75 per cent of the membership by enticing four independents and four KADU members plus the entire APP delegation to join the governing side. And in the local elections that followed, KANU did extremely well, winning all but one of the urban councils and a majority of the rural county councils. In October, 1963, KANU was able to secure important changes in the Constitution, giving the Central Government authority over the regional police and public services, together with emergency powers and a more flexible amending system. Thus, Kenya entered into independence on December 12, 1963, with a remarkable degree of political stability and national identification.[99]

Though Kenya came into independence with *"harambee"* (togetherness) not only as a political slogan but also as a real achievement, there were justifiable fears. On the basis of Kenya's turbulent history, certain questions obviously arose: Would those upon whom the responsibility for governing the country had been thrust be willing and able to use their power wisely? Would the new leaders act in such a way as to reduce the existing inter-racial and inter-tribal tension? Could the impatience of the African people for a better life be mollified so as to keep their frustration from bursting into violence?

The answers to these questions would, of course, depend on the extent to which the social environment was conducive to successful administration — in other words "elasticity of control," to use the concept introduced in the first chapter. This requires a cooperative relationship within government so that there can be delegation of authority to formally constituted local authorities (devolution) and to field agents and other subordinates (deconcentration). The next chapter will be concerned with the socio-economic impediments to the attainment of elasticity of control. But before going on, the relationship of these impediments to Kenya's history might be briefly recapitulated.

First of all, colonial rule left Kenya with European institutions but without a large trained and experienced elite to properly manage them. Insofar as such an elite existed, it largely consisted of Europeans and Asians (representing a small percentage of the population) rather than Africans. Not only had there been limited educational opportunity for Africans, but also limited political opportunity, inasmuch as African participation in political parties, functional associations, elections, legislatures, and communication media had been severely restricted. This meant that independence came before a basis for unity could be firmly established.

Second, colonial rule left Kenya with a fragile economy, with relatively little industry and dependence upon a small number of cash crops. While Kenya may have been economically stronger than most other African countries, it was unable to satisfy the popular demands and expectations aroused by political leaders: full employment, free education, free medical care, social security, superhighways, good housing for everyone, widespread ownership of automobiles, etc. What was most frustrating of all was the lack of a large indigenous business community, which could benefit from the opportunities of the private and public sectors.

Third, colonial rule left Kenya with divisions based on class, race, education, occupation, and religion. These were superimposed upon ethnic or tribal differences, often making these traditional cleavages much more severe. Adding to the existing social problems were the intellectual confusion and loss of pride engendered by colonialism. Because Africans under colonial rule were made to believe they were uncivilized and savage, they had great difficulty in overcoming an inferiority complex and in escaping cultural as well as economic neocolonialism. Certain traditional virtues (cooperativeness, generosity, concern for the community, respect for elders, and devotion to the land) were somewhat undermined by the vices associated with European rule: materialism, selfishness, conspicuous consumption, gambling, prostitution, alcoholism, etc.

No nation can escape the consequences of its history. Yet, while Kenya suffered much under colonial rule, it also gained the basis for progress: communication and transportation facilities, public health programs, the control of certain pests, an institutional framework, commercial and scientific agriculture, western education, the development of supra-ethnic ties and loyalties, urbanization, etc. While Kenya's basis for unity was weak, it did come into independence with a dominant party and leader. The existing African elite was certainly small, consisting mostly of Kikuyu living in Nairobi; but, being largely the product of mission schools that had been established in Kenya at the turn of the century, it had been imbued with a British public-school pride and code of conduct.[100] This African elite was aware of the fact that the economic and administrative system which was inherited, however inadequate, compared favorably to that of other emerging nations. Consequently, the leaders of Kenya were determined to uphold this system, with the sad experience of the Congo very much in the minds of all. Their ability to effectively organize and mobilize the administration was strongly affected by the nature of Nairobi's socio-economic problems, which were intensified by the process of transition from European to African rule.

# NOTES

1. Cf. L. W. Hollingsworth, *The Asians of East Africa* (London: Macmillan and Co., 1960), p. 47; George Delf, *Asians in East Africa* (London: Oxford U. Press, 1963), p. 11. Of the 32,000 Asian "coolies," 6,000 remained after completion of the railroad.

2. "No country could become a good working proposition," according to Lord Delamere in 1907, "until it had in its councils the people who live in the country, and are monetarily interested in it." Quoted, W. MacGregor Ross, *Kenya from Within* (London: George Allen & Unwin, 1927), p. 310.

3. *Ibid.,* p. 360.

4. Cf. Marjorie R. Dilley, *British Policy in Kenya Colony* (New York: Thomas Nelson & Sons, 1937), p. 163.

5. Cf. Richard K. P. Pankhurst, *Kenya: The History of Two Nations* (London: Independent Publishing Co., 1954?), pp. 46-57.

6. Quoted, Carl G. Rosberg, Jr. and John Nottingham, *The Myth of Mau Mau* (New York: Praeger, 1966), p. 39.

7. *Op. cit.,* p. 54.

8. Quoted, Ross, *op. cit.,* p. 381.

9. Quoted, Dilley, *op. cit.,* p. 156.

10. *Ibid.,* pp. 179-208.

11. *Ibid.,* p. 187.

12. Quoted, *ibid.,* p. 195.

13. Quoted, *ibid.,* p. 197.

14. *Ibid.,* pp. 174-75.

15. (London: Weidenfeld & Nicholson, 1964), p. 148.

16. Rosberg and Nottingham, *op. cit.,* p. 208.

17. *Ibid.,* p. 156.

18. Quoted, F. D. Corfield, *The Origins and Growth of Mau Mau* (Nairobi: Colony and Protectorate of Kenya, Sessional Paper No. 5 of 1959/1960), pp. 282-83.

19. Quoted, Rosberg and Nottingham, *op. cit.,* p. 226.

20. *Kenya: A Political History* (London: Oxford U. Press, 1963), p. 113.

21. G. F. Engholm, "African Elections in Kenya, March 1957," in W. J. M. Mackenzie and Kenneth Robinson, eds., *Five Elections in Africa: A Group of Electoral Studies* (Oxford: At the Clarendon Press, 1960), p. 399.

22. Cf. George Bennett and Carl G. Rosberg, Jr., *The Kenyatta Election: Kenya 1960-1961* (London: Oxford U. Press, 1961), p. 33.

23. *Freedom and After* (London: Andre Deutsch, 1963), p. 75.

24. Bennett and Rosberg, *op. cit.,* p. 36.

25. *Freedom and After, op. cit.,* p. 75.

26. Cf. J. E. Goldthorpe, *Outlines of East African Society* (Kampala, Uganda: Makerere College, the University College of East Africa, 1958), pp. 20-35.

27. Cf. John S. Roberts, *A Land Full of People, Life in Kenya Today* (New York: Praeger, 1966), p. 30.

28. Rosberg and Nottingham, *op. cit.,* p. 23.

29. Cf. D. H. Rawcliffe, *op. cit.,* pp. 19-26; L. S. B. Leakey, *Mau Mau and the Kikuyu* (London: Methuen & Co., 1952), *passim*; Rosberg and Nottingham, *op. cit., passim.*

30. Elspeth Huxley and Margery Perham, *Race and Politics in Kenya,* 2nd ed. (London: Faber & Faber, Ltd., 1956), p. 49.

31. Rosberg and Nottingham, *op. cit.,* p. 136.

32. *Ibid., passim*; Leakey, *op. cit.,* pp. 74-81.

33. For the situation at this time in Nyanza Province, cf. Bethwell A. Ogot, "British Administration in the Central Nyanza District of Kenya, 1900-1960," *Journal of African History,* Vol. IV, No. 2 (1963), p. 270.

34. According to the 1948 Census, the Kikuyu/Embu/Meru constituted approximately half of Nairobi's African population.

35. Cf. Engholm, *op. cit.,* pp. 391-462.

36. *Op. cit.,* p. 220.

37. *Op. cit.,* p. 79.

38. *Tom Mboya: Young Man of New Africa* (Garden City, New York: Doubleday, 1962), p. 216.

39. Bennett and Rosberg, *op. cit.,* p. 40.

40. *Ibid.,* p. 42.

41. Cf. Carl G. Rosberg, Jr., "Independent Kenya: Problems and Prospects," *Africa Report,* December, 1963, p. 4.

42. Cf. C. Sanger and J. Nottingham, "The Kenya General Election," *The Journal of Modern African Studies,* Vol. II, No. 1 (March, 1964), pp. 8-11.

43. John Nottingham, "The Development of Local Government in Kenya" (an unpublished article, 1964), p. 13.

44. Quoted, Mary Parker, *Political and Social Aspects of the Devel-*

*opment of Municipal Government in Kenya with Special Reference to Nairobi* (London: Colonial Office, 1948?), p. 174.

45. Cf. Desmond O'Hagan, "African's Part in Nairobi Local Government," *Journal of African Administration,* Vol. I, No. 4 (October, 1949), p. 156.

46. Cf. Parker, *op. cit.,* pp. 175-203.

47. *East African Standard* (E.A.S.), September 30, 1954.

48. Cf. O'Hagan, *op. cit.,* pp. 156-58.

49. *Op. cit.,* pp. 192-93.

50. *Op. cit.,* p. 158.

51. *Debates,* July 4, 1957, c. 1979.

52. *Annual Report,* p. 55.

53. E.A.S., May 5, 1962.

54. Leg. Co., *Debates,* July 14, 1961, cc. 2388-89.

55. *Op. cit.,* p. 189.

56. *Op. cit.,* p. 16.

57. Speech by the Commissioner for Local Government, Leg. Co., *Debates,* May 6, 1953, c. 30.

58. *Ibid.,* c. 40.

59. Leg. Co. *Debates,* May 30, 1957, c. 773.

60. *Ibid.,* c. 737.

61. *Ibid.,* c. 734.

62. *Ibid.,* c. 743.

63. *Ibid.,* c. 744.

64. Leg. Co. *Debates,* July 3, 1957, c. 1934.

65. *Ibid.,* c. 1927.

66. *Report of the Commission of Inquiry into Alleged Corruption or Other Malpractices in Relation to the Affairs of the Nairobi City Council,* December, 1955 — March, 1956 (Nairobi: Government Printer, 1956), pp. 25-26.

67. E.A.S., June 6, 1957.

68. E.A.S., June 22, 1960.

69. E.A.S., July 15, 1959.

70. E.A.S., July 20, 1959.

71. E.A.S., July 23, 1959.

72. Leg. Co. *Debates,* July 22, 1959, c. 111.

73. *Ibid.,* July 14, 1961, cc. 2353-54.

74. *Ibid.,* June 1, 1960, c. 1183.

75. *Ibid.,* July 14, 1961, cc. 2351-52.

76. *Ibid.,* c. 2374.
77. *Ibid.,* c. 2387.
78. E.A.S., April 9, 1959.
79. E.A.S., April 18, 1959.
80. E.A.S., May 21, 1959.
81. E.A.S., July 6, 1960.
82. Leg. Co. *Debates,* June 1, 1960, c. 1142.
83. *Ibid.,* December 9, 1960, c. 836.
84. *Ibid.,* July 14, 1961, c. 2369.
85. *Ibid.,* July 18, 1961, c. 2499.
86. E.A.S., November 23 and December 3, 1960.
87. E.A.S., February 10, 1961.
88. E.A.S., February 7, 1962.
89. E.A.S., March 6-7, 1962.
90. E.A.S., May 15 and July 11, 1962.
91. E.A.S., May 2, 1962.
92. E.A.S., December 30, 1955.
93. E.A.S., March 30, 1955.
94. House of Representatives, *Debates,* July 25, 1963, c. 1326.
95. E.A.S., October 25, 1961.
96. E.A.S., March 10, 1962.
97. E.A.S., February 1, 1963.
98. Cf. Sanger and Nottingham, *op. cit.,* pp. 8-9.
99. Cf. Rosberg, *op. cit.,* p. 5.
100. Cf. Rosberg and Nottingham, *op. cit.,* pp. 75-76 (the research work of David Koff dealing with the African elite of Kenya is here cited).

# 4 THE SOCIO-ECONOMIC
PROBLEMS OF NAIROBI

*The Slowness of Socio-Economic Progress*

"What is political change?" wrote M. Karienye Yohanna in the *Kenya Weekly News of* January 10, 1964. "In Kenya political change has meant political independence. But political independence is not a tangible thing and I am not in the least surprised to find a number of people here still wondering what has actually happened to us." For ordinary Africans in Nairobi, life following independence seemed not much better than before. Everywhere they turned, they encountered the discouraging sign, *"Hakuna Kazi"* (no work), despite the promise of the nationalist movement, *"Uhuru na Kazi"* (Independence and Work). And when a job was found, it still seemed to be *"kazi mingi; pesa kidogo"* (much work, little money). Too often the boss remained the same unsympathetic European or Asian as before, apparently oblivious of the changes that had taken place in Kenya. *"Ngoja kidogo"* (wait a little), begged the political leaders, but Africans were growing dangerously impatient.

A social and economic adjustment was needed — to correspond to politics. This would require rapid changes in a number of different directions but in a way that would not undermine the basis of socio-economic progress (which continued to be the presence of a large number of non-Africans). Above all, there was the need for Africans to feel "at home" in Nairobi. "I still feel uncomfortable here with a black skin," one of Kenya's leading intellectuals pointed out in a 1966 interview. "We have the feeling that we can't be ourselves in the city. We need to Africanize ourselves, but we have too much reverence for the European way — for the tie and coat and the schools that teach our children to be English ladies and gentlemen."

As independence approached, the "color bar" largely disappeared, hastened by the City Council's policy adopted early in 1962 of refusing tax concessions to organizations catering to one race only. However, the pattern of segregation that had developed during the colonial period could not suddenly be ended by legislation. Discrimination, it was alleged by KANU headquarters in Nairobi, was thereafter carried out in various subtle ways. "Advertisements carry no racial qualifications, but inquirers of the wrong race are told that the property has just been let."[1] In 1962, according to census data and information furnished by the City Council, 73 per cent of the total African population were living in the predominately African residential areas to the east and southeast ("Eastlands," it was called); 80 per cent of the Asians, in the Parklands-Eastleigh area or in the newer Nairobi South district; and 82 per cent of the Europeans, in the attractive elevated areas located a considerable distance north and west of the commercial section.[2] While Africans increasingly moved into the sections occupied by Europeans and Asians as they could afford to do so, "the racial communities of Kenya," to quote the 1965 Ominde Report on Education, "aided and abetted by an unfortunate town planning in the urban areas, still live unto themselves to a deplorable extent."[3]

The location and administration of educational and health facilities continued to be such as to discourage social integration. Schools in 1963 ceased to be designated "African, Asian, and European," but rather, "Schedule A, Schedule B, and Schedule C," and they were distinguished by their location in the city and by the fees charges (60/–, 182/–, and 579/– per annum respectively). By 1967 the number of African children attending the former European and Asian primary schools had risen to 2,869, but this constituted only about 5 per cent of African school-children in Nairobi. Needless to say, the education available in the Schedule B and Schedule C schools was of considerably higher quality than in the Schedule A schools, as is evident from the results of the Kenya Preliminary Examination. Similarly, the sixteen non-Governmental hospitals in Nairobi (containing more than half of the city's hospital beds) were too costly for all but a handful of Africans.[4] And what was true of educational and health facilities was also true of restaurants, clubs, and so forth.

What prevented social integration in Nairobi was the persistence with which lines of class and race converged. The income gap between the races had begun to narrow during the 1950's; between 1948 and 1960 the index of average earnings rose from 100 to 268 for Africans but only from 100 to 189 for Asians and from 100 to 199 for Europeans.[5] But the gap still remained alarmingly wide. In 1962, the aggregate earnings of Europeans in Nairobi were almost twice those of Africans, who were more than six times more numerous, and more than one and a half time that of Asians who outnumbered Europeans about three to one.[6] Thus, the average yearly income of African wage-earners in Nairobi then was about £142 ($397) as against £580 ($1,120) for Asian employees and £1,500 ($4,200) for employed Europeans. Whereas over 90 per cent of Africans in Kenya earned less than £120 ($336) in 1962 and less than 1 per cent earned over £400 ($1,120), the corresponding percentages for Asians were 11 and 68.4 and for Europeans, 1.5 and 92.2.[7]

What was necessary for social integration in Nairobi was the development of a large African business and professional class. But it was not easy to rectify the disadvantages suffered by Africans during the colonial period. During the ten years before independence more capital had been invested in European and Asian education, representing 3 per cent of the population, than in the education of the African 97 per cent.[8] Consequently, the number of Africans completing secondary school was extremely limited. In 1958, almost two-thirds of the Europeans and about 16 per cent of the Asian children completed the school certificate, while less than 1 per cent of Africans did so.[9] By 1962, only 0.7 per cent of Africans in Kenya (and 6.2 per cent in Nairobi), aged 15 years and over, had had nine or more years of education, whereas 81 per cent of Europeans in Kenya, in the same age bracket, were recorded by the Census as having completed this much education. Though African enrollment in primary schools increased substantially during the decade prior to independence (rising from one-third to over four-fifths of a million), only 15.7 per cent of the estimated African population of age 16 completed primary school in 1962 and only about 2 per cent entered secondary school.

By 1964, an estimated 51.6 per cent of the total high and middle level manpower employed in Kenya was African, but in the highest category (those occupations requiring university or higher education), only 22.7 per cent were held by Africans.[10] The pace of Africanization, however, was much faster in the public sector (where by February, 1967, 51 per cent of high level posts were occupied by Africans) than in the private sector. By 1966, Africans accounted for only 21 per cent of the country's total managerial category in the private sector; and they were a practically negligible component of the managerial staff of banks and motor firms.[11] Where Africanization was most inadequate was in the professional occupations. For example, in 1964 the percentage of Africans among lawyers in Kenya was 2.8; among physicians and surgeons, 4.8; and among engineers, 5.5.

The Africans were extremely vexed by the extent to which Europeans and Asians dominated commerce and industry in Kenya, particularly in Nairobi. In the years prior to independence (between 1946 and 1963) only 3 per cent of the registered companies had been owned by Africans, with a total value of only about £1 million by 1963 out of a total nominal capital structure of £139 million.[12] Though a small traders' loan scheme was initiated in 1956, the available administration and finance were inadequate. Moreover, credit was difficult to obtain since, under the paternalistic African Control Ordinance, debts in excess of £10 could not be recovered from an African unless the credit instrument had been signed before a Commissioner of Oaths or a District Commissioner. It is true that a few of the Kikuyu business groups became modestly affluent at various times, such as the Chicken and Egg Dealers (who in 1945 could afford to buy property in Nairobi worth £8,000) and the African Farmers' Cooperative Society (in which Charles Rubia, the first African to become mayor of Nairobi, got his start), but most of them had great difficulty surviving, often because of misuse of funds.

The neglect of African aspirations during the colonial period had somehow to be overcome. How to do this without damaging the economy was the primary concern of the Kenyan government after independence. Fear of the economic consequences made the government reluctant to attempt a radical redistribution of income. Mwai Kibaki had pointed out in 1963 that the proportion of rich people in Kenya was so small that a redistribution would not raise the standard of living.[13] And the 1965 Government publication *African Socialism and Its Application to Planning in Kenya* made it clear that African socialism in Kenya did not imply a commitment to indiscriminate nationalization.[14] Yet, stimulation of significant African participation in the economy without a real social revolution proved to be very difficult.

## The Expedition of Social Change

The Government tried various ways to help African businessmen after independence.[15] More capital was made available through the Small Traders Loan Scheme to Africans; and additional trade officers were employed to administer the scheme, particularly after 1965. By 1967, there were thirty-three District Trade Development Joint Boards and four Municipal Loans Committees, which made small loans to over 1,000 small businessmen. For the benefit of larger African entrepreneurs, the Industrial and Commercial Development Corporation was reorganized to provide credit and to encourage the commercial banks to do likewise. Also, various training programs were undertaken or expanded. And the Government repeatedly appealed to the big companies to put Africans into important positions and to provide them with shares, thereby giving them the experience and funds to establish their own businesses.

However, by 1966, it was clear that more drastic measures would have to be taken to overcome the existing imbalances in wealth and income between the immigrant and the indigenous populations. "It is discouraging to note," complained James N. Kenyanjui, the Chairman of the Kenya African Wholesalers' and Distributors' Organization, "that although four years have passed since Kenya became independent, the African is still not participating effectively in the economic progress of the country, especially in the area of trade."[16] Mr. Mwai Kibaki, the Minister for Commerce and Industry in 1966, noted that only about 7 per cent of businesses in Kenya were owned or controlled by Africans.[17] In July 1967, Mr. Kibaki told the National Assembly that out of sixty-three commercial enterprises in Kenyatta Avenue (one of the main avenues of Nairobi), there was only one wholly African business and two houses owned by the Kenya government.[18] Of these firms, thirty-one were operated by Asians, thirteen by Europeans, and the rest by overseas or local public concerns. "The Government cannot accept that businesses in the main streets of our urban areas will continue to be owned exclusively by non-Africans," Tom Mboya warned in 1966, adding that unless European and Asian businessmen made a greater effort to bring Africans into Kenya's commerce, their businesses might be taken over.[19]

In 1966, an official survey of private companies (of which only half had replied to the questionnaire) indicated that only about 20 per cent had an effective program for training Africans to take over responsible positions.[20] Many of these companies, it was charged, used Africans simply as "windowdressing." "Windowdressing will not do and will not be tolerated," the Government warned in a booklet outlining its policy on Kenyanization published in July, 1967. "The Government is asking for positive indications that serious efforts are being made to integrate Kenyans into commercial and industrial activity by appointing them to positions of responsibility."[21]

The fault, however, lay not completely with the non-African businesses. Many of the efforts initiated by private firms to train Africans proved fruitless. In 1968, the Institute of Bankers announced that of the 1,678 employed locally in the spirit of Kenyanization during the previous three years, 1,027 had left.[22] Despite an expenditure of £200,000 ($560,000), there had been a costly 61 per cent turnover. Those Africans, it seemed, with sufficient education and the proper attitude or outlook to benefit from this sort of training program were able to get grants to increase their formal education or to get better paying or more promising positions elsewhere.

The Asians were largely held responsible for the economic difficulties and the slow progress of African enterprise, despite the fact that the majority of companies registered in Kenya (and about two-thirds of the corporate wealth of the country) were controlled by Europeans.[23] While few Africans thought it possible to supplant the large European corporations, many wanted to replace the Asian traders, who controlled an estimated 80 per cent of Kenya's commerce. "Any African," writes John Roberts, "who has primary education and the slightest head for business sees the little neighbourhood duka with its jumble of brooms and cheap crockery, its tinned food and slightly stale chocolate, its sacks of dried chilis and lentils and beans, its charcoal stoves and kerosene lamps hanging like shrunken heads from the eaves, and he knows or believes that he too could be in the relative comfort and warmth of that shop instead of pushing his bicycle loaded with the vegetables that are his stock-in-trade through mud and dust, rain or shine."[24]

The African traders, it was contended, were forced to run through a gauntlet of malevolent Asian bankers or creditors, wholesalers, and landlords only to be eventually confronted by a conspiracy of Asian competitors anxious to drive them out of business in one way or another. So entrenched were the Asian traders that the initial effort of the Government in 1965 to put the wholesale and distribution business into African hands failed. The African agents of the Kenya National Trading Corporation, which was to be the sole outlet for most of the basic commodities used in the country, beginning with rice and sugar, resold their allocation to those very same Asian wholesalers from whom the agency had been transferred.[25]

In reality, however, the difficulties of the aspiring African businessmen could not be blamed entirely on the Asians. The major barrier to the success of Africans in business was their lack of formal education and, more important, of a sophisticated awareness of financial opportunities and dangers.[26] Another barrier, Peter Marris notes, was their lack of social contacts which would facilitate the obtaining of credit and the distribution of products.[27] Consequently, African traders tended to compete with one another, setting up all-purpose shops with minimal capital or credit near shops of the same sort in areas with limited market potential. Few of them kept proper accounts or showed an even elementary business knowledge. Many African businessmen preferred to split their profits among members of their extended families rather than ploughing them back into their businesses. And often they were expected to come to the aid of their relatives in cases of financial hardship and to employ them regardless of their ability.

In 1967, the Kenya Government attempted more forcefully than heretofore to rectify the social and economic position of Africans. To begin with, it announced its intention to purchase shop premises in the centers of towns through the Industrial and Commercial Development Corporation and to lease them at reasonable rents to African businessmen. The Nairobi City Council then took steps to oust non-African stand-holders from the City Market, following a letter from the Ministry of Local Government which stated that "the progress of African dealers in many municipal markets was being retarded by long-established non-Africans who were able to adopt extreme competitive trade practices in view of their large capital resources."[28] Less controversial (because of their paucity of numbers) was the City Council's decision at this time to give a 5 per cent bias to African manufacturers (i.e., to accept their tenders for contracts when no more than 5 per cent above those of their non-African competitors).

What really frightened the non-African population was the introduction in 1967 of legislation to tighten the entry requirements into Kenya for expatriates working in the private sector.[29] Only those who were essential to the national economy would be given work permits. Others were to be given short-term work permits which would not be renewed if their positions could be Africanized.

Though only 844 of the total European population then estimated to be 41,000 had taken out Kenya citizenship by the end of
1965, they were not really worried.[30] Most of them anticipated being bought out or retired under reasonably generous resettlement
and compensation schemes (with funds loaned by Britain and the
World Bank to be eventually repaid by Kenya). The Asian community, on the other hand, found the 1967 Immigration Bill very
alarming. Only about one-third of the Asian population of 185,000
were then citizens either by birth or registration. Forty thousand
had automatically become citizens and another 20,000 had registered for citizenship by the twelfth of December, 1965 (the last
day when it was possible to do so by those qualified for citizenship
at the time of Independence).[31]

According to the 1962 Census, almost two-thirds of the total
Asian population were born in Kenya. Most had never been to the
land of their ancestors in India or Pakistan, and they could not be
expected to adjust readily to life in these impoverished, overcrowded
countries. But the prospect of living in Britain was hardly more
pleasant for Asians who saw it as a strange, cold, unfriendly place.
The extent of British animosity became clear early in 1968 when
Britain enacted her stiff immigration curbs, limiting the number of
ethnic Asians with British passports who could enter the country to
1,500 workers a year plus their dependents.[32] Nearly 20,000 left
Kenya for Britain in the three months prior to this immigration
bill, almost a third of them in the last week of February. This left
approximately 160,000 Asians in Kenya. Since then, about 5,000
Kenyan Asians have annually departed for Britain.

The fear of the Asians stemmed not so much from the enacted
or proposed legislation as from the way in which policies were or
might be implemented. The Constitution of Kenya that had been
adopted just before independence very clearly disallowed racial discrimination of any sort. "Before there was no such thing as a nation, only several nations living side by side in one territory," the
1964 Ominde Report pointed out. "Now, however, the equal rights
of all citizens, unhindered by considerations of race, tribe, or religion, are not only openly acknowledged, but are also enshrined in
the basic law of Kenya."[33] Realistically, the hiring and promotion

practices of the civil service directly and indirectly favored Africans; and these practices were sanctioned in a number of official documents, including the Local Civil Service Salaries Commission, 1963 (the Pratt Report), *Highlevel Manpower Requirements and Resources in Kenya, 1964-1970,* and the *Development Plan, 1966-1970.*[34] Similarly, the statements of African leaders were ambiguous. For example, during the 1964 Parliamentary debate on the Citizenship Bill, the then Minister for Home Affairs gave a pledge that no citizen would be discriminated against in employment opportunities just because he did not have a black skin.[35] But Mr. Kenyatta was quoted as saying in August 1964, that "this is a black man's country, and everyone who wants to live with us must identify himself with the black man's aspirations."[36]

Yet, the more responsible leaders of Kenya recognized that the country remained dependent upon Europeans and Asians for its manpower and for its capital. Even members of the small militant opposition K.P.U. Parliamentary Group expressed concern at the alarming number of Asian immigrants to Britain early in 1968, though previously they had demanded outright Africanization in all fields.[37] John C. Roche had estimated in 1962 that 40 per cent of the scientific and technological positions in Kenya would have to be filled by Europeans and Asians for at least another decade.[38] In 1964, Calvin F. Davis estimated (on behalf of the Kenya government) that the shortfall in professional people (those in occupations requiring university degrees or post-secondary specialized training) would be more than 2,000 during the period, 1964-1970.[39] This study also indicated the need for more than 25,000 additional trained people for many specialized occupations.

Since only 22.7 per cent of the total high level manpower employed in Kenya in 1964 was reckoned to be African, any excessive departure of Asians or Europeans (more than 7 or 8 per cent a year from the public sector; more than 5 per cent from the private sector) was thought to be detrimental to the progress of the country.[40] For example, to fulfill the hope of providing secondary education for 50 per cent of the population of eligible age, nearly ten times as many teachers would be required.[41] Since Africans comprised only about 25 per cent of the secondary school teachers in Kenya, the departure of Europeans and Asians would simply increase the necessity and expense of recruiting teaching staff from abroad. In other highly skilled occupations, it was pointed out, the cost of replacing each departing European or Asian could amount to about 5,000 Kenya pounds worth of potential output and the potential loss of jobs for nearly ten additional unskilled or semi-skilled workers.[42]

Most non-Africans recognized that they would only be tolerated in Kenya if they proved themselves to be useful. For those Asians without much education or any special skills and for those Europeans unable or unwilling to accept their designated roles in Africa as teachers, advisers, or investors, life in Kenya would be very difficult. But it was also difficult for non-citizens to wait passively until they could be replaced, even for the 57 per cent of Europeans and the 23 per cent of Asians who (based on the 1962 Census) were in professional and managerial occupations. Of the 65,000 Europeans and Asians in the work-force in 1968, an estimated 50,000 were non-citizens. Many of them were frustrated by the Government's seemingly uncertain or inept handling of work permits and trade licenses. "Many expatriates are able to face this situation realistically," the *East African Standard* emphasized, "but those with families may naturally wonder why they should wait until they can be dispensed with, if they have a chance to make an advantageous move earlier."[43] It was also pointed out that those who were most useful to Kenya were the most likely to depart from Africa.

## The Problems of Social Change

The anxiety of non-Africans had a deleterious effect upon Kenya's economy even prior to independence. There was a fear not simply of their land and capital being confiscated or greatly reduced in value but, more generally, of a rapid deterioration of law and order and of public services and standards.[44]

Within two years after the 1960 Lancaster House Conference, the European population of Kenya declined by almost 10 per cent to 55,000. Many Asians also left or were in the process of doing so. The economic consequences of this exodus soon became apparent:

The investment rate fell by about 25 per cent from that achieved during the 1955 to 1960 period; deposits in the commercial banks, by 20 per cent; the purchase of agricultural machinery, by 17 per cent; the value of Kenya Government and High Commission stock, by 18.1 per cent and of industrial shares, by 32.5 per cent.[45] More than a third of the White Highlands, upon which the country depended for at least three-quarters of her exports, were for sale. And during 1961 and 1962, the value of the gross domestic produce rose by less than the annual increase in population, indicating a fall in real per-capita income. Such a decline in the economy was certain to exacerbate all of the other problems of Kenya.

The impact of the deteriorating economic conditions existing after 1960 had the most direct effect on employment. By 1963, employment was 14 per cent lower than it had been in 1960, which meant that the employed labor force consisted of only 535,000 out of a total population of nearly 9 million, of which the male labor force (defined as those actively seeking employment) was estimated to be 1.85 million.[46] There were, as of June 1, 1964, over 200,000 registered unemployed (over 40,000 in Nairobi).

A number of factors combined to make the unemployment problem an increasingly important concern of the Government in the first few years after independence: the results of the 1962 Census indicating a population growth of 3 per cent annually during the 1960's; the youthfulness of the population (half being under 16 years of age, as against about 25 per cent in England and other Western European countries); the rising number of primary school graduates (indicated by the increase of those taking the Kenya Preliminary Examination from 62,125 in 1963 to 18,146 in 1965); and the growing number of African women seeking employment.[47] It was not only necessary to eliminate existing unemployment and underemployment, but also to find jobs for 50,000 to 60,000 additional men who were expected to enter the labor force each year.[48] Altogether, there were an estimated 280,000 work-seekers in 1966, for which only 50,000 vacancies existed.[49] Since the number of work-seekers was projected to rise by about 10 per cent a year to 1970 and employment by less than 5 per cent a year, unemployment was expected to increase.

Because of the concentration of the wage-earning population in the urban areas, particularly Nairobi, the economic depression was most directly and painfully felt here. The great wave of building in Nairobi that had taken place in the decade prior to 1960, during which the population more than doubled to nearly 300,000, came almost to a halt by 1964. The contribution of the construction industry to the national income was only £4.3 million in 1964 as against almost £10 million in 1957. This decline produced an alarming increase in the rate of unemployment among African males in Nairobi from 3 per cent in 1959 to nearly 30 per cent in 1964.[50] Similarly, the Asian community, consisting of about 30 per cent of Nairobi's population, was hard hit.

What complicated the employment situation in Nairobi (and Kenya as a whole) was the fact that the average annual earnings of Africans rose at the rate of nearly 8 per cent per annum between 1954 and 1962.[51] This resulted partly from trade union pressure, partly from the growing policy of promoting Africans to more responsible positions, and partly from statutory requirements (raising the minimum monthly wage inclusive of housing allowances of a worker in Nairobi over the age of 21 from 73s 6d. in 1954 to 133s in 1962). Though somewhat justified by increases in productivity and prices, this wage increase apparently encouraged the use of more capital intensive methods by both the private and public sectors, thus benefiting the employed at the expense of the unemployed. This is indicated in a joint paper by Philip Ndegwa and O. D. K. Norbye, under the auspices of Kenya's Ministry of Economic Planning and Development: While the non-agricultural monetary gross product had risen between 1954 and 1964 by 7 per cent a year at current prices or by about 5 per cent a year at constant prices, the non-agricultural wage employment had risen by only 0.4 per cent a year.[52] Between 1964 and 1966 the rate of growth of average earnings was nearly three times that of employment; and output was expected to grow between 1964 and 1970 by nearly twice that of employment.[53]

In an effort to cope with the demonstrations and other manifestations of unrest stemming from unemployment, the Government reached an agreement in February 1964, under which Government and private employers promised to increase employment for a period of twelve months by 10 to 15 per cent in return for a moratorium on strikes by labor unions.[54] In addition, the Government made other proposals to stimulate employment, including irrigation projects and public works, land development and settlement schemes, self-help projects and cooperatives, youth and educational programs, etc. However, these measures seemed only a palliative, temporarily benefiting an estimated 15 per cent of the registered unemployed. What was obviously needed was a great increase in investment; but total investment in Kenya in 1964 was £20 million below the average level of £53 million required for the success of the 1964-1970 Development Plan.[55]

What significantly contributed to the unemployment problem in Nairobi was the ever increasing influx of Africans into the city after the lifting of Emergency restrictions in 1960. This extraordinary migration into Nairobi stemmed partly from the fact that, among the Kikuyu in 1960, 30 per cent were estimated to be landless and another 30 per cent on subeconomic holdings.[56] By 1965, the number of wage-earners in agriculture and forestry had fallen to 210,000 from 272,000 in 1960. The shortfall in agricultural jobs — then estimated to be nearly 100,000 — was associated with the distribution by 1965 of nearly one-third of the former White Highlands among some 30,000 Africans.[57] The process of transferring the White Highlands to Africans was of course politically and socially necessary, but it increased rural unemployment, insofar as the new African landholders lacked the resources to carry out the large-scale farming previously undertaken on the land.

This inability to stem the flow of Africans into Nairobi had been a cause of anxiety, and even despair, to the City Council even before 1960. In 1958, it announced that it would not consider further African housing projects until some measure of control of entry into the city for residential purposes was obtained. The limitations of this policy were then clearly pointed out by Tom Mboya:

> The City Council has failed to grasp the simple fact that so long as Nairobi remains the capital of Kenya, and in this context the main industrial centre of the country, the majority of able-bodied

persons all over the country will trek towards this large city for economic or social reasons. How would the English or Americans react to a control of entry into London or New York for whatever reasons?[58]

Yet, the proposal to control the influx of people into Nairobi could not be altogether dismissed by Kenyan leaders after independence, considering the persistent rise in urban population at the rate of 6 per cent a year. At this rate, the population of Nairobi was expected to reach 1,000,000 by 1982, representing 7½ per cent of the Kenya total as against 4 per cent in 1964.[59] This was the reason for President Kenyatta's threat in 1964 to confiscate the farms of those who left their land in the rural areas to come into the towns. "Such people," he exclaimed,

> distort the purchasing power of their relatives and friends, make them poorer and more miserable and also interfere with the social plans and provisions for the genuine residents of the towns. This is a clear waste of manpower and a definite obstacle to proper farming for the future. Any able-bodied man who exploits his relatives and friends in this manner is a disgrace to his manhood and to our society. Their friends and relatives must get rid of these people and stop feeding them.[60]

However, any "back to the land" movement required more than the threats that were made. There was, in addition to the problems of landlessness and rural unemployment, that problem posed by the 1960 *Dagleish Report*: "How can the inevitable attractions of the big city, with its apparent opportunities — both financial and material — which are at present so lacking in the African Land Units, be counteracted so as to draw away from Nairobi and Mombasa a large proportion of that surplus population which on security and social grounds is causing the Administration of the Municipal Authorities such disquiet?"[61] The lure of the metropolis irresistably beckoned many of the 15,000 who were expected to leave the rural primary schools each year during the latter 1960's, adding to the already substantial teen-age unemployment.[62]

Even those who had land usually found that their incomes were far less than that of wage earners. Statistics in Kenya in 1965 showed that the average wage earner earned twice as much total income and ten times as much money income as the average small farmer.[63] Between 1960 and 1966, the average income of African wage earners increased by 80 per cent while that of small farmers rose by only 20 per cent. In this regard, Nairobi was particularly attractive insofar as per capita income here was much higher than in the country as a whole.[64]

The Town Clerk of Nairobi noted in 1960 the wide range of problems associated with the swell of urban population which followed the lifting of the Emergency restrictions:

> The immediate problem was one of overcrowding in the African estates of the City, and the consequent increase in the water demands and pressures on health services and clinics. These led directly to an accelerating deficiency in the African housing rent account, and later in the year to proposals for rent increases. The presence of thousands of unemployed in the City was also reflected in the growth of unauthorized hawking and street trading and an increase in the crime figures. Tenants of Council housing were obliged to feed their newly-arrived tribal kin, and this led to increases in family costs.[65]

Crime rose in Nairobi by 36 per cent between 1959 and 1961 and a further 50 per cent by 1964 (most of it being thefts).[66] Much of the crime was a result of juvenile delinquency. In 1966, Mr. Otiende, the Minister for Health, noted that the number of children who appeared before the juvenile courts had increased from 161 in 1963 to 381 in 1965.[67]

This juvenile delinquency stemmed from the social conditions existing in Nairobi. In 1961, a "Survey of Problems of Child Welfare in Kenya" reported that some 1,500 African children between the ages of 8 and 15 were found in Nairobi every year trying to live by such means as illegal hawking or begging but were often near starvation.[68] By 1965, between 2,000 and 3,000 children were reported to have drifted into the city from other areas and to be without visible means of support.[69] In one Nairobi primary school, less than one-third of the boys claimed to know where they would be living at the start of the next school year.[70] The rest apparently moved among residents from their own village or clan, many of whom felt no moral responsibility or basic concern for these boys.

Prostitution or concubinage, particularly that involving girls between 13 and 16, was also found to be disturbingly high in Nairobi.[71] According to a 1962 study of the Child Welfare Society of Kenya, hundreds of African girls in Nairobi, many of them being as young as 9 or 10, were prostituting themselves for food or money. The desperation of these girls was indicated by the finding that about 60 per cent of those questioned were suffering from malnutrition.

Juvenile delinquency and prostitution in Nairobi indicated the extent to which traditional forms of protection were breaking down. Formerly it was assumed that Africans, if unemployed in the town, could always rely on their land in the reserves. With growing landlessness or semi-landlessness in Kenya, this assumption became dubious.

There was evidence that Nairobi Africans were losing their connections with the rural areas where over 80 per cent of them were born, despite the fact, according to a 1963 survey of African middle-income workers in Nairobi, that 60 per cent continued to remit to their home districts about 10 per cent of their income.[72] For the first time a significant number of unclaimed bodies was being found by the City Mortuary. Noting the existence of more than 250 beggars in Nairobi and about 2,000 other destitute individuals who needed to be restricted each month under the 1960 Vagrancy Ordinance, the 1963 *Report and Recommendation of Inquiry into Begging and Vagrancy* emphasized:

> It can therefore be expected that, if no steps are taken soon, the problem of begging and vagrancy will multiply as older persons, who may have been employed in Nairobi long enough that they are virtually de-tribalised and have no claims to land in their areas of origin, find they cannot hold their employment against rising competition from the younger ones. And of the younger ones who had had a measure of education and with it the incentive for modern life, a great proportion will be drawn to the cities where only a comparatively few will find employment.[73]

Begging and vagrancy in Nairobi were to some extent alleviated by the extended family system. Indeed, it was said that Africans encouraged their relatives to become "social parasites." "In every part of East Africa," exclaimed Tom Mboya in 1966, "one can witness the undesirable situation in which a member of a family whose income increases is suddenly and constantly besieged by demands for support from a large number of distant relatives."[74]

However, just as the ties with the rural areas were loosening, those binding the extended family system were weakening. As Africans viewed life in more competitive or individualized ways, it was likely that those family claims which seemed to frustrate individual achievement would be increasingly rejected.[75]

Officials in Kenya were anxious for the extended family system to be replaced by a strong nuclear family system. A favorable ratio of African men to women was established by the 1962 Census as 1.83 to 1 in contrast to disproportionate 9 to 1 ratio of African men to women before 1945. Yet, there was no evidence of a shift toward a nuclear pattern. In 1962, Mrs. E. E. Jackson, a former District Officer in Nairobi, noted that half of the boys in the Nairobi youth centers had neither contact with nor knowledge of their fathers.[76] She went on to write that, in the absence of compulsory marriage registration, "it is well-nigh impossible in the towns to tell who is married and who is not." In 1969, the Parliament of Kenya (consisting, it might be added, entirely of men) disallowed paternity suits to prevent women from getting a "nice ride"; but, to quote the *East African Standard,* "if the desires of the flesh are never to be cured by self-control, who is going to look after the unfortunate offspring?"[77]

A possible source of help for urban Africans was the traditional organizations (based on area of origin, kinship, or age-grade unit). At one time, there were reported to be as many as 500 of these societies in Nairobi which were primarily concerned with welfare and social functions.[78] According to G. F. Engholm, writing in 1957, they thereby helped to foster a sense of cohesion among the members of the respective tribes.[79] After independence, these tribal associations were discouraged by Kenya's leaders for fear that they might promote inter-tribal conflict and supplant the national party. "A worker's welfare should increasingly be the concern of the trade unions," a 1966 statement of KANU headquarters declared, "while a farmer or a businessman should look more to the associations and cooperatives formed by these groups. We cannot, on the one hand, oppose racial or Asian communal organizations while we support tribal groups."[80] Possibly as a result of official disapproval, the tribal associations in Nairobi apparently declined in importance after independence, at least as indicated by the small number which bothered to register.

Insofar as these traditional organizations proved inadequate, Africans in Nairobi might have supported actively the extraordinary number of European-type societies that existed within the African estates. But, as Tom Mboya pointed out in 1964, "almost all of them depend upon European women to do the work."[81] A short time later, Mboya took it upon himself to reprimand his fellow Members of Parliament for seeming to be unaware of the private centers in Nairobi, largely run by Europeans and Asians, that were attempting to help African cripples, beggars, juvenile prostitutes, and others in need. "We must begin to accept that one of the immediate responsibilities that devolves on the African community," he exclaimed, "is to begin to take an interest — and an active interest — in the unfortunates of our own community."[82] Yet, it has been difficult to draw upon a voluntary spirit to obtain workers and funds required by such charitable foundations as the Kenya Red Cross Society.

It seemed to be the prevalent opinion in Kenya that the problems of urban life were primarily the responsibility of government, using paid employees. This may have stemmed from the popular faith in the socialist ideals proclaimed by African leaders. The system of private charity which developed along functional or secular lines in Western countries was associated with capitalism. It was a way of dealing with the failures or casualties of modern competitive enterprise. Under African socialism, on the other hand, the human costs of modernization would be minimized and taken care of by a system of public welfare.

*Inter-ethnic Conflict*

By 1969, conflict among Africans had replaced that among the races as the outstanding source of tension in the affairs of Nairobi. This conflict involved class as well as tribal divisions, and it was intensified by the process of narrowing the racial gap in income and way of life.

While the Government was anxious for a large African bourgeoisie, able to cooperate and compete with the other races, it also desired "to plan development so as to prevent the emergence of antagonistic classes."[83] This proved to be very difficult to do. Particularly in Nairobi, an African elite was rapidly forming. Those who spoke English fluently gained in this way alone a higher status among the masses. In comparing Nairobi to Mombasa, an African secretary noted in the *East African Standard* in 1966 that "today you find so-and-so has become your chum and yet tomorrow the very same chum passes you by as if she did not know you from Adam. Such are the folk of Nairobi — a batch of squares, a bundle of snobs."[84]

The pace at which an African aristocracy was emerging, contrary to the prevailing spirit of African socialism, was, according to Oginga Odinga in his 1967 memoirs *Not Yet Uhuru,* the chief reason for his going into political opposition in 1966. "If Kenya started *uhuru* without an African elite class, she is now rapidly acquiring one," he wrote, adding: "Ministers and top civil servants compete with one another to buy more farms, acquire more directorships and own bigger cars and grander houses."[85] Odinga might have also mentioned the practice of using licensing to confer monopoly powers and benefits on a select group of African traders and businessmen.

Philip Ochieng, the African journalist previously quoted, claimed that the new class of African landlords and businessmen discriminated just as much against Africans as Europeans or Asians. Those who had fought for freedom, he wrote, "did not fight just so as to substitute White exploiters with Black exploiters. They fought in order to attain a new important economic freedom in their own country."[86]

A number of factors eased the tension of increasing social stratification among Africans in Nairobi.[87] Few Africans in the city broke completely their ties with their rural origins, or their links with members of their extended families, many of whom remained illiterate. Moreover, there was a growing African middle class of small businessmen, clerks, artisans, shop assistants, etc. who were able to bridge the extremes of "haves" and "have-nots." But the growing disparities in wealth and education so evident in Nairobi were certainly a cause of concern, at least on the part of the country's intellectuals, because of the likelihood that the "self-made" African elite of this generation would be the beginning of a self-perpetuating African aristocracy.

Even more disturbing to Africans in Nairobi than social stratification was the evidence of tribal discrimination. Indeed, it was the linking of the two social phenomena which so alarmed the people of Nairobi — the fact that, because of ethnic prejudice, certain tribes seemed to be getting ahead faster than others. There was great fear expressed of a domination of Kikuyus and Luos, as described by Tom Mboya:

> Some of our present difficulties in Kenya and some of the suspicions against the Kikuyu and the Luo arise from the fact that, although many of their leaders condemn tribalism, it is alleged that they meet secretly behind the scenes and plan a Kikuyu or a Luo approach to Kenya politics. The Kikuyu are especially accused of this. Fears of this sort have had an effect on relations between the tribes, and have sometimes produced tribalist reactions among other tribes. These fears have also been exploited by ambitious politicians for their own ends. Occasionally they have been used as propaganda to belittle good done by genuine Kikuyu leaders, and even to try to keep them out of national affairs.[88]

To understand the intensity of inter-ethnic conflict, the impact of colonial rule discussed in the two previous chapters must be re-emphasized. First of all, administrative units were set up in such a way as to coincide with ethnic units, with Africans employed as civil servants usually in their own tribal area.[89] In each section of Kenya, the British set up native courts, using the customary laws prevailing in the area and giving local chiefs or elders executive as well as judicial powers.[90] This meant that those who moved into a new area were generally considered ethnic strangers and, as such, prevented or discouraged from acquiring property and in other ways discriminated against and made to feel unwelcomed. Second, the location of schools, urban centers, and commercial undertakings was such as to benefit some ethnic groups more than others. Because of their proximity to European settlements, the Kikuyu, while more upset by colonial rule than other tribes in Kenya, were also more rapidly impelled towards modernization. Third, the colonial rulers consciously or unconsciously used one ethnic group against another. For example, the British recruited Kamba, Kipsigi, and Kalenjin tribesmen for army and police work against the Kikuyu, whom the British saw as their primary threat.

Possibly more significant than anything else was the denial of opportunities for trans-ethnic politics. By discouraging for many years African national parties, political organization, and newspapers, the British left the way open for ethnic parties, associations, and periodicals. Likewise, with the belated introduction of extensive African legislative representation through popular elections, local politics with an ethnic orientation prevailed. Since there were few experienced African administrators, judges, politicians, and military or police officers, there was a dearth of respected Africans who could mediate inter-ethnic disputes or could handle problems that generated inter-ethnic conflict. Moreover, most Africans lacked the integrative experience of formal education, including the learning of a common language, the forming of multi-ethnic friendships, and the developing of ethnically cross-cutting associations. In these and other ways, the socialization process which might have reduced ethnic ties was retarded.

The uneven impact of colonialism in Kenya caused the Kikuyu to lead the struggle for independence. Later, when Luo gained the leadership in this struggle, many Kikuyu were resentful. While the Kikuyu and the Luo leaders eventually joined together to form a nationalist movement, the party (KANU) which they established never completely lost its ethnic origins. As independence approached, the struggle to lead the anti-colonial movement was also seen as a struggle for the opportunities that independence presented. Consequently, certain leaders who feared that they would not adequately share in the spoils of independence aroused ethnic consciousness to gain support for their ambitions. Inasmuch as leaders sought ethnic rather than national support, they were viewed as ethnic spokesmen rather than as issue advocates.

With the coming to power of Kenyatta, KANU came to be increasingly dominated by Kikuyus. As such, it could hardly mediate inter-ethnic disputes. Likewise, because the struggle for political power was so intense, together with other reasons (poverty, illiteracy, inexperience, etc.), elections could not be used to resolve inter-ethnic conflict peacefully. At the same time, the legislature, the bureaucracy, the judiciary, the army and the police were no longer considered ethnically neutral. There was evidence that Kikuyu were using their political power in various ways for economic advantage. For example, of the Industrial and Commercial Development Corporation loans made up to April 1966, 64 per cent of the industrial and 44 per cent of the commercial went to Kikuyu, then comprising about 20 per cent of the adult male population.[91] Because there were no significant restraints on governmental action, it was feared that political power would be increasingly used by the Kikuyu to subordinate other ethnic groups, keeping them permanently in an inferior position.

While inter-tribal tension had always existed in Nairobi, the manifestations became more dangerous with independence than previously. These manifestations seldom involved the sort of street-fighting described by Mboya: "As soon as a Kikuyu saw a Luo, the first thing he did was pick up a stone and hit his head."[92] Nevertheless, because these two tribes (the Kikuyu and the Luo) most actively competed for political power, tension between them was most obvious. Consequently, the 1966 challenge to the leadership of Kenya presented by the Kenya Peoples Union, led by the former Vice President of Kenya, Oginga Odinga, was seen as a Luo conspiracy despite the fact that, of the nineteen representatives and nine Senators who followed Odinga into opposition, only five were Luo.[93] In any case, it was the Luo Members of Parliament who persistently charged the Government with tribal bias. "If tribalism remained," exclaimed Mr. Luke Obok in March 1968, "a ruling class would be created which would lead Kenya into conflict. The country was already heading for trouble because tribalism was being permitted to establish itself throughout the country."[94] Another Luo M.P. alleged in 1968 that nearly three-fourths of wage-earning jobs had gone to Kikuyu.[95] The implicit conviction that there was ethnic favoritism in job allocations was undoubtedly the greatest source of animosity in view of the existing urban poverty and unemployment.

As indicated in the previous chapter, Mboya was among those who worked hardest to diminish tension between Kikuyu and Luo. "He was a Luo," to quote Kenya's Vice President Daniel arap Moi, "but nobody could have been less tribal in outlook."[96] Of course, as the Member of Parliament for Nairobi, with its multi-tribal population, Mboya was particularly mindful of the need for inter-ethnic harmony. "Our task must be to eliminate tribalism and to forge a national consciousness," he exclaimed in 1966. "This is our greatest challenge and unless leaders can set out deliberately, persistently and conscientiously to remove tribalism, much of what we have achieved could be lost overnight."[97] For this reason he bluntly rebuffed the invitation to join an incipient Luo organization in the summer of 1965 by declaring: "While I am for harmony and unity among the Luo, I question the methods now being used by interested parties. Unity in this case must be positive, based on our integration into the Kenya nation and not as an isolationist, tribalist movement."[98]

The assassination of Mboya in the summer of 1969 was doubly unfortunate: it removed not only one of Kenya's most competent and experienced ministers, but also one of the most useful mediators of inter-tribal conflict. The pent-up malaise of the Luo people suddenly erupted into the most dangerous rioting ever seen in Nairobi. The eventual conviction of a Kikuyu for this assassination intensified the rumors of a Kikuyu plot to consolidate power.

Since 1969, the fears of growing Kikuyu power have been augmented by a number of developments.[99] All the institutions in which non-Kikuyu were prominent (Parliament, the cabinet, the trade unions, KANU, the national university, etc.) have been effectively neutralized. In the army, Kikuyu replaced Kamba as the top officers and became increasingly predominant in lower ranks. At the same time, as a counterforce to the army, a well-armed, largely Kikuyu paramilitary force of about 2,500 men (the General Services Unit) was organized. In this and other ways, political power (and, thereby, economic resources) has been increasingly dominated by a small number of the President's close associates, all of whom are Kikuyu and mostly from Kiambu (where Kenyatta's own clan originated).

## Conclusion

The socio-economic problems mentioned in this chapter (together with those of hawking and housing discussed in later chapters) have important implications for the administration of Nairobi, which will next be analyzed. Kenya, like so many other underdeveloped countries, suffers from what has been called "hyperurbanization" (a situation that exists when a nation's economic, cultural, social, and political institutions cannot cope with the numbers of people migrating to the cities).[100] In the case of Kenya, this situation has been worsened by existing inter-racial and inter-ethnic conflict stemming to a large extent from the colonial period. This, of course, adversely affects the attainment of elasticity of control — the cooperative relationship necessary for successful decentralization.

In Kenya, wealth continues to be largely in the hands of Europeans and Asians at a time when political power is in the hands of Africans. This means that the government is under great political pressure to diminish the racial disparities in standard of living. Yet, to do so without arousing dysfunctional racial fears is extremely difficult. Insofar as Europeans and Asians are frightened or forced into leaving Kenya, the economy inevitably suffers. While this is a fact recognized by the leaders, it is hard for ordinary Africans to understand.

What intensifies social conflict in Kenya more than anything else is economic scarcity. In other words, Africans express displeasure not so much at the skin color of Asians and Europeans as at their wealth in the midst of poverty. At the same time, the struggle for the existing limited resources also goes on among Africans. Amid poverty and unemployment, great pressure is put on those in power to distribute jobs and favors to kinsmen. As this happens, there is an intensified resentment of ethnic favoritism on the part of the politically disadvantaged. Thus, the struggle for resources in Kenya takes ethnic (and even sub-ethnic) as well as racial forms, undermining the government's capability of increasing resources to diminish social tension. This, as will be pointed out, has been a basic problem for the Nairobi City Council.

## NOTES

1. *East African Standard* (E.A.S.), July 19, 1966.
2. Cf. K. F. Craig-McFeely, *Planning Report No. 1: Population* (Nairobi: City Council, 1967), pp. 2-7; Dorothy M. Halliman and W. T. W. Morgan, "The City of Nairobi," in W. T. W. Morgan, ed., *Nairobi: City and Region* (Nairobi: Oxford U. Press, 1967), pp. 105-9.
3. *Kenya Education Commission Report, Part II* (Nairobi: Government Printer, 1965), p. 16.
4. Cf. Ministry of Economic Planning and Development, *Development Plan for the Period 1965/66 to 1969/70* (Revised Development Plan) (Nairobi: Government Printer, 1966), p. 316. With the decline of the European population, some of these hospitals became very much underused.
5. Cf. Dharam P. Ghai, "An Economic Survey," in Daram P. Ghai, ed., *Portrait of a Minority: Asians in East Africa* (Nairobi: Oxford U. Press, 1965), p. 99.
6. Cf. *Reported Employment and Earnings in Kenya, 1962* (Nairobi: Economics and Statistics Division, the Treasury, June, 1963).
7. *1964-1970 Development Plan* (Kenya: Government Printer, 1964), p. 34.
8. The Ominde Report, Part I (Nairobi: Government Printer, 1964), p. 1.
9. Cf. Guy Hunter, *Education for a Developing Region: A Study in East Africa* (London: George Allen & Unwin, Ltd., 1963), pp. 10-11, 20.

10. Calvin F. Davis, *High-Level Manpower Requirements and Resources in Kenya, 1964-1970* (Nairobi: Ministry of Economic Planning and Development, 1965), pp. 2-30.

11. Statement of Mboya, E.A.S., September 26, 1966.

12. Cf. J. Kamau, "Problems of African Business Enterprise," *Proceedings of the East African Institute for Social Research,* January, 1965, p. 5.

13. E.A.S., July 27, 1963.

14. (Kenya: Government Printer), 1965, p. 25.

15. Cf. K. S. N. Matiba, "African Businessmen Must be Realistic," E.A.S., July 25, 1967.

16. E.A.S., July 10, 1967.

17. E.A.S., December 16, 1966.

18. *Daily Nation,* July 26, 1967.

19. *New York Times,* May 6, 1966.

20. Robert Gavin, "Correcting Racial Imbalances in Employment in Kenya," *International Labour Review,* Vol. XCV (January-June, 1967), p. 75.

21. E.A.S., July 21, 1967.

22. E.A.S., February 9, 1968.

23. Kamau, *loc. cit.*

24. *A Land Full of People; Life in Kenya Today* (New York: Praeger, 1966), p. 114.

25. Cf. Matiba, *loc. cit.*

26. Cf. Mwai Kibaki, "The East African Community and the Growth of the African Trader," *Weekly News,* July 7, 1967, pp. 21, 34.

27. "The Social Barriers to African Entrepreneurship," *The Journal of Development Studies,* Vol. V, No. 1 (October, 1968), p. 33.

28. E.A.S., December 7, 1966. This action was declared unconstitutional in 1968 by the courts, E.A.S., March 9, 1968.

29. E.A.S., July 27, 1967.

30. Cf. Roberts, *op. cit.,* pp. 38, 93, 107.

31. Revised Development Plan, *op. cit.,* p. VIII. According to the E.A.S. of February 13, 1968, less than one-half of the 20,000 applications had been processed.

32. *New York Times,* March 24, 1968, p. 3. India subsequently also placed restrictions on immigration from Africa of Asians with British passports.

33. Part I, *op. cit.,* p. 12.

34. Cf. Gavin, *op. cit.*, pp. 61-77.

35. *Ibid.*, p. 65.

36. E.A.S., August 4, 1964.

37. E.A.S., February 8, 1968 and July 8, 1967.

38. "Human Resources for Economic and Social Development in Kenya," in *The Kenya We Want* (Nairobi: East African Printers Ltd., 1962), pp. 85-86.

39. *Op. cit.*, pp. 14-15.

40. *Ibid.*, pp. 8-9.

41. Article by Peter Kenyatta, E.A.S., February 7, 1967.

42. Cf. paper prepared by the Economics Department of the University College, Nairobi, E.A.S., March 9, 1968.

43. February 15, 1968.

44. Cf. Susan Wood, *Kenya: The Tensions of Progress,* 2nd ed. (London: Oxford University Press, 1962), pp. 12-13.

45. Cf. L. H. Gann and P. Duignan, *White Settlers in Tropical Africa* (Harmondsworth, Middlesex: Penguin Books, 1962), p. 136; International Bank for Reconstruction and Development (I.B.R.D.), *The Economic Development of Kenya* (Baltimore: The Johns Hopkins Press, 1963), pp. 22, 42; *Economic Survey, 1963* (Nairobi: Government of Kenya, 1963), *passim.*

46. Economics and Statistics Division of the Treasury, *Economic Survey, 1964,* pp. 39-43, 51-52; Revised Development Plan, *op. cit.,* p. 99.

47. Cf. Revised Development Plan, *op. cit.,* p. 53; the Ominde Report, Part II, *op. cit.,* p. 24; Joint Working Party of the Youth Department of the Christian Council of Kenya and the Christian Churches' Education Association, *After School What?* (Nairobi: Christian Council of Kenya, March, 1966), pp. 3-4.

48. Revised Development Plan, *op. cit.,* pp. 77, 257.

49. *After School What? op. cit.,* p. 27.

50. The 3 per cent unemployment rate is from A. G. Dalgleish, *Survey of Unemployment* (Nairobi: Kenya Government Printer, 1960), p. 19; the estimate of 30 per cent is a rough guess based on the 43,000 figure of registered unemployed in Nairobi in 1964 (not all of which actually lived in Nairobi or were genuinely unemployed) and the 1962 Census figure for adult African males in Nairobi.

51. Cf. *1964-1970 Development Plan, op. cit.,* pp. 16-17; I.B.R.D., *op. cit.,* p. 358.

52. E.A.S., October 1, 1966.

53. *Economic Survey, 1967,* pp. 84-88; Revised Development Plan, *op. cit.,* p. 257.

54. E.A.S., February 12, 1964. Under the arrangement signed by the Federation of Kenya Employers, the Kenya Federation of Labour, and the Government of Kenya, the Government agreed to increase employment by 15 per cent; the private employers, by 10 per cent.

55. Cf. the statement of Mboya, E.A.S., April 15, 1965.

56. Cf. Idris Cox, "Kenya Needs African Unity," *New Africa,* Vol. V, No. 4 (April, 1963), pp. 10-11; Dalgleish, *op. cit.,* p. 12. Altogether there were reported to be 150,000 African landless families in Kenya in 1962.

57. E.A.S., October 1, 1966; *The Economist,* January 21, 1967, p. 216; *Daily Nation,* July 19, 1967; Roberts, *op. cit.,* p. 130.

58. E.A.S., July 8, 1958.

59. Cf. E. P. Wilkinson, "Nairobi's Population Growth and the Problem of Housing" (a report to the Nairobi City Council, 1964), pp. 2-3; S. C. Lock, "Nairobi Area: Housing of Migrants" (Memorandum prepared by the Town Planning Adviser on the instructions of the Ministers for Local Government, Health and Housing, and Labour and Social Services, 1963), p. 2; Craig-McFeely, *op. cit.,* pp. 22-27.

60. E.A.S., September 12, 1964.

61. *Op. cit.,* p. 27.

62. *After School What?, op. cit.,* pp. 46-47.

63. H. Millar-Craig, Chairman, *Report of the Salaries Review Commission, 1967* (Nairobi: Government Printer, 1967), pp. 22-23.

64. *1964-1970 Development Plan, op. cit.,* p. 35.

65. (Nairobi: City Hall, March, 1961), p. 1.

66. Nairobi was one of the few major cities of the world to have had a reported drop in crime between 1965 and 1967, but the accuracy of these figures is difficult to determine. E.A.S., January 12, 1967. After 1967, the crime rate rose alarmingly.

67. E.A.S., June 30, 1966.

68. Humphrey Slade, Chairman (Kenya: Government Printer, 1961), p. 41.

69. E.A.S., August 2, 1965.

70. E.A.S., April 18, 1969.

71. Cf. *Reporter,* March 3, 1962.

72. (Nairobi: Directorate of Planning, The Treasury, July, 1964), p. 24.

73. Charles J. Ashby, Chairman (Nairobi: Nairobi Round Table No. 1, April 16, 1963), p. 2. The belief expressed here that there is a relationship between detribalization and the loss of land rights is probably mistaken.

74. E.A.S., August 20, 1966.

75. Cf. Peter C. W. Gutkind, "The Energy of Despair: Social Organization of the Unemployed in Two African Cities: Lagos and Nairobi (1st Part)," *Civilisations,* Vol. XVII, No. 3 (1967), p. 193.

76. "Family Problems in Urban Areas," in *The Kenya We Want, op. cit.,* pp. 85-86.

77. E.A.S., June 19, 1969.

78. Cf. Fred G. Burke, *Africa's Quest for Order* (Englewood Cliffs, New Jersey: Prentice-Hall, 1964), p. 50.

79. "African Elections in Kenya, March, 1957," in W. J. M. Mackenzie and Kenneth Robinson, *Five Elections in Africa: A Group of Electoral Studies* (Oxford: at the Clarendon Press, 1960), p. 439.

80. E.A.S., October 23, 1966.

81. E.A.S., April 13, 1964.

82. E.A.S., August 13, 1964.

83. *African Socialism, op. cit.,* pp. 12-13.

84. E.A.S., November 19, 1966.

85. (London: Heinemann, 1967), p. 302.

86. *Daily Nation,* March 2, 1969.

87. Cf. Roberts, *op. cit.,* pp. 78-92.

88. Quoted, Alan Rake, *Tom Mboya: Young Man of New Africa* (Garden City, New York: Doubleday & Co., 1962), p. 74.

89. Cf. Audrey I. Richards, *The Multicultural States of East Africa* (Montreal and London: McGill-Queen's University Press, 1969), pp. 1-30.

90. Cf. Eugene Cotran, "Tribal Factors in the Establishment of the East African Legal Systems," in P. H. Gulliver, ed., *Tradition & Transition in East Africa* (London: Routledge & Kegan Paul, 1969), pp. 127-146.

91. Peter Marris and Anthony Somerset, *African Businessmen: A Study of Entrepreneurship and Development in Kenya* (Nairobi: East African Publishing House, 1971), p. 71.

92. *Freedom and After, op. cit.,* p. 71.

93. Cf. Marco Surveys, *Kenya's Little General Election: K.P.U. Vs. KANU, 1966-1967,* Public Opinion Poll No. 15 (Nairobi: Marco Publishers, 1967), p. xi; David Koff, "Kenya's Little General Election," *Africa Report,* Vol. XI, No. 7 (October, 1966), pp. 57-60.

94. E.A.S., March 30, 1968.

95. Cited, Donald Rothchild, "Ethnic Inequalities in Kenya," in Victor A. Olorunsola, ed., *The Politics of Cultural Sub-Nationalism in Africa* (Garden City, N.Y.: Anchor Books, 1972), p. 302.

96. E.A.S., July 14, 1969.

97. E.A.S., October 6, 1966.

98. E.A.S., August 20, 1965.

99. Cf. Jim Hoagland, "Kenya's Crucial Issue: Who Will Succeed Kenyatta?," *The Washington Post,* Jan. 9, 1973, p. A12.

100. Cf. Bert F. Hoselitz, "The City, The Factory, and Economic Growth," *American Economic Review,* Vol. 45 (May, 1955), pp. 166-184.

# 5 THE ADMINISTRATIVE MALAISE

## Introduction

As was mentioned in the last chapter, the Kenyan economy in the 1960's continued to be dominated by Europeans and Asians while the polity was turned over to Africans. Likewise, the bureaucracy remained dependent upon European and Asian administrative and technical skills while being politically controlled by Africans. This produced the same sort of tensions within the government of Nairobi as existed within the general urban milieu, giving rise to inelasticity of control. In the earlier sections of this chapter, we will describe the situation that existed during the 1960's when most of the City Council's chief officers continued to be Europeans. In the later sections, we will describe what happened when Africans took over the chief officers' positions.

## Problems of Transition

The social and economic conditions facing the Africans who came into control of the City Council of Nairobi on the first of October, 1963 (several months prior to independence), would have taxed the ingenuity of even the most experienced and well-qualified politicians. Unfortunately, the background of these Africans did not augur well for the future.[1] Of the twenty-eight African Council members at this time, none had a university degree, though nine claimed to have had enough secondary school education to qualify for the General Certificate of Education and another eight claimed to have gone somewhat beyond primary school. In regard to the other members, the Senate Standing Committee that investigated the Nairobi City Council in 1964 "noted with grave concern that there were some councillors who because of their inability to read, write, or speak English were unable to follow Council proceedings and wondered how they were able intelligently to exercise their vote."[2]

Only three of this group of African Council members could be considered as active professional people and another three, as having executive experience in large firms. This situation reflected what is true of African society as a whole, "an almost complete lack of the middle-aged, semi-retired professional people who are so generally the backbone of British local councils."[3] Moreover, only six of the incoming African members had had prior experience on the Nairobi City Council, and two others, on some other local government council. The inadequate preparation of the African Council members frightened the Africans as well as many of the Europeans associated with the City Council. "Why did the British leave us in this way," moaned a newly elected African City Councillor, "without education, experience, or money? Why did they leave us in a house without furniture?"[4]

The situation was complicated for the inexperienced Council members by the new constitution which gave the City Council responsibility for an area of 266 square miles (instead of 35 square miles) and for additional services, of which education was the most important, previously handled by the Central Government. This added area contained a semi-rural population of 76,706 (according to the 1962 Census) with quite different problems from most of the people within the confines of Nairobi City proper.

The comparative complexity and sophistication of the municipal government being taken over presented both a challenge as well as an opportunity. Outside of Southern Rhodesia, no African city under British jurisdiction could match Nairobi during colonial days in affluence (the size of its budget in relation to the population served), in efficiency (based on the ratio of administrative costs to total expenditure), and in the extent to which it relied on professionally qualified people.[5] The economic importance of Nairobi can be seen from the fact that its proposed capital expenditure during the period 1964-70 amounted to £16.7 million, which was 12.6 per cent of the total amount to be spent by the public sector of the Kenyan economy. The Nairobi City Council could afford to spend far more than any other local authority in Kenya both because of the higher per-capita income of the population being served and because of its unique ability to borrow directly on the London Market. Consequently, between 1959 and 1962 Nairobi raised almost twice as much by loans as all other local authorities in Kenya combined (£7.8 million as against £4 million).[6] Though the City Council's stock-issuing ability was rather doubtful at the time of independence, it was expected to receive half of the amount to be loaned by Kenya's Local Government Loans Fund during the 1964-70 period.[7]

## The Committee System

The immediate effect of the City Council's coming under the control of inexperienced African councillors was the inordinate prolonging of committee meetings, upon which the working of an English-type local government depends. According to a veteran European member of the City Council, business that used to take two hours now took more than five. One officer (i.e., administrative official) claimed that he was spending 40 hours a month in committee, as against 20 hours a month under the old regime. This meant not only that the entire operation of the City government was seriously slowed down, but also that the chief officers of the City Council, who were required to attend these meetings, became very overworked. Even some of the Council members, particularly those with demanding businesses to attend to, complained about the waste of time.

In explaining the reason for the length of the committee meetings, one of the European officers suggested that it had to do with the African traditional practice of "talking a matter out." There were, however, more meaningful explanations having to do with the inability of the Council members to understand the issues that arose as well as the procedure or rules of order that were to be followed. "I could talk with the previous councillors in a way that I can't with the present ones," one of the more scornful of the European officers commented, adding: "Now when I mention 'stocks' to them, half think I am talking about animals on a farm, and the other half think I am referring to items in a store." This ignorance was also recognized by a number of the African councillors, one of whom frankly admitted that "we have little understanding of what the officers tell us, and we don't really understand what we are supposed to do." "Maybe," he went on, "the officers should help us by holding classes to explain the details of their jobs and problems."

Combined with this lack of understanding on the part of the Council members was their uncertainty about the extent to which they should rely upon the advice of the administrators. This uncertainty would have existed under the best of circumstances, but it was intensified by the fact that all of the chief officers at the beginning of the new regime were European hold-overs from the colonial period. Though many of them were quite capable, some were not inclined to be sympathetic with African problems and aspirations. Also, the fact that most of these officers had come from English local authorities rather than the Colonial Office (as did the District Officers who were sent to the rural areas to train Africans in running local government) partly accounted for their inability to see their role as "teachers" rather than simply as "administrators." Consequently, they viewed each additional African hired to be an officer as a burden rather than as a potential asset.

The City Council's officers were accustomed to exercising more influence than their counterparts in Great Britain, or so it was alleged in 1961 by W. Bestwick, the Organization and Methods Consultant:

> In the Nairobi City Council the heads of departments meet for one morning each week and more often, when considered necessary. It is understood that an agenda is prepared for each meeting

by the Town Clerk and consists of any items which any head of department considers should be discussed by all. Minutes of the meetings are prepared by the Town Clerk but are not circulated beyond heads of departments and the committee clerks. Recommendations to committees and the Council decided upon at these meetings then go forward as recommendations from the departments as a body.[8]

This meant, according to Bestwick, that, instead of ventilating differences of opinion openly in committees, as supposedly was the standard practice in Great Britain, the officers of the Nairobi City Council did so in secret meetings, thereby making the agreed-upon recommendations to the Council members more persuasive than they might otherwise have been.[9]

However persuasive the European officers had been during the colonial period, it was unlikely that they would be so well-received by an African council. Though sixty to sixty-five of these officers were to be retained under attractive terms until at least the middle of 1965, they had to endure the deep distrust of the African Council members.

The extent to which this distrust permeated the operation of the committees is indicated in the following remark:

> The African councillors simply won't trust us. They cannot understand why particular contracts are let to particular companies, and they won't accept the explanation that these companies are the most efficient. They feel that the officers are somehow being dishonest in their recommendations even after all the objections have been thoroughly discussed in the committees.

This distrust was thought by the European officers to be reinforced by the ignorance and inexperience of the African Council members. "The Councillors fail to understand the technical problems that we face in the building projects undertaken," one of them remarked, adding: "They want a maternity hospital completed in three weeks and flatly reject our opinion that it can't be done. They feel that we are sabotaging the project."

The same sort of attitude that is associated in the United States with the Jacksonian "spoils system" was said to prevail among the

City Council members. It was the opinion of one of the newly appointed African officers that "they cannot understand the need for skilled individuals. Anyone, they think, can supervise the laying of waterpipes or fill in forms as the officers do." Beyond this, there was the failure to understand how a large organization works. "They are putting pressure on us to raise the salaries of a certain group of employees," exclaimed one of the European officers, "not realizing how this would upset the entire pay-scale, endangering the morale of the entire staff!"

One early manifestation of this distrust of the officers was the ruling of the City Council prohibiting their officers from consulting officials of the Central Government on their own initiative.[10] If this ruling had been strictly enforced, it would have not only jeopardized good relations with the Central Government but also would have made the work of the Council's officers more difficult by preventing them from readily anticipating the reactions of those in the Central Government. With the extraordinary changes that had taken place at the time of independence, it became both increasingly necessary and difficult to keep the intra-governmental channels of communication open.

In any case, the officers constantly complained of a serious loss of freedom and flexibility, stemming from their inability to sense the feelings of the leaders at the various levels of government — their desires, motives, prejudices, etc. — in a way that previously could be done. What made the officers feel especially handicapped in this regard was the absence of strong committee chairmen, the sort who could work out with the officers acceptable policies which they would then take the responsibility to defend. "In the old days I could get to know the chairman of a committee so well that I always knew what I could get away with," one of the officers recounted. "Now I explain things to the chairmen I deal with, but they don't understand, or they refuse to support what is agreed upon and to give leadership."

The conduct and frequency of committee meetings was to some extent affected by the fact that the Africans who took control of the Nairobi City Council in 1963 were paid a "sitting allowance" of 50 shillings ($7) per meeting attended. Because some Council members sat on many more committees than others (thereby "earning" 40 to 50 pounds per month while some of their colleagues were only getting 15 to 20 pounds per month), the "sitting allowance" system was greatly resented. "The Council's main arguments," noted the 1964 Nairobi Standing Committee of the Senate, "were that a daily allowance led to councillors competing for appointments to as many committees as possible and involved the staff in extra administrative work in order to keep detailed records of attendances."[11] Moreover, the councillors soon learned that they could increase their income from sitting allowances by increasing the number of subcommittees on which they sat. In this way both the time and the authority of the officers were infringed upon, inasmuch as these subcommittees tended to get involved in functions (such as minor purchases) normally handled by the officers.

The Minister for Local Government until 1965 (Mr. Ayodo) resisted the demand of the Nairobi City Council for a flat monthly salary of £35 ($98).[12] Council members might not even bother to attend meetings under this arrangement, he argued, or else they would attend just the minimum number of required meetings to get their consolidated allowance. It was also asserted that if the Council members of Nairobi got such an allowance, members of local councils throughout the country would demand the same amount, thus intolerably burdening the already impoverished local governments of Kenya. An even bigger consideration in the mind of the Minister was the desirability of preserving the principle of voluntary service "so that a local authority councillor would not think he had obtained a job to support his family."[13] This raised the question of the extent to which Africans could be expected to appreciate an ideal already discarded or under attack in many countries as perpetuating the domination of the wealthier, more leisured class.

While endorsing the principle of voluntary service, the Nairobi Standing Committee concluded "that cognizance must be taken of the fact that the present Council was composed of councillors not wealthy enough to devote their services voluntarily" and, furthermore, "that the present system had resulted in an increase in the number of committees and subcommittees and the number of members per committee to the detriment of local government in the

Nairobi area."[14] Following the recommendation of this committee, the Ministry of Local Government agreed to a monthly pay-out of £20 ($56) to councillors and aldermen and of £30 ($84) to committee chairmen, provided that they attended at least three-quarters of council meetings and committee meetings to which they were appointed.[15] The Council members, however, continued to be dissatisfied.

In April, 1967, by which time the Council members were getting an allowance of £40 ($112) per month the General Purposes Committee resolved that allowances should be increased to £50 ($140) per month because of the high cost of living in Nairobi and the time-consuming character of Council work.[16] The committees met over 400 times per year, it was pointed out, and often the agendas for these meetings were so long that special meetings were required. In addition, there were subcommittee meetings to attend which were not taken into account in the enforcement of the 75 per cent attendance requirement. The Councillors also complained that they had to spend many hours beyond that officially required for Council business helping members of their electorate with their myriad problems. But the Hardacre Commission that met in 1966 was of the opinion that the current allowances were already too high and ought to be reduced.[17] Consequently, the Council's request in 1967 for an allowance increase was rejected.

*Africanization*

The fact that all staff positions would inevitably be Africanized had an obvious demoralizing effect upon certain of the remaining expatriate officers, as expressed in the following statement:

> No one cares anymore about his work. There is no teamwork. We used to think of our jobs here as lifelong. Now it is simply a matter of a year or two. Why bother?

Nevertheless, one of the leading African Council members claimed that the pressure for Africanization came not simply from Africans but from European staff as well. "Many expatriates indicate that they want to leave not only by word of mouth but also by being increasingly careless about their work."

Some of the European officers indicated a willingness to stay on, but lacking the security of long-term contracts, they were generally anxious to return to a desirable job in England while still young enough to do so. Actually, the more technically qualified officers could expect to continue with the City Council for the remainder of their careers though probably not as chief officers. They were worried more by the difficulties of raising a family under the trying social and economic conditions expected to prevail than by the alleged difficulties of working for an African government. The education of their children was the most troublesome concern of all.

The problem of replacing the European staff seemed to be the most pressing that the City Council faced. There was a need for people with a high level of training and experience (accountants, engineers, doctors, lawyers, health inspectors, etc.). Even during the colonial period, Nairobi had experienced difficulty in recruiting staff. Consequently there was a tendency to take junior officers from British local authorities, often with inadequate experience and overly anxious for quick promotion.[18] With rising salaries and opportunities in Great Britain and growing uncertainty about political conditions in Africa, it became increasingly difficult to retain those who were hired.

Mr. H. C. Beechey, the President of the Nairobi European Local Government Officers' Association, noted that of the 253 Europeans on the Council's staff at the end of 1954, only 98 remained in its employ in 1960.[19] This meant that at the beginning of 1961, 18 per cent of the Council's 1,100 posts, excluding manual workers, were vacant.[20] As independence approached, the complaints of the chief officers about insufficiency of personnel became ever more vociferous, combined as they were with the demand for measures to protect the pensions of the remaining staff. In 1962, Mr. A. W. Kent, the City Treasurer, pointed out to the City Council's Finance Committee:

> The shortage of experienced staff made it impossible to examine adequately all new projects and policies so that a considered financial and economic report could be presented to the Committee. Council's continued indecision as to the future security and pros-

pects of staff had undermined the morale of conscientious officers, and some at present in Council's service might be attracted elsewhere. This could be disastrous, particularly if any of the senior expatriate officers departed. The economic and political problems of the City's finance department were difficult, requiring greater skill and knowledge, when the staff situation at the senior level was desperate. . . . Whilst everything possible was being done by the remaining staff to keep the general control in operation, the majority of staff had been working long hours for such an extended period that it might lead to deterioration of their health and efficiency.[21]

How serious the staff situation had become by 1964 was indicated by the estimate that only 25 per cent of the protected staff (those expatriates given a special contract to remain after Independence) would renew their contracts when they terminated in 1965. This meant that by November, 1965, there would be between 200 and 300 vacancies that would have to be filled by the City Council.[22] "With three-fourths of the engineers employed by the City Council leaving," one African officer exclaimed, "the work is bound to deteriorate."

The exodus of staff had been anticipated by a number of the chief officers, but it was, wrote the Medical Officer of Health in 1960, "hoped that expediency during this period will not be made the excuse for the acceptance of staff of grossly inferior training and qualifications. Such a door, once opened," he warned, "would be very hard to close, although there may well be an attempt to force it by political pressures."[23] The saving factor, it was suggested, was the great respect in which Nairobi was held throughout Africa and the determination of the leading local and national figures to maintain the City's reputation. For this reason, argued Mayor Rubia, the imperatives of Africanization would have to be balanced against those of maintaining standards, keeping in mind that standards were relative, except where health and financial integrity were involved.[24]

In contrast to the Mayor's cautiousness concerning Africanization, the more militant Council members were generally insistent on "Africanizing" the Council staff as quickly as possible. "We would rather be independent than efficient," one African Councillor boldly insisted. And many doubtlessly agreed with the statement issued by the Chairman of the Localization Sub-Committee that "although the policy of Africanization has been fully accepted by the Council, its implementation has been long over-delayed." His conclusion that "very little indeed, if anything at all, has been done in this direction," would, however, appear odd in view of the fact that the percentage of Africans on the City Council's staff had by this time (April, 1964) gone up from the 12.3 that it had been in July, 1960, to 43.3, but it indicates the intensity of feeling on the issue.[25]

The militancy regarding "Africanization" stemmed only partly from a desire to rectify past racial discrimination. The high cost of keeping the expatriate officers was also a factor. For example, it was pointed out in 1966 that the European town clerk had a two-year contract at £5,000 ($14,000) a year plus a gratuity of 20 per cent of his total salary for the two-year period upon completion of his contract. This amounted to nearly twice the income of the African town-clerk whom he temporarily replaced.[26] However, the greatest stimulus for Africanization was existing unemployment. This meant that those responsible for appointing technical staff were less concerned with the qualifications required for the job than "jobs for relatives and friends."[27] It would be unfair, however, to suggest that the Council as a whole was completely oblivious to the need to prevent a serious deterioration in the quantity and quality of its staff.

In its 1964 estimates, the City Council had set aside £125,000 for a "localization and training programme," under which more than 100 members of the staff were taking various courses (mostly at the University College, Nairobi and the Kenya Institute of Administration, Kabete).[28] But this was not enough. In the spring of 1964 four Nairobi African Council members, together with the newly appointed African Town Clerk, went to England to interview Kenyan students there (estimated to be about 2,000) and others who might be interested in working for the City Council, but they found only twenty-six candidates for the more than 200 positions they were hoping to fill. The reason for this was not only the paucity of Africans doing technical subjects but also the fact that many of them were already committed to working for the Central Government, the East African Common Services Organization, or private business. Though this trip to recruit staff was rather fruitless (and, as such, open to criticism), it certainly made the Council members more aware of the difficulties involved.

Since the number of qualified Africans was so limited, the City attempted to offer attractive salaries. What was available, however, left much to be desired, including "one chap with a vague law degree from India who left the Attorney General's Office without even giving notice or arranging for repayment of the salary advance made to him."[29] The strict limitations on the salaries that could be paid frequently made it difficult to keep those who were hired. "Some cases occurred during the year," wrote the City Education Officer in 1966, "of competent Headmasters leaving the profession for occupations which considerably enhanced their salaries."[30] A similar complaint was made in September, 1966, by the City Engineer in reporting that seventeen "key" men during the previous twelve months had left for better salaries elsewhere. This, he declared, "was an alarming rate of staff depletion at a time when Council had accepted the challenge to extend services."[31]

In its effort to speed Africanization, the City Council sponsored a number of students for education abroad with the understanding that they would work for the City Council when they returned. It also hired Africans as "shadows" — people who supposedly were to observe and perform the work of the positions they were training for under the direction of the officers they were eventually to replace. But neither of these programs were altogether successful.[32] The sponsorship of students abroad was expensive. Moreover, it proved to be difficult to check on what they were studying and how well they were doing, and there was no way to require these students to work for the City Council when they returned to Kenya. While the attachment of trainees to local government authorities in the United Kingdom was valuable if the students gained all-round experience, the periods of stay were felt to be usually too short for much benefit of this sort. When people were ready to work for the City Council, it was thought best to give them a definite job to do and then to hold them strictly responsible for their performance. There was a tendency for "shadows" to do more "observation" than "performance" and thereby to lose the experience of really having to face responsibility for particular tasks.

The most successful method of training, the City Council found, was the sponsorship of students at the Kenya Institute of Administration (an institute established in 1960 a short distance from Nairobi with the help of British and American funds and personnel). The program here was residential, carefully supervised, and of approximately one year's duration, which seemed to be the most suitable length of time. Also very useful were schemes of in-service training for staff, including formal lectures and help with various aspects of work or study, with time-off for preparation prior to the taking of professional examinations. Attachments to British local authorities or private firms were considered to be desirable for officers who were already professionally qualified but who needed specialized study or additional experience in certain aspects of their work. Thus, in 1967, four graduate engineers were sent by the City Council to work for British firms for periods of two to three years, financed jointly by the firms and the City Council.[33]

Among the impediments to Africanization (as of 1967) was the lack of formal training programs in Kenya for the final levels of certain professional examinations that were particularly relevant to Kenya. For example, the City Council attempted unsuccessfully to hire full-time instructors in accounting. When finally an advanced accounting course for officers of local authorities was scheduled to commence, it had to be cancelled for lack of qualified applicants. Consequently, all eight of those who attempted in 1967 the final examination for accounting failed. It was discovered that most of those who applied for eight available positions in a computer programing course in 1967 (seventy in all) lacked the basic education to benefit from the instruction. "The higher school certificate people got places in university," commented the City's Chief Accountant, "leaving us with only four people to undergo training; and, of course, not all of these will actually finish the course or work for the Council."

The City Council could not avoid using relatively untrained and inexperienced Africans for many positions. This meant that more people had to be hired without a corresponding increase in output. Between 1963 and 1965 the salaried staff, exclusive of manual workers and teachers, increased in size by about 50 per cent (from 1,385 to 1,993) while the expenditure of the City Council went up by about 20 per cent (from £3,650,701 to £4,415,717), excluding that for education which was added in 1964. In the legal department seven lawyers were employed in 1966 whereas three had done the work prior to independence. And in the Accounting Section, it required six African adding machine operators to do what four Europeans used to do. This did not necessarily mean any loss of effectiveness or any increased expenditure. "Though only 10 per cent of the draftsmen and clerks here are satisfactory," reported one of the officers in the Town Planning Section in 1966, "we have managed to reorganize the work to take this into account. What we have done," he explained, "is to downgrade their positions and salaries so that we have been able to carry on with no more a financial burden on the Council than before." This, however, was not always the case. "Even with twice the staff that we used to have," complained one of the engineers, "it takes us now a few weeks to inspect and approve structures that we once were able to do in a few days."

The insistence on putting Africans into top positions, often without regard for their experience or ability, meant that they were sometimes overly dependent on their European subordinates for the reports and decisions that needed to be made. In the City Council in 1966 the work of the Council continued to rest largely on the 114 Europeans and the 276 Asians (who together made up 20 per cent of the salaried staff excluding teachers and manual workers). This fact did not altogether escape the notice of some of the members of the National Assembly who complained that Africans who were given new jobs acted as "figureheads" while the real job was being done by expatriate officers.[34] "There can come a time when the African civil servant is nervous to assume responsibility: he wants someone else to plan for him," wrote Odinga in 1967, adding: "Some seem to prefer to work with expatriates because they prefer strangers to know their weaknesses rather than their African brothers."[35]

During the first few years after independence, the European officers of the City Council bitterly complained about their inability to discipline their African subordinates. The African officers, however, faced a similar problem — one that was intensified insofar as these officers lacked experience or ability. Those newly appointed to leadership positions also faced the difficulty of separating their social life from their business or professional milieu. "It is not easy for us to order our people about, particularly our relatives or friends," one of the African officers pointed out.

Some of the African officers had trouble delegating responsibility because they lacked confidence in the ability and loyalty of their subordinates. In its report on the Kenya civil service, the Millar-Craig commission noted that there was "room for a greater sense of loyalty within the service itself, as between one civil servant and another."[36] According to an African local authority chief officer, many junior employees wanted promotion to executive posts though they had no qualification. When their wishes were not fulfilled, they branded the officers as "Black colonialists worse than Europeans" and tried to secure the support of disgruntled politicians to oust them.[37] To curtail the practice of subordinates taking complaints and information of various sorts directly to the Council members, the General Purposes Committee in 1965 recommended that Members of Council deal only with Chief Officers and Deputies on administrative matters because "everything should be done to encourage the loyalty of officers, first to the Department head and through that head to the Council and then to the citizens and rate-payers."[38]

The African officers were often more vulnerable to pressure by the Council members than were the European officers. Most of the European officers felt that their advice was generally accepted when it was properly presented. "I have had to simplify my arguments," one officer mentioned, "to make them more forceful." "The councillors realize that I have a great deal of experience and know what I am doing," another officer pointed out, "and they respect me for that." The African officers, on the other hand, lacked the same degree of confidence in themselves; and the Council members were sometimes quick to take advantage of this weakness, particularly when appointments were being considered. Consequently, in its 1964 report, the Nairobi Standing Committee of the Senate noted "that the relationship between officers and councillors was not altogether happy and considers that this has resulted from a misunderstanding or unwillingness of councillors and officers to appreciate the division of their responsibilities as policy-makers and administrators."[39]

The complaint was frequently made that the new African officers were unimaginative. "They tend to memorize rather than to think," according to an instructor at the Kenya Institute of Administration, "which is especially sad because of the desperate need here for innovation. They are so busy learning the routine aspects of their work that they only get a superficial grasp of it." This meant that some of the African officers could not cope well with sudden or unexpected difficulties. Moreover, there was a surprising fidelity to the colonial arrangements from which Kenya had supposedly been liberated. The reason for this, John Roberts suggests, is that "in Kenya the first African professional men had nothing African to copy, since there was no traditional bourgeoisie. . . . They did the only thing they could — they followed European examples."[40] The Nairobi Council members were aware of the need to develop their own way of doing things. Consequently, they resolved "that it is unnecessary that this Council should be bound by rules of procedure which are embodied in the system which we inherited from abroad and that our regulations should be framed in such a way as will reflect our local conditions."[41] In practice, however, they hardly encouraged the sort of innovation that would have been most constructive.

It was also suggested that the operation of the Nairobi City Council was more adversely affected by the inadequacies of the lower than the higher levels of the bureaucracy. "We often get work done only to have it bungled [by delay or improper handling] by stenographers, administrative assistants, or clerks of some sort or another," one of the officers stressed, adding: "The Councillors persist in hiring people who are obviously incompetent and then fail to understand why we are not as efficient as before."

It was more than once alleged that the files of the City Council were in a mess. "We sometimes lose money," one of the lawyers exclaimed, "because information about debts to us are mislaid for several years." The clerks had to be constantly supervised, and everything had to be checked and double-checked. "We can tell a European secretary to write a letter rejecting a request, and she will know how to do it," a European officer of the City Council explained, "but this can't be done with an African or even an Asian secretary." Many Africans in high positions also used expatriates for positions of stenographer and copy-typist despite the high salary demands and criticism that they had to face. The shortage of competent clerical help (particularly, of stenotypists) was so great that the Senate had to be adjourned for twenty-five days in 1965.

Petty corruption was as big a concern to the senior staff as incompetency, and it necessitated a tiresome form of vigilance, made all the more difficult by the lack of supervisory personnel. "Thefts, shortages of cash and other irregularities were increasing and involved the Council in considerable expenditure," concluded the General Purposes Committee on the fourth of March, 1966.[42] "Whereas we used to get one or two fidgets a year before independence, we now get one or two a week," one of the European officers commented. A typical incident was the one reported to the Finance Committee on March 17, 1965:

> A shortage of cash had been found in the collections of a Clerk/Cashier. The current receipt books had disappeared and the exact amount had not yet been established but was at least Shs. 298/–. Investigations were proceeding and the Clerk had been suspended from duty and the matter handed to the Police.[43]

What was remarkable about so many of these cases of irregularity was the naiveté of administrative personnel. As one of the European officers pointed out, they indicated a failure on the part of the African employees to understand the workings of a sophisticated bureaucracy, particularly the audit process. Moreover, few Africans seemed to think of their jobs as part of a life-time career, ending with a pension. Instead, the "here today, gone tomorrow" attitude was prevalent. Consequently, they were prepared to take the sort of risks that more experienced, career-minded civil servants would have avoided. Other factors, however, were obviously involved. According to a report of the Senior Civil Servants Association of Kenya, most thefts were committed by junior officers who had heavy family responsibilities which could not be met by the salaries paid to them.[44]

The problem of administrative impropriety was obviously linked to the general problems of administration. By June 1964, standards had dropped so drastically that, in the words of a European officer:

> Salaries almost didn't get paid last month, and many didn't get paid correctly. The ledgers were prepared only as a result of a great effort on the part of the Treasurer. The accounting system is breaking down so that rent collection is becoming more difficult, particularly when this defect is combined with the effort of councillors and others to protect those in arrears. Rent arrears are up to 12 per cent now, and bills owed by merchants to the Council are not being paid for the first time.

After investigating numerous complaints about the service provided by the Graduated Personal Tax Section, the Organization and Methods Officer in 1965 expressed the opinion that over 90 per cent of the complaints were justified.[45] Among his conclusions were:

> (i) The present system is too inflexible. (ii) Systems currently employed are too cumbersome. (iii) Staff, particularly at senior levels, is inadequate. (iv) Collection rate is suffering because of poor systems and procedure. (v) A breakdown in the normally good relations with the public. (vi) Poor physical workplace conditions. (vii) An overloaded machine system. (viii) A disappointing lack of leadership from senior staff.

While the Graduated Personal Tax Section was reported to have ironed out many of its administrative kinks by 1967, other sections of the Treasurer's Department continued to be mismanaged. Under these circumstances, it was difficult not only to prevent peculation but even to identify it. For this reason Nairobi's senior resident magistrate in 1972 dismissed charges against a former clerk of stealing rent money from the City Council, pointing out that the council's ledger books contained no columns for receipt numbers and that a cashier's keys could be used by employees generally so that it was impossible "to hold a cashier responsible for receipts issued under a certain key."[46]

Despite all the problems of Africanization mentioned, the City Council succeeded in collecting an estimated 80 per cent of its potential revenue in 1965, raising the total income of the city to over £5 million (as against about £3.5 million in 1963).[47] This led the Acting Director of Social Services and Housing in 1965 to write: "Needless to say the change over to local officers had no adverse effects on the normal high standards of efficiency as the prophets of doom had predicted; in fact everybody worked hard during the year; efficiency increased and standards were improved and continue to improve."[48] A more balanced point of view may have been expressed by the City Treasurer in his annual report for 1966. "I would not wish it thought," he wrote, "that I do not have confidence in the sections to cope with what lies in front of them, and I must pay tribute to the entire staff, particularly the leaders of the various sections, for the way in which they have continually struggled to maintain both the output and the standards of what is really a very large sized business organization."[49] At the same time, he warned:

> By the time the localisation programme is complete, over 70 of the department's most experienced officers will have left within the space of three years. In the nature of things, their successors will take some time to develop to the same degree of knowledge and facility in the work. This in turn throws a greater load on the senior men who now run the department. I think that with vacancies arising from changes in staff, and with absences due to study leave of the rising younger men, the present period is one of great difficulty.[50]

### Racial Discrimination

A persistent source of contention was the definition of Africanization — did it mean "Kenyanization," "Localization," or "Blackenization?" Asians were especially concerned about this. They comprised close to 25 per cent of the City Council's staff prior to independence. During the colonial period they had worked hard to gain these positions in the face of an often hostile European-controlled council. In the past, the Asians argued, the European elite had failed to recognize that nearly one-third of the population of Nairobi (holding more than one-third of the City's wealth) was Asian. However, with the departure of European staff after the Lancaster House Conference of 1960, the City Council was forced to rely increasingly upon Asians, who comprised nearly half of Kenya's professional people, for the middle-level technical and clerical positions.

With the coming of an African City Council, the Asian employees realized that they were in a far more vulnerable position than were the Europeans who could usually leave without much difficulty. The Asians, on the other hand, felt trapped — equally uncertain of their future in East Africa and of their reception in other countries such as Great Britain, India or Pakistan. For these Asian employees, the definition of "Africanization" accepted by the City Council was of crucial importance. "If it means 'Black Africanization,'" one of the Asian officers pointed out in 1964:

> we might as well leave at our own convenience rather than that of the Africans. Otherwise, we might be dismissed when there won't be any opportunity for us. On the other hand, if the policy of the Council is "Kenyanization," then there is the incentive to take up Kenya citizenship. We really don't want to leave, but we don't know what to do now.

In the absence of a non-racial staff association (the declared objective of the Nairobi Asian Local Government Staff Association), the Asian employees had to rely on the ten remaining Asian Council members, three of whom occupied committee chairmanships. These Asians were useful to the Council partly because of their political experience but also because of their contacts with the business community. As one of the Asian councillors put it: "We manage to get what we want by helping the Africans get what they want." It was no secret that the Asian Council members were willing to help their African colleagues financially. Indeed, it was an Asian supporter of KANU who publicly agreed to put up the funds (£300) for the deposits of the thirty candidates sponsored by KANU for the 1963 City Council elections.[51]

Nevertheless, the Asians associated with the City Council realized that African hostility to them could not be readily overcome. It was alleged that the African Council members preferred to employ Englishmen from Europe at great expense on short contracts rather than local Asians on permanent terms. While the Asian Council members were reconciled to the dismissal or supersession of Asian employees of the Council "in the interests of Africanization," they insisted upon fair compensation in accord with the 1963 Kenya Local Government Officers' Superannuation Fund Rules. In March, 1964, the Asian Council members managed to obtain reconsideration of the recommendation of the General Purposes Committee that "localisation" be defined as "Africanization."[52] It was hoped at this time, according to one of the Asian Councillors, that African leaders would realize "that racial discrimination is unconstitutional and embarrassing for international relations and opposition to South Africa."

The racial policy of the Council was debated again in the September, 1964 General Meeting. At this time the chairman of the Council's Localisation Sub-Committee declared that if too many Asians (particularly artisans) were put on permanent terms, it would be difficult to Africanize their posts.[53] To this, Mr. V. P. Mandal angrily replied that some of the artisans referred to had been on the staff for many years and that, when they were engaged, there were no African artisans who could even tighten a screw. He went on to suggest that, while it was right for Africans to take over the jobs for which they were being trained, the emotional attitude displayed by some councillors over this matter would have a bad effect on efficiency and discipline among Council staff.

By 1965, the number of Asians employed by the City Council had decreased to 276, which was little more than half the number employed in 1963. In 1967, however, the Asians still comprised 30 per cent of those at the senior staff level (those earning over £804 per year).[54] Despite the fact that they were considered essential for the efficient administration of the City, the Council was determined to dismiss those who were not citizens of Kenya. In the case of the City Treasurer's Department, this meant the loss in 1967 of more than one-third of the seventy-three Asian staff members, including many occupying key supervisory and supporting positions.[55] "Africans first," was declared by the Mayor to be the policy of the Council, adding: "On its own staff the Council has Africanised all posts except when the Council could not find an African readily."[56]

As time went on, the Asian Council members became at least publicly reconciled to the departure of Asian staff members. For them it was significant that Mr. Naranja Desai, who had been Chairman of the Staff Committee and one of the most vociferous of the Asian Councillors in protecting Asian employees, was not renominated by KANU for candidacy in the 1964 municipal elections.[57] His approach had obviously been too antagonistic to succeed. It was better, they felt, to work behind the scenes for Asian interests and to win from Africans recognition of their usefulness rather than benevolent sympathy. At the same time the African Council members began to emphasize quality of administration rather than Africanization. This point was clearly made by Mr. G. K. Kariithi, the Permanent Secretary in the President's Office and head of Kenya's civil service in May, 1967:

> Most of the controlling positions are now occupied by our own people. From now on our task is to consolidate. We must concentrate on improving the quality of our service. For this is a national imperative to prove that Njuguna, Okello and Mwakio are as capable as Smith, Patel and de Souza. If we cannot do this, then Africanisation as a policy will have failed.[58]

## Tribal Discrimination

To many non-Kikuyu, the "Africanization" carried out in 1963 and 1964 by the City Council was viewed as "Kikuyuization" because, of the twelve Africans named to top positions, ten were Kikuyu, and five other officers were being "shadowed" by Kikuyus. The qualifications of the candidates chosen were frequently emphasized by Mayor Charles Rubia, who, as a Kikuyu, was very sensitive to this issue. Those who attack the Council for appointing a Kikuyu, he was quoted as saying, "are forgetting — it is not because he is a Kikuyu. We are considering — and I think the Government is doing the same thing — we are considering every case on its own merit."[59] The Mayor's defense of the appointment process was accepted by a number of the Council members of other tribes. "The Kikuyu are chosen for important positions in the City Council," asserted a committee chairman (a Kamba), "because they are the best qualified. Otherwise, they would not have been chosen; and, if they prove unsatisfactory, they will be dismissed."

The Kikuyu Council members, however, occasionally defended the appointment of Kikuyu on a more emotional basis. "Nairobi is a Kikuyu town," one of them declared in an interview. "Therefore, it is right that the local administrators be Kikuyu. Kisumu and the Nyanza region, on the other hand, are for the Luo, and no Kikuyu would have a chance there." Still more complacent was the remark of another Kikuyu Council member: "The truth is that tribal prejudice is inevitable and may not be altogether bad. There is always prejudice of some sort, and it can lead to pride, which is a good thing." This sort of argument was sympathetically received by one of the European officers who pointed out that tribalism was no more obvious in Kenya than in Great Britain: "As a Scotsman, I would have a harder time getting a job with a local authority in England than an Englishman, and vice-versa."

In regard to staff appointments, the consensus of the European officers was that, with certain notable exceptions, the choices made were neither unreasonable nor grossly unfair. This did not mean, however, that tribal considerations were not taken into account. Even when Council members rationally rejected tribal prejudice, they were sometimes forced to take tribalist positions because of the pressure of their fellow tribesmen.[60] Friendship, family relationship, and political activity were also taken into account in appointments. In any case, the appointment procedure was open to criticism. For this reason, the 1964 Nairobi Standing Committee of the Senate "felt that much of the trouble in the Nairobi City Council today stemmed from their system of appointment which had led to allegations of corruption, tribalism, and brotherization."[61]

The Luo were the most vocal in accusing the leaders of the City Council of tribal bias. They complained that most committee assignments as well as most top appointments were going to Kikuyu. The Kikuyu therefore received more money and a better chance of getting jobs for their fellow tribesmen. "All should be equal in the Council," protested one Luo Councillor in an interview: "After all, we were all elected."

In assessing the validity of this charge of "tribalism," the tribal breakdown of Nairobi must be kept in mind. (According to the 1962 Census, the largest tribes here were: Kikuyu, 43 per cent of the African population; Luyia, 17 per cent; Luo, 16 per cent; and Kamba, 15 per cent.)[62] Of the 28 African Council members in October 1963, there were 17 Kikuyu, 6 Luo, 3 Luyia, and 2 Kamba. Thus, it would appear that the Luyia and Kamba, rather than the Luo, were underrepresented. Of the eight important committees in the Council during the period from October, 1963 to June, 1964, only one was chaired by a Luo, but then only two were chaired by Kikuyu, despite the fact that the Kikuyu made up a majority of the Council members.

Since the Luo were most disturbed by the fact that so many important staff positions went to Kikuyu, controversies in Council meetings tended to be based on the Luo-Kikuyu rivalry. As might be expected, a tribal outlook was more evident in less technical considerations than in such matters as public health. In any case, tribalism was combined in very complicated ways with other sorts of conflict having to do with personalities, ambitions, and issues. According to a reliable European informant, part of the conflict that existed for a time between the Finance Committee and the Education Committee stemmed from the fact that the chairman of one was a Kikuyu and of the other, a Luo. It was also alleged that the Luos constantly went behind the Mayor's back to air their grievances with the Minister for Local Government, thereby fomenting trouble between the Mayor and the Minister.

The extent to which the Luo gained the support of the other tribes in their opposition to the "Kikuyuization" of city administration was uncertain. Some of their behavior, it was felt, "got the backs up of the other tribes." Later it was seen as part of the K.P.U. or Odinga's effort to disrupt the entire country. "The trouble with the Luos is that they are very arrogant," asserted one of the KANU leaders, "but we will isolate the bad ones." Yet, as one of the African officers pointed out, "the accusation that we are being chosen on a tribal basis is a very serious one if it undermines confidence in our decisions and advice." Tribalism might be temporarily muted or suppressed, but it could not be lightly dismissed as a "passing phenomenon" as some African leaders suggested.

## Problems of African Management

In summarizing the administrative problems of the Nairobi City Council during the transition to African control, the key word would appear to be "distrust." The various racial and ethnic groups into which the Council members and employees were divided did not trust one another. Those associated with the City Council were distrustful of those associated with the Central Government. This distrust was invariably reciprocated and, thereby, reinforced.

This distrust manifested itself in a number of dysfunctional ways. To begin with, it impeded the communication processes necessary for administrative efficiency. An example of this was the ruling prohibiting the officers of the City Council from consulting officials of the Central Government on their own initiative. Another example was the effort of the Minister for Local Government in 1966 to channel all communication between the City Council and the Central Government through the Ministry of Local Government. Likewise, the chief officers of the City Council were constantly trying to prevent their subordinates from communicating to the Council members information that would undermine their positions.

Another manifestation of distrust was the inordinate prolonging of committee meetings, upon which the functioning of the Nairobi City Council depended. Demands were often imposed upon the administrative officers which were unfeasible or improper, but the officers' protests were considered by the Council members as evidence of insubordination. In this way, the technical decisions or advice of the officers came to be viewed as biased or racially motivated. Their sphere of autonomy was thereby reduced, causing them to lose the freedom and flexibility needed for operational effectiveness. At the same time, their professional pride and confidence, as well as the respect of their subordinates, were diminished.

Using the terminology introduced in the first chapter, we can see the causes of political inelasticity in the functioning of the Nairobi City Council. So long as the chief officers remained Europeans, the Councillors were unwilling to delegate to them sufficient authority to perform effectively their duties, one of which was to guide the Councillors in their decision-making. This meant that the capability of the chief officers was reduced as the control over them tended to be excessive. But control over the officers was also at times inadequate, insofar as the Councillors lacked the experience and knowledge to provide effective guidelines and supervision. With the replacement of European chief officers by Africans, greater elasticity of control might have been expected. Unfortunately, the consequences of political inelasticity actually became increasingly evident in many aspects of Nairobi's municipal government.

While it is always difficult to determine the quantity and quality of output in public administration, there was a clear indication that the Nairobi City Council was becoming decreasingly efficient. A road was estimated to be costing twice what a similar length of road had cost prior to independence. A private contractor could put up a building for fifty per cent less than what it cost the City Council to construct. The City Engineer in 1971 admitted that he could not manage well his labor force of over 3,000 persons and his cash flow of £2 million per annum.[63] While the work-load in 1971 was expected to be double that of 1970, there was not the professional manpower to organize, design, and implement the various schemes. It was therefore imperative that more work be given to consultants. In any case, the City Council simply could not undertake much of what it had done in the past.

In 1961, the officers of the Nairobi City Council estimated that about one-third of the Council's income would be spent that year on manpower (£1,160,000 out of £3,500,000).[64] Ten years later, a team of consultants pointed out that 55 per cent of the Council's total revenue was being spent on manpower and that this percentage was increasing.[65] These consultants then noted that "the Council's current planning and control of manpower resources tends to be un-coordinated, haphazard, or, in some areas, virtually non-existent." While there were insufficient staff in some sections, too many existed in others. Moreover, lacking a proper system of job-titles, those doing similar jobs in different departments found themselves earning unequal rates of pay, thereby creating a persistent source of grievance. This resulted in pressure to upgrade jobs or to create extra job titles, but this process of random upgrading or promotion further distorted the salary and hierarchical system. Employee frustrations were intensified by the Establishments Section, which was "well-known for its capricious and callous treatment of just about everybody."[66] Expatriates were particularly unhappy at arbitrary and inconsistent decisions in regard to housing allowances.

In 1961, the Nairobi City Council employed 4,259. By 1971, the number of employees had more than doubled, including the additional ten per cent required by the Tripartite Agreement. Yet, some departments were insisting upon a personnel growth rate of as much as 25 per cent each year, despite the effort of the City Treasurer to restrict the annual establishment growth rate to below six per cent. This caused the City Council in 1972 to propose the construction of an additional office building costing £650,000. While some departments, such as education, or the Cleansing Section of the Public Health Department, could have used more manual workers, other departments were obviously wasting labor. In the Public Works Section of the City Engineer's Department, for example, many employees were reported to be working only two or three hours a day.

The public was made most aware of the Council's administrative incompetence by persistent newspaper accounts of irregularities in the Graduated Personal Tax Section of the Treasurer's Department. In April 1970, it was reported that £100,000 in Graduated Personal Tax could not be accounted for. Ten employees of that section were dismissed at this time, though six of them were later reemployed in another section. The next year, it was revealed that a number of families had been evicted from City Council housing, after being falsely accused of nonpayment of rent. Apparently, a certain amount of the money collected by the Council's officers had never reached the coffers of the Council.

It was estimated in 1971 that between one and two million pounds were owed to the Council, including £106,401 in rents and

£537,731 in water and conservancy charges, but inadequate records obscured the exact amount. The trouble could not be overcome, Dr. Kiano (the Minister for Local Government) noted, until the Council's administrative machinery was improved. He was concerned, not only with "the fact that some persons who had already paid have received these notices but also the very question as to how a tenant can be in arrears of Sh. 9,000, Sh. 10,000, Sh. 11,000, and he or she has not been receiving notices of being in arrears until one day the axe comes down."[67] Dr. Kiano might have added that the difficulty of collecting debts was increased when the guilt of nonpayment was spread among Councillors, Council officers, top civil servants, and even Ministers.

One of the most illustrative examples of persistent sources of trouble for the City Council was the Transport Depot Section of the City Engineer's Department. The drivers in this section were constantly being reprimanded for carrying unauthorized passengers, using their vehicles for private purposes, and for failing to check engine oil and the conditions of their tires. "It has become an almost daily practice for some drivers to arrive at sites between one-fourth of an hour to two hours late," the Assistant Organization and Methods Officer reported in 1970.[68] Then, instead of starting their day with their tanks full of gasoline, the drivers would at unexpected times need to return to the Depot to obtain more fuel. There was generally poor coordination between the Transport Depot and the user sections, preventing an efficient utilization of vehicles. And the fact that instructions were not written down for drivers added to the confusion. Corruption pervaded the Transport Depot. Allegations of malpractices in 1967 led to the suspension of the Transport Manager and the resignation of his assistant, and in 1972, to the dismissal of the Transport Inspector.

Because of the misuse or overuse of vehicles, many of them were being repaired more often than they were being used, particularly the forty per cent over five years old. But while at least thirty needed to be repaired each day, the Maintenance and Servicing Section of the Transport Depot could only manage eight a day. This meant that it often took a month to repair a vehicle, upon which an estimated average of ten men depended for their work. Moreover, because of the shortage of qualified mechanics, supervisors, and in-spectors, workmanship tended to be poorly planned and performed. Lacking a mechanical or electrical engineer, the Council was paying to outside garages more than $2,000 per month for the repair of wiring, starters, and generators. Altogether, it was estimated that forty per cent could be saved in repair costs. Added to the delay and cost of repairs was the difficulty of obtaining local purchase orders for spare parts, and the reluctance of some suppliers to fill orders because of their complaints about delays and mistakes in payments. Bills would often be held for three months without action, haphaz-ardly filed in drawers, eventually to be overpaid or underpaid. On the other hand, what was ordered by the Purchasing Section was often incorrect or overpriced. At the same time, tools and parts were constantly being lost because of the inadequacy of stock records.

However justified the City Council had been in Africanizing its top administrative positions, the deleterious repercussions of having inexperienced chief officers were by 1972 undeniable. These weak-nesses were more apparent in some departments than in others. Probably the strongest department was that of education, led by an officer who exuded professional competence, despite his lack of a university degree — a fact which had made his initial appointment in 1968 somewhat controversial. His office, according to Frederick Temple (a perceptive critic of the City Council's administration), was covered with projections of pupil populations, building needs, and operating costs and revenues until 1980.[69] This thoroughness of planning provided "a buffer of expertise against political pressures." Added to this was the prestige derived from the success of the City's Education Department in accommodating about 85 per cent of Nairobi's school age children (which meant a doubling of enroll-ment between 1963 and 1972), in racially integrating the school system, and in guiding a high percentage of students through the Kenya Preliminary Examination. While there continued to be com-plaints about the incompetence or negligence of some of the school principals and supervisors, the chief officer generally set the tone and style for the rest of the department. Unfortunately, the other department heads, who by the end of 1970 were all Africans, could not establish a similar basis for elasticity of control. Thus, they were unable either to protect or expand their own spheres of influence. Their troubles will be the subject of the next section.

## The African Chief Officers

Even one of the most qualified of the African chief officers, N. S. Mwenja, the Chief Engineer from 1965 to the end of 1970, could not escape the consequences of his inexperience. In 1968 he agreed to the payment of overtime to employees within his department, a practice then uncommon in the Kenyan civil service.[70] Soon employees throughout the Council were demanding this payment, causing or threatening trouble for recalcitrant officers. But they also quickly learned to take advantage of the opportunities presented, especially in the absence of proper organization of work, supervision, and control. Workers would dawdle during the day so that they would have to work overtime to catch up. In the Cleansing Section of the Public Health Department, it was reported "that employees who absent themselves from duty without permission during any one month, do in fact claim more overtime to compensate for the days deducted, so that their pay packets are unaffected, or even fatter."[71] The cost of overtime amounted to an estimated £30,000 in 1969 and continued to be a drain on resources until the practice was curtailed in 1972.

As did other African officers, Mwenja allowed himself to be pressured into overruling his administrative subordinates responsible for hiring manual workers. This eventually caused him to have to spend much of his time doing the work of a personnel administrator. He then found himself directly confronted by Councillors anxious to find jobs for relatives, friends, or constituents. Having abandoned a proper system for hiring workers, he increasingly had to surrender to this pressure. Consequently, the situation prevailed that "you had to know a Councillor before you could get a job."[72] Likewise, the permission of the councillors was necessary to dismiss or discipline an employee. Thus it was that chief officers, such as Mwenja, lost control over their departments. The power of the Nairobi branch of the Local Government Workers Union was also a factor in this regard. Some of those with union positions were fully convinced that they did not have to do any work at all.

Despite a decade of intensive Africanization within the City Council, the bulk of the technical work continued to be performed by the remaining Asians and Europeans, particularly the non-citizens numbering about 150. For example, of the 55 doctors employed by the Health Department in May, 1971, only five were citizens. In the Treasurer's Department, the only two fully qualified African accountants were the Treasurer and the Deputy Treasurer. The other accountants were employed on contract or temporary terms. However valuable these expatriates were, the fact that they seldom stayed more than three years reduced their usefulness. They often left just when they were most needed. The constant turnover of senior staff meant that there could be little building of experience or awareness of precedents — the knowledge of past cases that facilitates decision-making. Moreover, there were fewer available administrators, such as K. F. Craig-McFeely, the Chief Planning Officer, who had over many years of work with the Council established reputations engendering real trust and useful contacts with important people in the Ministries or the private sector.

While the chief officers remained heavily dependent on the advice of these expatriates, they often lacked the necessary experience to be able to evaluate this advice. They therefore tended to avoid or postpone decision-making, moving instead from crisis to crisis, hoping somehow that difficulties would disappear by themselves. Occasionally, they would reject the advice of these expatriates on quite petty or irrelevant grounds, belittling or disregarding their contributions or taking credit themselves for suggestions and accomplishments. At other times, they would try to command the obedience of expatriates, or question their motives in such a way as to hurt their pride. They might suddenly be asked to cancel a vacation or a leave-of-absence that had long ago been planned, or asked to do things that were clearly corrupt or for the special benefit of leading officials or politicians. When this happened, the expatriates often ceased to care anymore about their work.

As hard as they tried, the chief officers could not hide their incompetence from Councillors, colleagues, and subordinates. It was recognized that some of them had gained their positions largely as a result of political favoritism. Insofar as positions were gained by political pull, politics rather than competence was seen as the way to get ahead. But at the same time, politics could also be the source of their downfall. Being insecure, the chief officers had to be more concerned with the political implications of proposals than with their legitimate merits. In other words, less important than the desirability of recommendations was their being acceptable to Councillors and Ministers. Their lack of self-confidence prevented the officers from really asserting their authority. Consequently, they had to rely upon their personal contacts rather than on their professional expertise to gain agreement.

Since the officers seldom had reputations based upon solid achievement, they suffered from lack of respect. Thus it was that the Councillors unanimously rejected the recommendation of the chief officers in April, 1971, following a cholera scare, to burn down all food kiosks in Nairobi. They preferred the opinion of a foreign expert that burning was unnecessary, despite the Mayor's warning to them that "you are digging your own graves."[73] Likewise, the officers were vulnerable to demands made upon them by politicians, subordinates, etc. For example, if the chief officers could have developed some rational system for personnel management, they could have gained greater control over the hiring, promotion, demotion, and dismissal of employees. As it was, they tried bureaucratically to obfuscate such decisions, refusing to disclose letters of suspension, termination, or warning because "of the possible embarrassing nature of these letters and the dangers of court suits having to do with slander or defamation of character."[74] This convinced some Councillors and union officials that these decisions were being unduly influenced by considerations of friendship, tribalism, or family ties. Of course, it was common knowledge that Asian citizens were being denied top-level positions in the City Council because of racial prejudice against them. But there were also a few well-known cases of Luo being denied promotion to the level warranted by their successes in qualifying examinations. Under the circumstances, personnel decisions become more politicized than they might have been. For example, the Kenya Local Government Workers' Union claimed in 1972 in the Industrial Court in Nairobi that the Nairobi City Treasurer had personal interests in a case in which a Luo accountant had been dismissed from the Council in 1970, allegedly for misappropriating funds, and then not reemployed after being cleared by a court of law.[75]

For all the reasons mentioned, the chief officers found it difficult to delegate responsibilities to their African subordinates, or to inspire them to better performance. Some of these subordinates had, like their superiors, gained their positions as a result of political maneuvering and, as such, were not respected for their competence. Occasionally they would resort to various strategems to hide their inadequacies (such as the officer who threw away seven letters having to do with a particular Graduate Personal Tax problem because of his uncertainty about the answer), but they were seldom successful. In any case, insofar as these officials took advantage of existing opportunities to profit from their positions, their advice could no longer be considered disinterested. Likewise, when they appeared to undermine the chief officers through forms of political intrigue, the burden of work could not be shared.

Because of the lack of delegation, levels of bureaucracy were often bypassed to get to the top. Any agreement reached with a deputy officer had to be renegotiated again with the chief officers. This explains the tendency of union officials to ignore the industrial relations officer, preferring to deal directly with the Town Clerk.[76] Indeed, the official chain-of-command appeared to be meaningless inasmuch as officials were bypassed, afterwards being confronted with unexpected decisions.

The inability of the chief officers to share their responsibilities meant that they were inevitably overwhelmed by the details of administration. For example, the Chief Engineer had to go to Europe himself to interview candidates for vacancies, an activity he considered unpleasant as well as a waste of time. One officer referred to his activities as "crisis management." "We plodded along a difficult river with innumerable cataracts which haunted us like a passion," admitted Mr. C. N. W. Siganga, the Director of Social Services and Housing, in his 1967 Annual Report.[77] As Temple points out, "the problems associated with keeping the Council running on a daily basis seem to be sufficiently taxing that little time or energy is left for thinking about the future."[78] Typical in this regard was the Public Health Department in which "one official admitted that the department does not plan well, that it has a difficult time seeing even three or four years ahead."[79]

Ideally, the head of a department should be like a good orchestra conductor, able to bring harmony out of the variety of instruments played. But few could give the necessary guidance. This prevented subordinate officials from knowing what they were going to be doing next, or what they were supposed to be doing. In a 1972 interview, one senior official confessed that he was given things to do by default, or else he undertook tasks on his own initiative, hoping afterwards for approval. Another official pointed out that there was no realistic work schedule because of inadequate consultation. This meant that it was difficult to know how seriously to take assignments. An additional complaint was that "decisions in my sphere are taken by others, while other people's work is thrown on my lap." When work was completed, it was sometimes rejected without any reasons given. Or else, there was no feedback so that officials felt themselves working in a vacuum. Likewise, there was insufficient coordination among sections within the departments. Within the Engineering Department, for example, one of the top quantity surveyors (the officials responsible for estimating costs) claimed that his section could have substantially reduced the maintenance costs of the buildings put up by the Council had its services been properly utilized. This also contributed to the feeling of isolation on the part of officials, undermining that *esprit de corps* so necessary to the functioning of any organization.

Just as there was insufficient coordination among sections within departments, there was also inadequate coordination among departments. In July, 1972, the chief officers had to be reprimanded by the General Purposes committee for bringing to the standing committees too many unscheduled items, having failed to discuss these items among themselves and with the chairmen and Mayor.[80] The chief officers no longer encouraged or permitted their deputies to

meet among themselves to lay the groundwork for interdepart-
mental meetings. Consequently, when the officers met together, the
administrative preparation necessary for agreement had not been
worked out. Time was therefore wasted on insignificant items or
petty recriminations. Agreements that were finally reached among
the officers would sometimes be disavowed or ignored in the standing committee meetings, or else not followed through in any effective way. Memoranda sent from one department to another tended
to be misplaced; staff papers or other relevant information not circulated; and reports neglected. The Organization and Methods Officer was particularly unhappy that his reports were not read by the
officers or brought to the attention of the Councillors. It took two
years for the Council to get around to acting on the O & M report
having to do with the excessive use of overtime. Likewise, the
Traffic Engineer was convinced that the hostile press reaction to his
proposal for installing traffic signals in place of certain major traffic
circles resulted from the failure of the other officers to provide the
necessary support.

The absence of coordination was most obvious in the preparation
of the budget, particularly the capital program.[81] The relationship
between budget requests and expenditure capacity (considering the
administrative difficulties previously mentioned) became so unrealistic by 1970 that capital program estimates were up to ten times
larger than what was actually spent. While the Ministry of Local
Government reduced considerably the capital program, the City
Council was left with three times the amount it could realistically
spend. To finance its 1970 capital program, the City Council bor-
rowed £2 million at seven per cent, but it then had to invest much
of this money temporarily at five per cent to minimize losses from
holding the funds which could not be used.

The pressure to inflate the capital program came largely from
councillors who were anxious to have social halls, health centers,
and roads for their wards. The Chief Medical Officer and the Social
Services and Housing Officer were most obliging in this regard,
giving in completely to these demands without indicating their long-
term practical implications (in terms of money and qualified per-

sonnel). The City Treasurer might have been expected to exercise sufficient leadership to force the officers and the councillors to set limits and priorities, but his own limited experience and technical knowledge prevented his doing so. The existing social halls, it might have been pointed out, were not being fully utilized, and better use could be made of school auditoriums. The possibility of multiple-use facilities or *harambee* projects (using voluntary labor and supplies) could have been considered. Instead, S. K. Mbugua, who became City Treasurer at the beginning of October, 1970, allowed the budget estimates for 1971 to exceed the figure for 1970 by more than forty per cent (rising from 10.25 to 14.75 K £ million).

It was frustrating for a number of the more knowledgeable officials and councillors to work within a system in which there was so little regard for norms of efficiency. While lip-service was paid to maximizing output and limiting input, there seemed no real desire to save money. For example, when it was pointed out that St. Mary's Hall (a hostel for women maintained by the Council) was losing money by employing 32 servants to take care of fifty girls, few showed concern. At a time of great unemployment, it was almost unpatriotic to suggest the dismissal of redundant or incompetent employees. And, after all, the bulk of the urban income continued to come from the European and Asian property owners, who were represented by only two councillors. Moreover, in a society which emphasized cooperation and harmony, the aggressive, maximizing administrator could hardly be appreciated. The achievement of efficiency, in other words, inevitably led to the situations of conflict, stress, and isolation which most administrators wanted desperately to avoid.

This toleration of waste and inefficiency could not help but affect morale. It certainly undermined the work of budgetary comptrollers and efficiency experts. Inspectors and supervisors also found themselves in a difficult situation. Why should diligence be required of all employees when so little was expected of some? Inasmuch as competence was deemphasized, tribalism, friendship, and other traditional considerations could be stressed, thereby reducing administrative effectiveness.

Since control over the budget was not properly exercised by the leading officers and committees of the Council, it was left up to the Ministry for Local Government. However, the Ministry did not have the personnel to do this job as quickly and carefully as was desirable. In 1972, the work had to be done by the top European official in the Ministry, and it could not be completed until June, too late for many projects to be carried out. Part of the delay was caused by the grossly inflated nature of the budget submitted by the Council (up from K£5,116,000 approved in 1971 to K£11,379,000). Half of the capital expenditure estimates had to be cut, including most of the health clinics and social halls that had been proposed. It was hoped that this action would have the effect of forcing the Council to make its proposals more realistic, thereby strengthening the position of the City Treasurer's office. Yet, the Chief Medical Officer continued to want a number of medical clinics and dispensaries that, even if built, could not be staffed or equipped. The councillors insisted that social halls were their "first priority" (more important than schools, clinics, roads, sanitation facilities, or anything else), seeing the European official's veto power as neocolonialism.

The Nairobi City Council had over the years maintained that, because it was different from the other Kenyan municipalities in size, scale of operations, complexity of administration, and rate of growth, it should not be supervised to the same extent as other local authorities. "It is not important for the Ministry to have to be consulted on the minutiae of its detailed estimates," argued E. L. Jones in 1970. "It is not important that, having approved a multi-million pound budget, the Ministry should have to approve a supplementary estimate for a new typewriter if specific provision had not been made for that one item."[82] But as a sign in one of the offices of the City Council acknowledged, "trust must be earned; not demanded."

So long as the financial affairs of the Council were mismanaged, controls were likely to be excessive. Similarly, Smith and Stern pointed out, the Council would have to develop and institute comprehensive manpower plans to convince the Ministry of Local Government to reduce the current level of controls which were causing delays, frustration, and inefficiencies.[83] The Ministry, it was noted, was responding to the Council's current practice of uncritically accepting the recommendations of the section heads for additional staff by automatically reducing all requests for establishment increases. This led to serious understaffing in some sections, such as the Transport Depot, with detrimental results for the community. However, an improvement in relations with the Central Government would have to await the improved performance of the City Council. In other words, if elasticity of control were to be operational between the Central Government and the City Council, it would also have to be operational within the City Council itself. However, it was also clear that elasticity of control within the Nairobi City Council would necessitate an improvement in inter-governmental relations. For this reason, the next chapter will be devoted specifically to the impact of inter-governmental relations in Kenya upon the functioning of the City Council.

## NOTES

1. The sources used for this information include: Marco Surveys Ltd., *Who's Who in East Africa,* 1963-64 (Nairobi: Marco Surveys Ltd., 1964); the files of the *East African Standard* (hereafter referred to by the initials E.A.S.); the files of the Public Relations Officer of the Nairobi City Council; and personal interviews.

2. The Hon. C. K. Lubembe (Chairman), "Report of Nairobi Standing Committee 1964," Government of Kenya Printer, p. 10.

3. Ursula A. Hicks, *Development from Below: Local Government and Finance in Developing Countries of the Commonwealth* (Oxford: At the Clarendon Press, 1961), p. 494.

4. Unless otherwise indicated, all quotations in this chapter are based on the interviews conducted during my stays in Kenya. They are, of course, merely an approximation of what was actually said.

5. Cf. Hicks, *op. cit.,* pp. 214, 220-21, 242, 249-250, 402, 450.

6. Cf. H. C. Seely, "Local Government Development Finance (Kenya)," *Journal of Local Government Administration Overseas,* Vol. III, No. 4 (October, 1964), pp. 191-97.

7. *1964-1970 Development Plan* (Kenya: Government Printer, 1964), pp. 100-101.

8. *Organizations and Methods Report, No. 11, The Overall Administration of Nairobi City Council* (Nairobi: City Hall, March 20, 1961), p. 14.

9. *Ibid.*, pp. 36-37. This allegation was heatedly denied by the Chief Officers in an amusing addendum, "The Busy Councillor's Guide to the O & M Report."

10. *Minutes of Proceedings,* Vol. XXXI, No. 7 (January, 1964), p. 1075.

11. *Op. cit.*, p. 10.

12. *Ibid.*, p. 8.

13. *Ibid.*

14. *Ibid.*

15. E.A.S., October 8, 1965.

16. *Minutes of Proceedings,* April, 1967, pp. 1756-57.

17. *Report of the Local Government Commission of Inquiry* (Nairobi: Republic of Kenya, 1966), p. 58. Also, cf. Sessional Paper No. 12 of 1967, p. 24.

18. Cf. Alan Rose, Chairman, "Report of the Commission of Inquiry into Alleged Corruption and other Malpractices in Relation to the Affairs of the Nairobi City Council, December, 1955 – March, 1956" (Nairobi: Government Printer, 1956), pp. 8-13.

19. E.A.S., January 29, 1960.

20. E.A.S., January 28, 1961.

21. *Minutes of Proceedings,* Vol. XXIX, No. 10 (April, 1962), pp. 1355-56.

22. E.A.S., April 18 and 22, 1964.

23. *The Thirty-First Annual Report of the Medical Officer of Health, 1960* (Nairobi: City Hall, 1966), p. 1.

24. E.A.S., January 5, 1965.

25. Cf. the Staff Committee's Resolution, *Minutes of Proceedings,* Vol. XXXI, No. 9 (March, 1964), pp. 1536-39.

26. E.A.S., May 26, 1966.

27. The 1964 Nairobi Standing Committee (*op. cit.,* p. 10) also points out that Council members did not understand the meaning of the technical qualifications required.

28. E.A.S., April 28, 1964.

29. Statement of a European officer during an interview.

30. *Annual Report,* p. 30.
31. Works Committee, *Minutes of Proceedings,* September 9, 1966, p. 576.
32. Report of the Treasurer, *Minutes of Proceedings,* September, 1966, pp. 556-57.
33. *Minutes of Proceedings,* September, 1967, pp. 155-56.
34. E.A.S., February 24, 1967.
35. *Not Yet Uhuru* (London: Heinemann, 1967), p. 248.
36. *Report of the Salaries Review Commission, 1967* (Nairobi: Government Printer, 1967), p. 95.
37. *Daily Nation,* April 14, 1967.
38. *Minutes of Proceedings,* May 2, 1965, p. 1505.
39. *Op. cit.,* p. 2.
40. *A Land Full of People: Life in Kenya Today* (New York: Praeger, 1967), p. 88.
41. *Minutes of Proceedings,* May, 1965, p. 2201.
42. *Minutes of Proceedings,* p. 1676.
43. *Minutes of Proceedings,* pp. 1870-71.
44. E.A.S., November 9, 1967.
45. (Nairobi: City Hall, 1965), p. 10.
46. *Daily Nation,* August 30, 1972.
47. Cf. A. St. J. Hannigan, "Some Aspects of Local Government in Kenya," *in* The British Institute of International and Comparative Law, *East African Law Today* (London: Stevens & Sons, Ltd., 1966), p. 96.
48. (Nairobi: City Hall, March, 1966), p. 1.
49. (Nairobi: City Hall, 1967), p. 8.
50. *Ibid.,* p. 6.
51. E.A.S., August 27, 1963.
52. E.A.S., March 4, 1964.
53. E.A.S., September 2, 1964.
54. E.A.S., March 29, 1967.
55. *Annual Report, op. cit.,* p. 3.
56. E.A.S., August 9, 1967.
57. Other factors may have been involved here. Cf. chap. 7.
58. *Daily Nation,* May 4, 1967.
59. Quoted, Roberts, *op. cit.,* p. 70.
60. Cf. *ibid.,* pp. 70-71.
61. *Op. cit.,* p. 13.

62. Cf. *Kenya Population Census, 1962* (Nairobi: Economics and Statistics Division, Ministry of Finance and Economic Planning, Advanced Report of Volumes I and II, January, 1964). The other tribes of Kenya form a relatively insignificant proportion of the population of Nairobi.

63. Amos J. Nga'ang'a, *Annual Report* (Nairobi: City Hall, April, 1971), p. 1; Nairobi City Council, *Minutes,* Vol. XXXVIII, Public Health, Education and Social Services Committee, 2nd July, 1971, pp. 2747-48.

64. "The Busy Councillor's Guide to the O & M Report" (unpublished comments by the Chief Officers on W. Bestwick's O & M Report No. 11), Nairobi City Council, 20 March, 1961, p. 10.

65. G. S. Smith and W. M. Stern, *Nairobi City Council: The Introduction of Manpower Planning* (Nairobi: Inbucon International Ltd., November, 1971), pp. 2-6. This is referred to as the Inbucon Report.

66. Hunter Morrison, "The Site and Service Scheme: Problems General and Specific," Nairobi Urban Studies Group, July 30, 1971.

67. The National Assembly, *Official Report,* Vol. XXIII (Part I) Second Session, 21st May, 1971, c. 693.

68. Mark Manyonyi, *Organization and Methods Report on the Transport Depot Section of the City Engineer's Department* (Nairobi: O & M Section, October, 1970), p. 4; Nairobi City Council, *Minutes,* Vol. XXXIX, No. 10 (May, 1972), Works Committee, 8.5.72, pp. 2161-62.

69. Frederick T. Temple, "Planning and Budgetting for Urban Growth in Nairobi," Nairobi Urban Studies Group, February, 1972, pp. 12-14.

70. S. N. Michiri, *Overtime in the Nairobi City Council* (Nairobi: O & M Department, 1970); Z. Kariuki, Chairman, "Summary of the Working Party Report on Overtime in the Nairobi City Council," Nairobi City Council, July, 1972.

71. Mark Manyonyi, *Organization and Methods Report on Unauthorised Absences in the Cleansing Section of the Public Health Department* (Nairobi: O & M Department, March, 1972), p. 3.

72. Cf. statement in Parliament by Mr. B. M. Karungaru (Embakasi), E.A.S., July 21, 1972.

73. Cf. Julius Kinothia, "The Risks Nairobi's Councillors are Running," E.A.S., April 27, 1971.

74. Nairobi City Council, *Minutes,* Vol. XXXVII, Staff Committee, 15.5.70, p. 1915.

75. *Daily Nation,* October 12, 1972.

76. Smith and Stern, *op. cit.,* p. 12.

77. (Nairobi: City Hall, 1968), p. 1.

78. *Op. cit.,* p. 15.

79. *Ibid.,* p. 9.

80. Nairobi City Council, *Minutes,* Vol. XXXIX, No. 11 (July, 1972), p. 2643.

81. Temple, *op. cit., passim.*

82. "Review of the City's Financial Position (City Treasurer's Memorandum)," Nairobi City Council, 18 September, 1970, p. 14.

83. The Inbucon Report, *op. cit.,* p. 10.

# 6 INTER-GOVERNMENTAL RELATIONS

*Introduction*

While the City Council was primarily responsible for coping with the great population influx into Nairobi during the 1960s, its capacity to deal with the situation was limited. "There must be a national plan — whether it deals with industry or other aspects of the economy, or whether it deals with begging and destitution," Mayor Charles Rubia emphasized in 1962. "Nairobi cannot do much about these problems in isolation."[1] Nevertheless, as the Mayor himself readily admitted, such considerations were not of much consolation to those who were faced "with the harsh unyielding reality of empty pockets and empty bellies."[2]

The City Council's policies regarding its social and economic problems invariably needed the approval and support of the Central Government, causing much frustration for the City Council. For example, the City Council desired as early as 1964 to reduce school fees, eliminating them altogether by 1970, but this plan was opposed by the Minister of Education because of the pressures this would bring for free universal primary education throughout Kenya. Since less than half Kenya's children, aged 7-13, were enrolled in primary school, as of March 31, 1965, free primary education was both desirable and politically attractive. However, it was simply not financially feasible, entailing, according to the 1964 Ominde Report, the expenditure of almost twice the amount currently being spent on education by the national government, assuming no increase in teachers' salaries and other costs.[3]

At other times the City Council suddenly found itself burdened by arbitrary decisions of the Central Government. In June, 1965, President Kenyatta unexpectedly announced that there would be free out-patient treatment of adults and free in-patient treatment of children at Government clinics and hospitals. Within a short time thereafter, the use of health centers and hospitals increased by 500 per cent and 25 per cent respectively.[4] In Nairobi, the overall attendance at the City's dispensaries increased by approximately 90 per cent. What occurred, according to Dr. J. Kabiru, Nairobi's Medical Officer of Health, was a situation approaching chaos until some measures were taken to alleviate the problem.[5] Indeed, the health care of Africans in Nairobi's clinics and hospitals had previously been bad enough, considering that an out-patient at a City Council Health Center got on average less than a minute of a doctor's time and mothers were discharged within 24 hours of childbirth.[6] Not only were the medical personnel in short supply, but also, it was alleged by Kenya's Minister for Health, lacking in training and experience and even in responsibility and dedication.[7] Consequently, despite an obvious need for more health centers and a medical school in Nairobi, plans for them had to be postponed in 1966 because of a lack of staff and finance.[8]

The personality and behavior of the mayors of Nairobi had a profound impact upon Kenya's inter-governmental relations. For this reason, the mayoralty of Charles Rubia (1962-67) will be discussed in detail in this chapter, including a series of major and minor episodes which established important precedents and guidelines for future relations between the City Council and the Central Government. At the same time, the roles of the various participants in local government (ministers, mayors, councillors, and civil servants) became more clearly defined. Before specifically discussing Rubia's mayoralty, some of the general problems of decentralization in Kenya will be indicated. The last section of this chapter will deal with the situation since Rubia.

*The Problems of Decentralization*

While the Nairobi City Council was much affected by the policies of the Central Government during the colonial period, it maintained a considerable amount of independence. With the coming of
an African government, the City Council's sphere of autonomy was
expected to be drastically reduced. It was even suggested that the
administration of Nairobi might be placed entirely in the hands of
the Central Government as, for example, Washington, D.C. Though
it was decided in 1963 to grant the City Council much of the status
and responsibilities of the seven regions that were then set up, this
authority was carefully circumscribed at the insistence of the Ministry for Local Government in the realization that Nairobi's incoming African council and staff would need a great deal of help and
direction.[9]

Under the 1963 Constitution, the Minister for Local Government
gained the right to approve the City Council's estimates, together
with the other means of control normally exercised by the Central
Government over local authorities under the British governmental
system. Moreover, all matters related to Nairobi were to be reviewed
by a standing advisory committee of the Senate, consisting of one
Senator from each region (chosen by all other Senators from that
region) plus one other Senator appointed by the Minister for Local
Government as chairman.[10] This committee was obliged to submit
an annual report to the Senate and the Minister on the administration of the Nairobi area. The Office of District Commissioner remained as another connecting link between Central and City governments. While formally under the Ministry for Home Affairs and
mainly concerned with law and order, the D.C. was expected to
cooperate closely with the other ministries in supervising the administration of governmental policies.

Very soon after the Africans came into control of the City Council, a conflict developed between it and the Ministry for Local Government. Partly involved here was a clash of personalities, including
conflicting ambitions, temperaments, viewpoints, and expectations
regarding deference and perquisites, all of which was intensified by
the fact that the Minister was a Luo and the Mayor, a Kikuyu.

Even if the Minister had been a Kikuyu, he would almost certainly have clashed with the Council members over such matters as allowances and, more generally, the functions of the Ministry and the Council. Insofar as the roles of the various participants in local government (Minister, Mayor, Council members and civil servants) remained undefined and unclear, this conflict would be intensified. As one observer noted, "the Mayor is not sure what a mayor ought to do, and the Minister is not sure what a minister ought to do." The situation was made all the more difficult by the social and economic problems faced by Nairobi and Kenya as a whole.

According to the Mayor and his supporters in the City Council, the Minister was far too ready to interfere in the City Council's business: he procrastinated in approving the Council's expenditure proposals and appointments; he needlessly vetoed things that the Council wanted to do; and in various ways he humiliated the Mayor and the Council. Instead of giving constructive advice and help to the Council (which was supposedly the practice of British and former Kenyan ministers), the Minister was accused of trying to run the City Council and, when that was not possible, of trying to frustrate it. "Why doesn't the Minister let the City Government carry on by itself until it proves irresponsible or incompetent?" asked one of the Mayor's close associates, adding: "After all, it is the officials and councillors of the city who are financially responsible for what goes wrong, not the Minister." It was alleged that the Minister, instead of advising on the larger aspects of policy or expenditure, preferred to pay attention to such petty affairs as the request for an extra typewriter or a small additional travel allowance for recruitment of staff.

Mayor Rubia detailed his criticism of the Ministry of Local Government in a memorandum presented in July, 1966, to the Local Government Commission of Inquiry:

> At present the Council prepares and carefully considers its revenue estimates and is required to submit them for detailed approval to the Ministry. This process took over 4 months last year. This delay means that there is an annual hiatus in the progress of major schemes, while even minor improvements have to be

crammed into an unnecessarily shortened period. It would appear that the emphasis is being placed at the wrong point. The Minister of Local Government should have general control over the Council's capital programmes and should give the Council general policy directions. But having done this, the Council should be left to work out the details. On the other hand, capital schemes (which in the opinion of this Council are of greater importance than the revenue estimates) do not appear to have the attention they deserve from the Minister or even from the Government as a whole. The Minister should give closer consideration to the Council's capital programmes and should only give general direction of policy on revenue matters.[11]

Mayor Rubia went on to note that the slowness of the Minister to approve an increase in house rentals for some of its middle-class housing estates had caused a loss of revenue for the Council of over £2,500. "Any alteration of fees," he added, "which are included in a by-law are often delayed even longer." Similarly, the approval of tenders from other than the lowest bidders (even for items or services costing less than £100) was taking so long, it was claimed by one of the officers, that some construction projects had to be cancelled because contractors had meanwhile made other commitments.

In support of this position, the City Council repeatedly appealed to Government that it no longer be required to get the Minister's approval for estimates and the fixing of fees for goods and services, and that in other ways its powers be substantially increased.[12] The Minister for Local Government, however, remained unconvinced, arguing that the Council members were for the most part too inexperienced to be fully trusted as yet and that increasing Africanization of the staff would necessitate further governmental guidance. Mr. Sagini, who became Minister for Local Government in 1965, was particularly concerned about the procedure for the acceptance of tenders for goods and services. "There are allegations of bribery and corruption or irregularities in the tender procedures," he charged at the 1966 annual meeting of the Association of Local Government Authorities at the Nairobi City Hall, adding: "There is a certain amount of dissatisfaction among some traders who deal with local authorities, and generally I am far from satisfied that all is well."[13] While the Minister was not speaking specifically about the Nairobi City Council, he was aware of rumors that some of the Council members were demanding "kick-backs" from those tendering for contracts.

Unfortunately, the Minister for Local Government was in no position to give the sort of guidance that might have been useful to the Council because, to a large extent, he faced the same sort of problems as did the City Council. The 1966 Report of the Local Government Commission of Inquiry noted that out of an establishment of 60, there were 16 vacancies within the Ministry.[14] Moreover, only 5 of the 31 engaged in audit work were of senior capacity. This inadequacy of staff was especially serious because of the inability of most local authorities in Kenya to prepare their own final accounts. Consequently, the Ministry was in some cases seven years behind in its audit work, thereby greatly reducing the effectiveness of this control. "It will probably be several more years before the present audit staff of the Ministry are able to complete the audit of all accounts up to the end of 1964," concluded the Commission, "and by this time the audits for 1965 and subsequent years will then be in arrears."[15]

Under these circumstances, the City Council did not feel itself obliged to treat the Minister with the deference that he might have expected or desired. The City Council in its 1966 "Memorandum of Evidence to the Local Government Commission of Inquiry" boldly asserted that it could "justly claim that its efforts, and the efforts of its predecessors, have made Nairobi as attractive a capital city as to be found anywhere in the world and that its local government services compare very favourably with those of any other city of similar size."[16] Consequently, argued the Mayor, "it should not be subject to the same detailed control as smaller authorities who may not have the necessary professional and technical officers, but should be subject only to broad policy guidance and left to work out implementation on its own."[17] "The fact is," declared an African alderman of the City Council, "the Minister simply wants to make himself look important by interfering in the affairs of the City Council, since he cannot get over the fact that our budget is many times that of his, and that his staff is not as good as ours."

The City Council was impatient not only with the alleged incompetence of the Ministry of Local Government but also with that of the Central Government as a whole. For example, pay increases and promotions for those in the school system had to be approved by the Public Service Commission as well as the Education Ministry through a very time-consuming procedure. Another complaint was that the City Council was not consulted in the decision-making of the Government. This point was forcefully made by the Town Clerk in his 1965 *Annual Report:*

> The City Council is the authority for primary education in Nairobi. The tax-payers of the City pay for the whole of this service and no contribution is received from the Government; and yet the terms of service and salaries of teachers are fixed without any consultation whatsoever with the City Council or any other local authority. It is important that the Ministry of Education acknowledge that the cost of teachers and education at the primary school level is borne by local taxes and that the Council should be granted some say in the determination of the salaries of teachers.[18]

The City Council was so dissatisfied with its relations with the Education Ministry that it requested in 1966 to be made "responsible as agents of the Government for secondary education in Nairobi so that the planning and administration of primary and secondary education is under the control of one authority subject to the general directions of the Government."[19]

The officers of the City Council were frequently upset by the lack of direction from the Central Government which could give guidelines to public policy. "There is no direction from the Government as a whole — no such thing as collective responsibility," a European officer exclaimed in an interview, adding: "It is, therefore, much harder now than in the old days (and then it could be difficult enough) to know if a minister is speaking for himself or for the cabinet or for the legislature or for some other group." Consequently, to quote another European officer: "Often Councillors pretend to have been instructed by individual legislators or ministers, proclaiming that such and such is Government policy, without anyone being sure just what this means."

What might have been useful to the City Council — and indeed was requested at the hearings of the 1966 Local Government Commission of Inquiry — was some form of liaison body between the Central Government and the Council. The Nairobi Standing Committee of the Senate did not properly fulfill this function, having failed to meet after 1964. "It did not ask for the Committee to be appointed and was not represented on it," asserted the Mayor on behalf of the City Council.[20] Instead, the Mayor proposed "a Standing Conference composed of representatives of the Council and the Ministers concerned, advised by a Working Party of officers."[21]

Mayor Rubia also proposed in 1966, perhaps with tongue-in-cheek, a seminar for Members of Parliament "so that they can be instructed on how to conduct their relations with local authorities."[22] This might have the effect, he maintained, of enabling the City Council to correct allegations made in Parliament and to answer questions which were within the jurisdiction of the local authority. The Mayor was here referring to the criticisms made in Parliament of the salaries and conditions of employment of particular Council employees. What might even be more useful, according to the Mayor, was a way for the Council to comment on bills affecting local government before Parliament. This matter came up in April, 1967, when the Council took issue with an amendment proposed in Parliament requiring the Minister's approval for the naming, numbering, re-naming, or re-numbering of streets in the City.[23] The Council was at this time accused of "threatening civil disobedience," to which it replied that "in commenting on the Act the Council felt that some of its provisions encroached on matters that are best left to local authorities."[24]

The difficulties of the Central Government mirrored as well as intensified those of the City Council. First of all, the socio-economic conditions of Kenya were such that the leaders were simply overwhelmed by the problems they faced. Secondly, there was the possibility that, to quote an officer in the Ministry for Local Government, "an 'old boys' network,' which would facilitate communication among the politicians," had not yet been built up. Relations were certainly hampered by tribal cleavages within the Central

Government, so much so that the Prime Minister in 1964 had to send around a circular in regard to the tendency of Ministers to make their departments tribally homogeneous. When one visited the Ministry of a Kikuyu member of the Cabinet, it was claimed in a 1965 Parliamentary debate, so much Kikuyu was spoken that one had the feeling of being in a Kikuyu village.[25]

During the first four years after independence, the national leaders of Kenya showed very little respect for the semi-federal constitution under which they were operating, feeling that it was forced upon the country by the departing colonial power in return for independence. Moreover, they had neither the patience nor the legal resources (lawyers, clerks, investigators, and so forth) to carry out the complicated procedures required to work the constitution. This caused, among other things, an increasing burden of legal work to fall on the understaffed Attorney General's Chambers, from which the output was slow and uncertain. Arising from this situation was the complaint made in 1967 by an officer of the City Council that three years had elapsed since the validity of the by-laws concerning the collection of fines for parking-meter offenses had been challenged successfully in court. Since these by-laws remained unchanged, he exclaimed, "we have issued £25,000 of fines which we can't collect."

In the years after 1963, the Government increasingly bypassed parliamentary and judicial controls. "In many important respects," wrote Yash P. Ghai, the Associate Dean of the Faculty of Law of the University College at Dar es Salaam in 1967, "whole sections of the Constitution have been suspended; and the suspension has been in effect for so long that they have ceased to have any influence on the practice of law and administration, and remain sad reminders of earlier hopes."[26] This meant that the necessary procedural consensus for spontaneous cooperative action was missing.

African leaders in Kenya increasingly worked within a context of law they neither accepted nor understood. "When we came to Cabinet meetings," noted the former Kenya Vice-President Oginga Odinga in his autobiography, "we were faced with decisions that had been taken outside by a group of the Ministers acting as a caucus, with or without advisers — we were never told."[27] Since many of the ministers were unsure of what the official policies of the Government were, even minor matters had to be referred to the Cabinet. Finally, when decisions were taken and laws enacted, N. S. Jones Carey, a former Permanent Secretary to the Kenyan Ministry of Lands and Settlement, points out, they rested upon the faith of African administors "that a government decision, by the very fact of being taken, had somehow solved a problem, without appreciating the need to make it effective by positive action; as though a Cabinet decision in some magical way became known to the people and an expression of their own will."[28]

## The Personality of Charles Rubia

The relations between the City Council and the Central Government were very much affected by the personality of Charles Rubia, Nairobi's first African mayor. He had initially gained the position in July, 1962, at a time when most of the members of the City Council (23 out of 37) were still Europeans. As a suave, facile, intelligent person in his early forties, educated at the Alliance High School (the most famous in Kenya) and having had unusual business experience and responsibility, Rubia was considered to be a fairly "reasonable chap" by his European mentors. From membership in the Nairobi General African Ward Council, Rubia had been first appointed to the City Council in 1957, and next to the Kenya Legislative Council from 1958 to 1960, from which he was elected by the Council members directly to the aldermanic bench. He then became Deputy Chairman of the Finance Committee (one of the most important of the City Council's committees) before attaining the mayoralty. Despite this experience, doubts about Rubia's ability persisted. "When I took over," Rubia recalled at the time of his retirement as Mayor in the summer of 1967,

> there was a lot of pessimism in the minds of many people, especially the non-Africans, as to whether the civic affairs of the capital would be well-conducted by an African. I should confess that I had no prior experience at all in mayoral work or even that of the deputy mayor's office. But I was determined that not only would the Nairobi City Council's affairs be maintained, but, most

important, the people of Nairobi should observe an improvement in the task of providing public services.[29]

As Mayor, Rubia quickly built up a large following, particularly among his fellow Kikuyu. This was surprising since he had never fought a general election and had never been considered as an outstanding nationalist. Indeed, by allowing himself to be nominated to membership of the Legislative Council in 1958, Rubia had aroused the animosity of Tom Mboya, the top African political leader of this period. And in City Council affairs, Rubia took a relatively conservative position to the chagrin of some of the African members. Consequently, Rubia was probably more highly regarded by Europeans than by Africans when he first became Mayor; and this soon led to his receiving an impressive number of well-paying directorships, ranging from the Kenya Bus Services and the Kenya Broadcasting Corporation to the Development Finance Company of Kenya, making him one of the country's wealthiest and most influential Africans. All this success had the effect of giving the short stocky Mr. Rubia the appearance of a rather pompous figure in his large, official, chauffeur-driven limousine, ever ready to take offence at any supposed slight to his mayoral dignity and anxious to use his position to further his career in national politics.

The obvious adroitness of Rubia, his experience, his dignified and commanding presence increasingly overawed the other African Council members, conscious as they were of their own inadequacy. It was surmised that part of the power of the Mayor stemmed from his ability to take advantage of the confusion prevalent in the committees following African political ascendancy. According to an informant: "The Councillors wait for the Mayor to come, until he speaks, they waffle along." The alleged slowness of the committees to act and to coordinate their decisions led a group of Councillors sympathetic to the Mayor to propose in 1965 that his executive powers be expanded, enabling him to make certain appointments and take some actions without having to refer them to the committees.

This proposal to increase the executive powers of the Mayor and, in addition, to extend his term of office to five years, was strongly criticized in an *East African Standard* editorial:

If a mayor is given executive powers, there is the possibility of overlapping with the Town Clerk's powers, undermining his authority, not to mention the other chief officers in the jobs as managers. The Mayor is the most respected member of a council and chief citizen during his term of office. He . . . cannot be expected to understand the professional and technical problems of the departments, which must be left to the control of the chief officers under the general policy decisions of the council sitting in open session. In the final reckoning, all councillors are elected by the public to serve the public. This is the acknowledged principle of election by popular vote, applicable to the M.P.s and municipal councillors. If executive authority is to be vested in the mayoral office, would it not eventually become the repository of all power?[30]

Although the Mayor was never formally given the power he sought, many of the Council's officers were convinced that he increasingly attempted to exercise more power than he officially possessed. One of them suggested that Rubia may have brought back from his 1963 tour of America an inflated conception of the role of mayor — one far different from the largely honorific character of the traditional British mayoralty.

The European officers were particularly alarmed by the behavior of the Mayor because of their feeling of insecurity and uncertainty following the advent of an African council in 1963. They had originally hoped that the Mayor would help overcome the distrust manifested by the African Council members. However, instead of supporting the officers, it was felt that the Mayor openly humiliated them to enhance his popularity among the Africans. For example, Rubia, according to one of the engineers, demanded that construction work on a certain project be completed in a fortnight, overriding all objections by shouting: "You are employees of the City. I am the Mayor. Your job is to obey my instructions." While this forceful treatment of the officers may have impressed the African Council members, it was thought to lower the morale not only of expatriate but of African officers as well. Even more ominous, in the view of the European officers, were the Mayor's demands which seemed to disregard regulations and priorities, such as roads paved to the homes of certain leading politicians, "even insisting at times they be closed to outside traffic." While these demands may have had the support of the Council and the Central Government, they forced the officers into positions they found ethically questionable.

The Mayor, it should be noted, was seen in a somewhat sympathetic light even by some of his critics. "The Mayor is very conscious of his position, and he doesn't want to lower the prestige of his job," one of the Mayor's aides explained in a 1964 interview. "He is anxious to be as good as his European predecessors, but his troubles come from the nature of the political situation here in Kenya. He and the other African leaders are too inexperienced to be sure of the limits of power and responsibility that come with the positions they hold." Another difficulty, it was pointed out, was the inability of African leaders to know what could or could not be done on the part of administrators. "For example, we used to have six months to prepare for a state banquet. Now we are lucky to get three weeks, resulting in an unavoidable series of errors and misunderstandings."

## The Case of the A.I.D. Loan

Both the Mayor's sympathizers and opponents often predicted that Rubia's numerous clashes in 1964, beginning with his colleagues and officers within the City Council and extending beyond them to many of the country's top leaders, would inevitably cause his downfall. To illustrate the sort of conflicts that arose, one might start with what occurred during the City Council's negotiations with the American Agency for International Development (A.I.D.).[31]

For several years the City Council had been attempting to obtain a loan to heighten Sasumua Dam, from which Nairobi draws much of its water. While there were other sources of funds, A.I.D. seemed to be the most promising with regard to quantity of funds and generosity of terms. A.I.D., however, insisted that only American contractors should be allowed to tender for the work and that American consulting engineers would have to "vet" the design and check on progress of the work during construction. It was estimated that these conditions would add as much as £325,000 ($910,000) to the cost of the scheme. Considering that the total proposed loan amounted to less than £800,000 ($2,240,000), the cost entailed by the A.I.D. conditions was thought to be exorbitant. Moreover, these conditions seemed to reflect adversely upon the competence of the local contractors and, indirectly, the entire City Council and Kenyan Government. As such, they were vehemently rejected.

In April, 1964, the City Treasurer, A. W. Kent, and the Chairman of the Finance Committee, Isaac Maina, were sent to Washington, D.C. to conclude negotiations with A.I.D. for a loan of £750,000 ($2,100,000) for the expansion of the Nairobi water supply.[32] Though the delegation was to be joined there by the Minister of Finance, they were instructed to report back to the Council the results of their discussions rather than to finalize the negotiations at this time.

While from one point of view, Kent and Maina were the proper choices of the Council to be sent for this important business, from another point of view, they were not. Kent had been with the City Council for almost two decades and was generally recognized as a highly capable person, having been awarded the coveted Order of the British Empire. Yet, his personality was considered to be abrasive, having irritated many officers and councillors over the years. Had it not been for his extraordinary ability, Kent would have been dismissed very soon after the Africans came into control of the Council. In any case, it was inevitable that he would come into conflict with Mayor Rubia who was anxious to establish his own authority within the Council. The animosity between the two men flared into the open in the General Council meeting of January, 1964, when it was alleged that the Treasurer showed insolence in answering one of the Mayor's questions.[33] Kent then had to make a humiliating public apology to the Mayor and the Council. An indication of the distrust of Kent was the Mayor's proposal in 1965 that the Chairman of the Finance Committee countersign all cheques — a proposal objected to by Kent as interfering with the Council's financial administration, including the practice of signing cheques by machine.[34] Though Kent was later supported on this particular point by the Ministry of Local Government, his position was in other ways undermined.

Isaac Maina, the Chairman of the Finance Committee, was also the object of the Mayor's hostility, though a Kikuyu with similar education and experience to that of the Mayor and a member of the Council since 1958. Maina's troubles with Rubia stemmed largely from the fact that his background and genial personality enabled him to challenge the Mayor's authority in a way that no other councillor could. Indeed, Maina took advantage of Rubia's difficulties in the fall of 1964 to contest the Mayoralty, but he took his step at the wrong time and was eventually forced out of the Council.

As it turned out, Kent and Maina were able to gain a considerable concession from the American officials in Washington, amounting to a major deviation from the usual A.I.D. requirements. The agreement reached was that:

> If U.S. firms bid £500,000 ($1,400,000) or less, the contract would be awarded to the U.S. firm submitting the lowest responsive bid regardless of whether a local firm had submitted a lower bid. If no U.S. firm submitted a responsive bid within the £500,000 ($1,400,000) cost estimate, the contract would be awarded to the lowest bidder, whether U.S. or local.[35]

Since the estimate referred to of £500,000 was the one originally calculated by Council's consulting engineers and submitted to A.I.D., it was considered a fair estimate based upon East African prices and, as such, unlikely to be met by an American firm. Thus, in its amended form the loan was thought by many of those concerned with the negotiations to be advantageous to the City Council because only $3\frac{1}{2}$ per cent interest would be charged (of which 3 per cent was eventually to be returned to the Kenyan Government) and this loan was repayable over 25 years with a "grace" period of three years.

This proposed contract with A.I.D., however, was flatly rejected by the City Council, thereby disregarding the arguments of Kent, Mr. James Gichuru (the Minister for Finance), and other respected figures. In its meeting of May 27, 1964, the Finance Committee resolved that "whilst this Council is anxious to obtain a loan to heighten the Sasumua Dam, it regrets that it is unable to accept the condition laid down regarding contractors," adding: "This Council has no objection to American contractors tendering for the work in open competition with local contractors."[36] This resolution was later amended in such a way as to allow any nation, including one from the Communist Bloc, to compete for the job to be undertaken through the American loan — something that the American Government was then unlikely to accept.[37]

According to those interviewed, the Council's response resulted from a combination of all the factors that have been discussed but, particularly, from the attitude of the Mayor. Rubia, it was asserted, wanted to do the negotiations in Washington himself with the City Advocate, but he was ill when the matter was initially discussed by the Council. Moreover, for the Mayor to have too boldly insisted upon personally representing the Council in Washington would have been out of place, considering the persistent British concept of the mayor as "coordinator" and "supervisor" rather than as "director" or "manager." Anyhow, the Mayor was thought to have opposed the loan because he feared that the prestige associated with it would be garnered by others, including his rivals.

Kent may have hardened Rubia's opposition, it was pointed out, because he was back from Washington for two weeks before seeing the Mayor about the loan. Maina, however, was considered equally at fault. Instead of returning directly to Nairobi to defend the loan, he went to London to be with the team then recruiting employees for the City Council. When the loan finally came to be considered, according to an African City Council member: "Maina was confused and not able to explain to us what had happened." This information was corroborated by one of the officers most knowledgeable about the situation:

Maina failed to appreciate just what was involved — the fact that the American negotiators were tied to conditions laid down by Congress and that, despite this, a very good deal had been arranged. Anyhow, Maina was too uncertain of himself to sell the loan to the African Councillors, and the Mayor, for reasons probably of personal rivalry with Maina, saw to it that the loan was rejected.

The complexity of the loan agreement might also be mentioned, running into 143 pages with all sorts of ramifications. This complexity may have raised doubts in the minds of some of the Council members, particularly those who were convinced that money was easy to get from such countries as China and the Soviet Union.

The Minister for Local Government was, of course, concerned about the rejection of the loan by the City Council. "The Government has the right to require the Council to reconsider its decision on the A.I.D. loan," declared a veteran official in the Ministry for Local Government, adding: "He [the Minister] can simply take over the negotiations with the American Government if the City Council fails to use good judgment." However, the Mayor was fully determined to let the Minister know that the loan was none of his business. "Recently the Minister for Local Government wanted to see the dam that was to be enlarged through the loan," related one of the officers of the City Council, "but the Mayor not only refused to go with him but also refused to provide him with a car for his trip." This obviously did not improve the relationship between the two men.

It was reportedly the insistence of the Finance Minister that forced the City Council to reconsider its rejection of the A.I.D. loan proposal. Thus, the proposal was finally signed in December, 1964, and approved by the Kenyan Senate in October, 1965 (after having been rejected at the Second Reading). As it turned out, the successful low tenderer was a California firm which, to the embarrassment of A.I.D., proved not to be altogether reliable. Nevertheless, work on the dam was carried out, and eventually came to be counted by Mayor Rubia as one of his major achievements.

Despite the successful outcome of the loan agreement, the entire affair was for a time politically embarrassing to all concerned. The lines of communication between the City Council and the Central Government became more strained than previously. The authority of Maina, who had failed to show leadership, and of Kent, who had carried the brunt of the burdensome negotiations, appeared weakened. More important, it was feared that the Council's handling of this matter made future attempts to borrow money from abroad far more difficult.

*The 1964 Resignation of Mayor Rubia*

On September 15, 1964, Charles Rubia resigned from his position as Mayor of Nairobi. This action aroused considerable tribal passion, thereby threatening the unity of the national political party, provoking the KANU youth wing into angry demontrations and the Kikuyu women of Nairobi into their piercing ululating cry in front of the City Hall. What was so surprising to the public was that Rubia's resignation came only a few months after he had been overwhelmingly backed by Council members for a third term, indicating the high regard in which he was held.

Rubia was increasingly concerned by what he felt to be the slighting of his mayoral dignity, so much so that at one point during a 1964 visit by the Emperor of Ethiopia, he was reported to have threatened to boycott the proceedings.[38] It was his opinion that the Mayor should have precedence in all ceremonies in the City after the President. The Cabinet Ministers, on the other hand, maintained that they were entitled to the more exalted positions beside the President. In this and other ways, according to Rubia, the Cabinet members, particularly the Minister for Local Government (Mr. S. O. Ayodo), were attempting to minimize the status of the Mayor and the Council as a whole. "The Council cannot understand," Rubia exclaimed, "why the normal precedence of the Mayor as followed in other parts of Africa, India, the United Kingdom and other foreign countries should not be observed in Kenya, and consider that the matter should be put beyond doubt by appropriate legislation."[39]

In his disputes with Rubia, Ayodo, being a Luo, felt doubly disadvantaged in a government as well as a city dominated by Kikuyus. Moreover, he had no previous experience as a cabinet member or even as an administrator and was relatively young in age (33, when appointed in 1963). Prior to his election to the Legislative Council in 1963, Ayodo had been a secondary school teacher, following his graduation in 1955 from Lincoln University in Pennsylvania. The Minister's lack of experience, according to one of his European subordinates, made him overly dependent upon a staff that was rapidly losing its very capable British personnel. At the same time, he did not know enough to be able to evaluate the advice given him or to make decisions with perspicacity and confidence.

The showdown came over an apparently trivial matter: a registered letter from the Senior Local Government Inspector requiring Mayor Rubia to disclose in confidence details of any business transactions in which he was engaged in the Nairobi area, so that any debt on his part to the City Council could be ascertained. This request was brought about by the disqualification of a councillor for having a debt to the City Council outstanding for more than two months. By October, 1964, ten other Council members were expelled from the Council for the same reason.

The Mayor, however, felt that the technicalities of the law (a carry-over from a British local-government statute) were being used by the Minister to embarrass him for political and ethnic purposes, using as an excuse the existence of a small bill (amounting to about $22) that had been overdue for more than three months but which, the Mayor claimed, had only recently been brought to his attention. This, Ayodo firmly denied:

> In ordering this inquiry, the Minister was acting in the interests of local government and was not motivated by political or tribal jealousies. This Ministry is therefore disappointed to learn that the Mayor has taken this inquiry as a personal affront to his dignity.[40]

Superficially, the issue here was the manner of treatment of the mayor. According to Rubia, a European mayor would not have been treated in such an insulting way. Instead, the Minister, if he wanted any information from the mayor, would have taken the request personally to him instead of sending a letter by registered post.[41] Unfortunately, claimed Rubia and his supporters, certain Ministries are still run by imperialists. "The bureaucracy," to quote the editor of one of Kenya's newspapers, "must be taught that they cannot pry and probe with impunity into the affairs of honest men in a free society; that they cannot bring a civic leader and a city into disrepute over a trifling matter of a few shillings."[42]

Ayodo was not slow to defend himself against this attack. "If anybody is going to suggest that in this type of case the Mayor should have preferential treatment in application of the law, I would find it difficult to agree with him," he told the House of Representatives, adding that anybody who calls the Minister an imperialist "could himself be the biggest imperialist of all."[43] A still more caustic comment on what had taken place came from Hilary Ng'weno, the editor of the *Daily Nation:*

> Perhaps the concept of the Mayor as the First Citizen of the City is quite unsuited for the place and the times in which we find ourselves. Perhaps a Minister of the Government takes precedence over the Mayor in any function in which the two are present. Perhaps Nairobi should have no Mayor at all. All these are considerations which the Government should take seriously.[44]

Within a month after the Mayor's resignation, Mr. Kenyatta, as Prime Minister acting on behalf of his cabinet, withdrew the disqualification notices from the eleven Council members to whom they had been served. Later the ordinance having to do with debts to the City Council which had initially caused the trouble was also deleted. The way was thus opened for Rubia to offer himself for reelection as alderman and subsequently for Mayor, and this was done with considerable fanfare. But Rubia's victory was less than complete. At the same time that he re-instated the Council members, Kenyatta was careful to uphold the decision of the Minister for Local Government that had brought about the Mayor's resignation, noting quite pointedly:

> The Government is convinced that in this whole matter the blame must lie with the weaknesses in the administration of the City Council. It has been shown beyond doubt that the city administration is lax and in some cases just careless.[45]

It was, of course, hoped that the Mayor-Minister rivalry would be curtailed following the Prime Minister's intervention, but this was not to be the case. In his reelection speech of November 4, Rubia warned of "cold war factions at work," including the perpetuation of tribalistic cults, class interests and group loyalties of an inimical nature.[46] "Call it the day-dream of Rubia if you like — I would like to believe that I am wrong," he exclaimed, emphasizing that Kenya must not allow itself to become "another Vietnam."

The intention here was obviously to intimidate the Minister for Local Government, but this was not so easily done. In deploring the Mayor's "vague and misleading" utterances, Ayodo countered:

> It would seem that the Mayor has forgotten that the purpose of the City Council is to provide services to the public. The Council was created by the Government and is therefore controlled by the Government. The Ministry exercises control on behalf of the Government and it is the duty of the Ministry to ensure that the Council conducts its affairs in the public interest.[47]

To restore relations between the City Council and the Ministry, it was decided in January, 1965 to have Mr. Ayodo switch positions with Mr. L. G. Sagini, the Minister for Natural Resources. Sagini was born in 1926 at Kisii (which also designates the Bantu-language group in the eastern part of Nyanza Province) and had graduated from Allegheny College in the United States prior to becoming an Education Officer and later a Minister for Education.

Although Sagini was a more experienced administrator than Ayodo, he seemed unable to improve significantly the relations between his Ministry and the City Council. Rubia continued to disregard the Minister for Local Government, going instead directly to the Kikuyu ministers and, particularly, to President Kenyatta for support of his projects. So concerned did Sagini become about this practice that he required in 1966 "that all communications with his Excellency the President, other Ministers and/or Ministries should be channelled through the Ministry of Local Government unless prior authority has been given by his [Sagini's] Ministry to deal direct on specific subjects."[48] This sort of stipulation, however, was not likely to be respected by the majority of Council members who happened to be Kikuyu and, as such, was practically impossible to enforce.

## The Dismissal of Waiyaki

The man caught in the middle during the controversy between the Mayor and the Minister for Local Government over the debts of City Council members was Mr. Kimani Waiyaki, who had been appointed on probationary terms in May, 1964 as Nairobi's first

African Town Clerk. Waiyaki had gained this position at the insistence of the Mayor and the Kikuyu Council members in preference to a Luo lawyer with experience in the Advocate's Section of the City Council. Waiyaki had no prior experience in local government, but he had qualified as a barrister in London and had served with the East African Common Services Organization. Moreover, he was a brother of Dr. Munyua Waiyaki, who was a leading Kikuyu politician and a descendant of the famous Chief Waiyaki, renowned as an early opponent of British colonialism.

At the committee meeting in October, 1963, when Waiyaki's name was first put forward for the position of town clerk, three of the Luo Council members walked out, claiming that tribalism had determined the Council's recommendation.[49] This allegation of tribalism was later redirected at the Minister of Local Government when he hesitated to confirm Waiyaki's appointment after expressing concern about Waiyaki's lack of administrative experience. "The City Council were however insistent that Mr. Waiyaki was the man they wished to appoint and the Government therefore concurred," Mr. Sagini later explained in the House of Representatives.[50]

It was generally felt among the European officers of the City Council that Waiyaki's competence as a town clerk left much to be desired. Exclaimed one of them:

> He is useless as a town clerk. He doesn't know anything, and he doesn't want to do anything. He neglects to attend committee meetings and doesn't stay when he does attend. When he went to London with the group recruiting staff, he refused to stay with the Councillors and disappeared for three days with a woman he knew there. When he was recently reprimanded by the Mayor for leaving a committee and not returning as he had promised, he told the Mayor to talk to Kenyatta who was responsible for his being appointed as town clerk in the first place.

What was frequently admitted, however, was that Waiyaki was useful as an intermediary between the European staff and the African Council members. "Waiyaki has proved to be very useful because he will accept advice," it was suggested. "Through him, information has been fed to the committees; and it will then be accepted to an extent that it wouldn't be coming directly from the European officers."

To be fair to Waiyaki, it must be remembered that the position of town clerk is considered the most difficult as well as the most important in an English-type local government. It requires a combination of legal knowledge, administrative skill, and political acumen — a combination unlikely to be possessed by one as inexperienced as Waiyaki. "He was in a difficult position," one of the European officers pointed out. "He needed to depend on Europeans, and this fact could be used to embarrass him, particularly by the Mayor." Lacking confidence in himself, Waiyaki "was arrogant with the Councillors, always trying to show off his little knowledge of law," an African officer contended, adding: "The problem with Waiyaki was that he lacked tact. He wanted to dominate. He failed to realize that the councillors are our employers." Indeed, it was the line between the roles of politician and administrator, vague in any case but particularly obscure in developing countries, that complicated the situation for Waiyaki.

During the Mayor-Minister crisis of 1964, the pressure upon the Town Clerk made his position hardly tolerable. This was acknowledged by Waiyaki in January, 1965, when it appeared that he would not be retained by the City Council: "It has been my duty as Town Clerk and head of administration continually to admonish and check individuals who feel that they are above the law, and this has made me extremely unpopular."[51] Waiyaki was accused at this time of having used the evidence of debts to embarrass his enemies within the Council, particularly the Mayor.

While the handling of the debts obviously lowered the prestige of the Town Clerk within the City Council, it caused the Government to emphasize his position vis-à-vis that of the Mayor. This was indicated in a directive to the City Council, stating that the Town Clerk was the chief executive officer of the Council and, as such, he should not seek administrative advice from the Mayor, chairmen of committees or councillors.[52] Moreover, he would have sole authority for the issuance of press statements relating to Council affairs and to decide what matters should be placed on Council agendas.

The possibility of the Town Clerk undermining the Mayor's position certainly alarmed Rubia and his supporters in the City Council. By the beginning of 1965 when he took over as Minister for Local Government, Sagini noted that relations between clerk and council had so deteriorated that "I considered it my duty to intervene and ask the Council to defer discussions of the Town Clerk's confirmation for three months so the matter could be discussed in a calmer atmosphere."[53] Meanwhile, Waiyaki refused to resign (whereupon his car was allegedly stoned by the Mayor's supporters), and he insisted that the Government set up a formal commission with full legal power to go into the affairs of the Council at all levels.

The decision of the City Council's General Purposes Committee to dismiss Waiyaki appeared quite disturbing to all concerned, coming as it did so soon after the Council's unseemly conflict with the Ministry of Local Government which had led to the Mayor's dramatic resignation and reinstatement. "Though it is no part of our duty to judge precisely what has gone wrong in Nairobi City Council affairs," editorialized the *East African Standard,* "clearly something is amiss."[54] Waiyaki boldly implicated the Mayor in his public statement without actually mentioning him:

> Because some influential members of the Council are trying to run affairs with an eye to popularity, and without strict regard for the law, the Council's administration is declining and could well become chaotic if improper interference with the administrative machine continues.
>
> Too many members are ignoring accepted procedure; integrity in staff appointments is declining, and I had to warn staff against the prevalence of seeking the support of influential members of the Council who seem prepared to help them in matters of promotion and advancement.[55]

The Council members were embarrassed and angered by Waiyaki's statement to the press, and they quickly reacted by forbidding chief officers to approach the press before exhausting the existing grievance procedure.[56] They further undermined Waiyaki's position by transferring the Establishments Section (which has to do with the control of staff) from the Town Clerk's Department to that of the City Treasurer, despite Waiyaki's assertion that the transfer was not only contrary to his advice, but also in disregard of Local Government Regulations.[57] You cannot overrule my authority, he argued, "unless you have consulted an expert." "I do not like threats," the Mayor countered in a reply that was readily supported by the Council. This rebuff suffered by the Town Clerk was the prelude to the vote which terminated Waiyaki's appointment.[58]

The Minister for Local Government was not in a position to protect Waiyaki's position, but, in conjunction with the Senate's Nairobi Standing Committee, he did investigate and report on the problems of the Nairobi City Council. This report made some general observations on the working of the committee system and the inexperience and lack of education of many of the Council members, in addition to the unhappy relationship between Council officers and members and between the Ministry of Local Government and the City Council.[59] The overall import of the "Report of the Nairobi Standing Committee 1964" was to emphasize the prerogatives of the Ministry of Local Government and the officers of the City Council as against those of the Mayor and the Council members. At the same time it recognized the difficulty of formally defining the boundaries of positions in local government:

> The proper relationship between councillors and officers is the key to the success of local government administration. But relationship is not a matter that can be legislated for. It is something that must develop from a constructive desire to understand and accept each other's functions and responsibilities.[60]

### The Rolls-Royce Affair

Mayor Rubia did not escape unscathed from his clash with Waiyaki. To replace Waiyaki, the Council temporarily turned to a European, D. M. Whiteside, who had been Acting Town Clerk prior to Waiyaki's appointment. But the costliness of this move was soon seized upon by Rubia's critics, pointing out that Whiteside was to be paid an amount nearly twice what Waiyaki had received. Mr. J. M. Shikuki in the House of Representatives claimed that this sort of action could lead to frustration among the educated Africans who were being by-passed in preference to non-citizens.[61]

In his characteristic way, Rubia vigorously replied to this attack by Members of Parliament. M.P.s should not voice their criticism, he exclaimed, "in a haphazard manner by questions and answers put to obtain the greatest publicity and to do the utmost harm to the Council."[62] At the same time he threatened to have the Council or the Nairobi Standing Committee "obtain details of the salaries of permanent secretaries, financial, economic, and other advisers to the Government and of similar posts in semi-governmental organizations so that a fair comparison between these salaries and the salaries of the principal officers of the Council can be made."

It was Rubia's decision to purchase a Rolls-Royce, even more than his dismissal of Waiyaki, which exposed the Mayor to criticism. Rubia sought to obtain a Rolls-Royce soon after becoming Mayor, considering it the only car really dignified enough for the head of the most important city in East Africa. After all, the Mayor argued, what was important was not so much his personal dignity as the dignity of Nairobi, emphasizing that the car was not for his personal use alone but for the use of the City.[63] He also contended that a Rolls-Royce was actually economical because it was guaranteed to last for many years.

The Ministry for Local Government rejected the Mayor's request for a Rolls-Royce when it was initially broached in November, 1963. Again, in May, 1965, the Ministry refused to agree to the spending of £7,000 ($19,600) for a new Rolls-Royce, after a technical report indicated that the vehicle he was then using was in good shape and that the defects complained about (leaks and electrical shocks) could be repaired.[64] But finally in January, 1966, the Minister for Local Government (then, Mr. Sagini) was prevailed upon to authorize the Council to purchase a Rolls-Royce costing £10,850 (including a 30 per cent tax) "which is in keeping with the dignity of the Mayor of the capital city of the Republic of Kenya."[65] He then announced in the House of Representatives that the car would be arriving within a month.

A storm of protest almost immediately followed the Minister's announcement. "When people come to Nairobi looking for a job, they are asked for their 1964 tax," exclaimed Mr. Martin Shikuku in the House of Representatives, adding: "All this money goes to the City Council to enable the Mayor to have a £10,850 Rolls-Royce so that he can drive nicely and say he is the greatest man. We do not believe in people's dignity at the expense of the poor man."[66] Perhaps the sharpest criticism came from the African editor of the *Daily Nation,* pointing out that the sum of money set aside for the Rolls-Royce could feed a village of 200 people for eight years, could build a hospital, and could buy a fleet of cheaper cars. "Is Kenya so rich that she can afford a luxury Rolls-Royce of the type which is not even used by the President of the U.S.?"[67]

Joining the protest against the purchase of the Rolls-Royce were the Kenya Students' Union of the University College of Nairobi and a number of labor unions. "Our unions are ready at any time to support the fight against the City Council of Nairobi about this extravagant expenditure at a time when people are still living in slums within the City," warned one of the labor union leaders.[68] This threat was underscored by the decision of the Nairobi City Council branch of the Kenya Local Government Workers' Union (consisting of all employees with the exception of those on supervisory grades) to engage in a "slow-down" and possibly a strike unless the car was returned and an inquiry into City Council finances undertaken.[69] At the same time that he announced this decision, Mr. J. Karebe, the General Secretary of the Kenya Local Government Workers' Union, revealed that the Minister for Local Government had approved the additional expenditure of £2,100 for six motorcycles (together with drivers' costs and maintenance) to escort the Mayor on official occasions.

On February 8, 1966, there occurred what was described in the *East African Standard* as "one of the most heated debates ever to take place in the Kenya House of Representatives" on the Rolls-Royce affair.[70] Leading the attack was Mr. D. N. Ngala. "As a taxpayer to the Council, I am thoroughly fed up and disgusted with the action taken by the Council," he asserted. "This is daylight robbery of the taxpayers," he went on. "It is a sure way of losing the confidence of our own people." The widespread outrage manifested in this debate could not be ignored by the Government. Before a week had passed, Mr. Kenyatta ordered by special decree that the purchase of the Rolls-Royce be stopped.

The whole episode of the Rolls-Royce caught the City Council and the Mayor by surprise. According to Rubia, there had been "interference from international quarters" to promote the controversy, led by the newspapers.[71] "My view is that because of the success of the City Council, some people do not like you. They have felt insecure in their political careers because of the Council's unity and success," he told the City Council members. "As far as I am concerned, an inquiry is very welcome," he concluded, "but I do not want foreigners and fellow travellers dictating to us. People are taking advantage of our hospitality and exploiting the situation to divide us."

Rubia appeared to be particularly upset by the poll conducted by the *East African Standard* in which 97 per cent of those questioned indicated their disapproval of the Rolls-Royce purchase. The *Daily Nation,* however, responded that Kenyatta's disallowance of the purchase was the clearest evidence of the ability of the people to use "constitutional methods of influencing policies and questioning performance."[72] In any case, it suggested that "those who have been made the custodians of public bodies, corporations, and funds must be careful about the means in which they use public money."

Privately, some of the Council members blamed not so much the press as the Luo enemies of the Mayor (particularly among the trade union leaders) for stirring up the controversy. It was also pointed out that the Ministry of Local Government deserved some of the blame. Indeed, the Minister, Mr. Sagini, had to acknowledge before the Senate that he had been pressured into authorizing the Roll-Royce purchase. "I do not want to say I support this and I do not want to say I oppose it," he told the Senators.[73] In view of the Minister's earlier approval of the purchase, his statement to the Senators seemed to the Council members an act of weakness as well as betrayal. Yet, as the editor of the *East African Standard* pointed out, it was unfair of the Council to "first say that its decision must be accepted by the Minister and then, when the public protested, try to avoid responsibility by blaming the Minister for submitting to the Council's demand."[74]

*The Mayor's Recoupment*

To some extent, the Rolls-Royce Affair had the effect of solidifying the Council's support of the Mayor. A minority of the members had opposed the decision to purchase the Rolls-Royce, the Mayor admitted in his address to the Council on February 10, 1966.[75] "Yet once a decision had been taken," he noted, "the Council exhibited unity during the past two weeks of frustration." This unity, emphasized the Mayor, did not mean that disagreement was suppressed but that "we have developed a very rare quality to disagree and yet remain loyal to the cause." At a special meeting the City Council later reassured the Mayor "that this Council deplores the unfair attacks made on it and its Mayor by some Members of Parliament and hereby reiterates its full confidence in the integrity, loyalty, and able guidance of its Mayor, Alderman Charles Rubia."[76] Thus, while somewhat chastened by the Rolls-Royce episode, the Council members were not demoralized. They were, instead, more than ever determined to prove their integrity and competence.

By the summer of 1966, Mayor Rubia had regained some of the prestige lost during the Rolls-Royce affair. Partly this resulted from the success of the Council in withstanding a challenge from the emerging Kenya People's Union. Rubia had earlier indicated his desire to resign for reasons of health, but he agreed to stand again because, as he explained in his acceptance speech, "he had been made aware that he formed the basis for unity in the Council."[77] If he refused to take office again, it would amount to "running away when the battle gets hot." Of much more significance for the Mayor was the improved performance of the Council, as he pointed out in his statement to the Council on the thirtieth of June, 1966:

> Last year, I described the business of the Council during my third year of office as hectic. This year has not been quite so hectic. Rather, it has been a period of consolidation. Members of the Council have applied themselves to the work of their Committees with diligence and an increasing sense of responsibility. They have learned much in the short time since Uhuru, and it is a sign of maturity in municipal administration that meetings do not last as long as they did. I have been happy to note too the cordial

partnership established between members of the Council and the staff. In particular, the expatriate officers recruited last summer have settled down wonderfully well.[78]

Many of those interviewed in the summer of 1966 attested to the validity of the Mayor's remarks. "The overall atmosphere of the City Council has become much more relaxed," observed a European officer, adding: "Committee meetings are now much shorter. It is rare for a committee meeting to last more than a few hours whereas previously, six hours was not uncommon." There was also, it was agreed, a much more cooperative relationship between the African Council members and the European officers who remained in important positions.

It was the view of one of the recently hired European officers that the City Council members were no less responsible in behavior than those he had associated with in Britain. "The Councillors actually work harder here," he remarked. "Instead of just a few hours in the evening, they devote many hours to the work of the Council. They really are concerned with the problems of their constituents and with those of the City. They still have much to learn, and they can be a nuisance at times, but they are doing the best they can." The extent to which the African Council members had mastered Council organization and procedure evoked the surprise and admiration of a veteran European Council member. "We underestimated their quickness to learn," he admitted.

The good relations that emerged between European and African officers — as indicated by the cheerful way in which they discussed mutual problems over lunch — was one of the outstanding developments that occurred during Rubia's period as Mayor. The obvious improvement in staff morale was partly facilitated by the retirement of some of the more distrusted or disgruntled European officers and their replacement by men who proved to be not only highly competent, but also able and anxious to work with African colleagues and Council members. E. L. Jones, who replaced Arthur Kent as Treasurer in 1965, was a particularly fortunate choice.

While, as mentioned in the last chapter, the African officers generally lacked experience and confidence in themselves, some of them came to be increasingly respected by the African Council members and, thereby, able to exercise a useful degree of influence that was much appreciated by their European colleagues. The tactfulness and political skill of J. P. Mbogua, the Director of Social Services and Housing from 1964 to 1967 before being elevated to Town Clerk, was often cited in favorable contrast to Waiyaki "who would take sides on various matters and would publicly criticize and argue with the officers, instead of working out in private grievances with the officers before presenting statements to the Council or the public."

The Mayor was given a great deal of credit for the improved performance of the Council even by his most severe critics. He had showed courage and good judgment in retaining a considerable number of the more competent European staff members and in hiring others to replace some of those who had left. Moreover, Rubia became increasingly willing and able to support the officers when they needed it. "The Mayor has matured over the years," observed one of the officers. "He can now be relied upon to defend us and to get the Councillors back on the right track." The Mayor's support of the officers was eventually reciprocated, adding to his influence among the Council members.

The Mayor's effectiveness was also enhanced by his effort to placate the various races and tribes in the City. While he proclaimed that the policy of the Council was "Africans first," he insisted that the City Council was opposed to racialism.[79] The truth, as seen by the non-African Council members, was that the Mayor attempted to moderate the existing racial discrimination in the affairs or decisions of the Council. The pressure for Africanization was obviously irresistible; but, as Councillor Mandel (an Asian) explained in 1966 in defence of the Mayor when he was attacked in the House of Representatives, "we are very careful in Africanizing posts when it is thought a new man could not do the job as efficiently."[80]

During his earlier years of office, Mayor Rubia was constantly charged with being a "tribalist." However, an informal process began to emerge with regard to incipient tribal conflict. The Mayor showed great patience and skill, according to informants, in negotiating with the representatives of the various tribes and in reaching acceptable compromises. Conflicts remained, it was pointed out, but they were worked out within the Council. There was a growing realization of the danger of going outside the Council, thereby lowering the prestige of the Council in the minds of Government and the general public and making issues so emotional that they became difficult to resolve. The Mayor could afford to be magnanimous in matters of patronage, some argued, having politically eliminated those who had most threatened him in the past. Nevertheless, it was recognized that the Mayor occasionally went out of his way to be fair — for example, in insisting that the one K.P.U. member of the Council (a Luo) be treated in accord with the prescribed rules, however repugnant these rules might appear to some of the members. Rubia's close association with his Deputy Mayor, Isaac Lugonzo, whom he groomed as successor despite a different tribal origin, was also considered to be useful in reducing tribal tension.

The wealth of the Nairobi City Council continued to be impressive, with assets amounting to nearly £24,000,000 ($67,200,000) by 1966, which was more than twice the Council's external debt. "Without trying to overstress the City's standing," the Town Clerk (Mr. D. M. Whiteside) wrote in March, 1966, "it is necessary to note that Nairobi has a higher rating in the London money market than Tanzania, Uganda, or Zambia."[81] In November, 1966, the Nairobi City Council was praised by the *Times* of London for redeeming its stock "on time and in full" — an achievement which also won the praise of the editor of the *East African Standard*.[82] Such publicity, of course, redounded to the benefit of the Mayor.

The prosperity of the City Council enabled it to undertake a considerable number of improvements in the areas of Nairobi where the African population was concentrated, including the expansion of piped water, water-borne sanitation, electricity, lighting, telephones, parks, schools, sporting and entertainment facilities, etc. The paved roads, according to Rubia, may have been what was most appreciated by the public:

> Eastlands was somewhat neglected, and one of my ambitions when I became Mayor was that my African brothers and sisters

should have better roads in the areas where they live and where they are predominant. Today it is a cause of pride on my part that, except for the Pumwani area, which is in fact going through re-development, all roads in the Eastlands area are tarmaced, as are most of the paths.[83]

These improvements not only increased the popularity of the Mayor among the general public but also gained him the respect of the political leaders. The City Council members were especially respectful of the Mayor insofar as they were beholden to him for benefits to their constituents. They soon realized, an Asian Council member pointed out, that opposition to the Mayor would be punished. "The things they want in their locations just won't get done." Moreover, as Rubia became an increasingly powerful member of KANU, the Council members looked to him for the advancement of their political careers.[84] The fact that most of them lived off what they earned as Council members was probably a factor in this regard.

## Rubia's Legacy

By the end of Rubia's fifth and final term of office in the summer of 1967, the progress achieved by the City Council of Nairobi was apparent. While potential conflicts remained, institutional methods and procedures were beginning to develop which might prevent these conflicts from spreading and engulfing the political system as they had previously done. Likewise, there were still many administrative problems to be overcome at the time of Rubia's resignation, but they were then much less serious than at the time of his first inauguration.

The achievements of Rubia can only be appreciated by recognizing the difficulties that he initially faced: the ignorance and inexperience of most of those who had come to power, inter-ethnic and inter-racial tension, the lack of qualified civil servants, and the need to rely upon men associated with a despised colonial regime. In the process of having to deal with grave social and economic problems, there was the need to adapt an institutional framework transferred from a completely different political and cultural setting, giving rise to confusion over roles and responsibilities.

As was mentioned in the last chapter, the control exercised by the Council members over the officers tended to be both excessive and inadequate at the same time, thereby intensifying mutual frustration and conflict. Between the Central Government and the City Council, exactly the same situation prevailed — one associated with "inelasticity of control." Moreover, as conflict worsened within the City Council, it also adversely affected inter-governmental relations, exacerbated by Rubia's personality, as illustrated by the episodes presented.

During the course of Rubia's mayoralty, the conditions for elasticity of control improved as the relationship among those associated with the Nairobi City Council became more harmonious. Some of the more distrusted of the European staff members and the less competent African officers were "weeded-out." Those who remained worked well together, and their cooperation facilitated their rapport with Council members. The Council meetings subsequently became shorter and less emotionally charged.

As the staff became Africanized, the pressure for Africanization decreased. At the same time, the remaining European officers came to be viewed as "our men" rather than as "holdovers" from the old regime. As their experience and confidence increased (bolstered by the continued prosperity of the City Council and by the popularity of some of the projects and services undertaken), the Mayor and the leading Council members were more willing to support the officers. This support enabled the officers to be more assertive in decision-making, dealing with the public, guiding subordinates, and advising or even criticizing Council members. Thus, staff morale, as well as performance, were enhanced.

Rubia, during his final year as mayor, was generally viewed both as a formidable and a reasonable leader — one who could be petty and arrogant and yet willing to listen to all sides before reaching decisions, which he then often tenaciously supported. You knew where you stood with Rubia, it was said; and, if he was on your side, you could count on him. While inter-racial and inter-ethnic tension remained, it became less obvious and disruptive. Europeans and Asians were pleased at Rubia's willingness to retain the more competent non-African officers and to recruit others as they departed. At the same time, he pleased the non-Kikuyu Council members by providing them a certain share of privileges and patronage. Moreover, he was seen to work closely with his non-Kikuyu Deputy Mayor, Isaac Lugonzo, who was destined to be his successor.

## The Mayoralty of Isaac Lugonzo

Mayor Lugonzo, during his term in office from August, 1967 to February, 1970, was actually considered more likeable than Rubia, certainly less threatening and vindictive.[85] Indeed, his genial personality, as much as anything else, possibly accounted for his various attainments, including, in addition to the mayoralty, the chairmanship of the Kenya National Football League and the general managership of the East African Power and Lighting Company. While not a forceful or innovative leader, Lugonzo was unwilling to be dominated by Rubia, who continued to try to control the Council until his election to Parliament in December, 1969. In his conflict with Rubia, Lugonzo relied increasingly on his Deputy Mayor, Margaret Kenyatta, the President's daughter, who had manifested a certain animosity towards Rubia since entering the Council in 1964. Involved here, more than issues, was a factional rivalry among Kikuyus, particularly those from Kiambu versus those from Murang'a. Lugonzo also gained the support of the non-Kikuyu Council members.

Although Lugonzo was a relatively popular mayor, he was in many respects less effective than Rubia. While his problems were not altogether of his own making, they did weaken his control over the City Council and lessen his protection from ministerial pressures. Many of the factors which had operated to facilitate elasticity of control during Rubia's mayoralty became less efficacious under Lugonzo, thereby hindering the City Council's performance. As the capacity of the City Council was reduced, the work of the Ministry of Local Government was also hampered, giving rise to increasing inelasticity of control.

Lugonzo's problems partly resulted from the continued departure of experienced expatriate staff and the increasing difficulty of recruiting replacements. This was most forcefully pointed out by the

City Treasurer E. L. Jones in November, 1969, noting then the imminent departure of two assistant city treasurers, the chief account ant, and the assistant chief accountant.[86] In addition to filling these vacancies, the City Treasurer indicated the need for at least nine more accountants. "For a period around May last," he wrote, "our accountancy strength was reduced to about one-third of normal, just at a time when work on the 1969 accounts should have been at its peak."[87] The problems of obtaining these accountants, he emphasized, were intensified by the persistent shortage of local accountants and by evidence that the city's salary scales and other perquisites were no longer attractive to experienced British accountants.

The Council's inadequate terms and conditions of service were also emphasized by Dr. Kabiru, the Medical Officer of Health, noting that of the sixteen African doctors recruited by the Council at various times, only four remained by the end of 1969.[88] By 1971, Council's salaries were 30-50 per cent lower than those offered by the central government for comparable positions and even less competitive with the salaries paid by the large private firms.[89]

The lack of staff had a number of ramifications. It meant that the quality of services in many areas could not be maintained. "Neglected areas are developing in the outer parts of the City," acknowledged the City Treasurer in September, 1970, "and the volume of public complaints at delays and non-performance is constantly increasing."[90] The need for at least seventeen engineers, together with subordinate technical staff of all grades, it was pointed out in the summer of 1970, meant the possible abandonment of projects involving a total of £6,249,000.[91] The City Engineer's Department in 1971 was operating with only sixty per cent of its permitted staff in the top fourteen grades, preventing it from utilizing more than twenty per cent of the funds initially requested for the year.[92] The effect on staff morale was equally severe. For example, the Cleansing Section of the Public Health Department never recovered from the absence of a cleansing superintendent during 1967 and 1968. This delayed the hiring of additional workers and impeded the effort to discourage the excessive drinking and absenteeism of employees. By the middle of 1970, the cleansing services were described as being at the stage of breakdown.[93]

What worsened staff morale and discipline during Lugonzo's term of office was the increasing tendency of councillors to interfere in matters of personnel administration, thereby undermining the authority of the chief officers. "The Section Heads," according to the February, 1969 minutes of the General Purposes Committee, "were often afraid to take any action for fear that they would not ultimately have the support of Council."[94] The culprits were being exonerated, the minutes pointed out, and the chief officers made to appear ridiculous. A stronger mayor, it was suggested, would have done more to support the chief officers.

However, in his last months of office, Lugonzo had to contend with 21 new councillors. Many of them were primarily beholden to Rubia for their KANU nomination in August, 1968 which, with the disqualification of all KPU nominees, meant automatic election to office for four years (later extended an additional two years). These new councillors seemed generally less educated than their predecessors and, therefore, less able to follow the explanations of officers and to participate usefully in debate. Instead, they appeared mainly concerned with the allocation of jobs, contracts, housing, and licenses, all of which redounded to their material benefit.[95] The lack of an opposition party and the low turnout at municipal elections (usually less than ten per cent of the adult population) meant that they were under limited political pressures to behave otherwise, impelling the Town Clerk to note in his 1969 *Annual Report*:

> It should be of immense concern to the Government that its capital city has ceased to have general public interest in matters of representation. That very few people bothered to come forward and vote needs examination. . . . There must be something seriously wrong in a system where a candidate is returned to Council with only 65 votes in a ward with 6,536 registered voters. . . . It is not, of course, the intention in a report of this nature to enter into debate on party politics, but the results of the elections just quoted appear to indicate that there is need to revitalise the party's contacts at the grass root level to ensure that a mature meaningful democratically elected Council is maintained. It could even be beneficial to engage in an exercise which explores possibilities of attracting businessmen, the University lecturers, the private doctors,

the practicing lawyers, etc. to ensure that they have a share in the running of the government of our Capital City.[96]

The harshest criticism directed against Lugonzo was his failure to protect the interests of the Council against adverse decisions of the Central Government, the most serious of which was the requisitioning of half the city's income from the Graduated Personal Tax, beginning in 1968. Previously, about 25 per cent of the G.P.T. collected by the City Council had gone to other local authorities under a complicated arrangement by which a percentage was returned of the tax of those who lived (or who had families) in other areas part of the year. Now the City Council was expected to lose an additional 15 per cent of its estimated income.

While the Central Government acknowledged the budgetary implications for the City Council of this sudden decision at the end of 1967, it contended that the Nairobi City Council was already too wealthy in comparison to the other local authorities of Kenya, most of which were in serious financial trouble. The Government also felt that there was a great danger in unduly concentrating economic development in Nairobi. To neglect the other parts of the country would augment political dissatisfaction and an excessive shift of population to the already overcrowded urban areas. "The inference was that Nairobi's development was proceeding too quickly and should therefore be slowed down so that others could catch up."[97]

The Central Government's requisitioning of the City Council's G.P.T. income came to have an increasing effect on the Council's capability. A large number of proposals had to be postponed or drastically curtailed, including street light installations, multi-storied car parking facilities, road construction and improvement plans, sewage and drainage schemes, and community or social-hall construction programs.[98] Likewise, there were no funds for new health centers, clinics, and dispensaries. The City Council was only able to finance 34 per cent of its approved school building program for 1969, resulting in an accommodation crisis in certain schools. At a time of increasing housing shortage, the Council had to reduce by 50 per cent its expansion program for new housing. It also had to cut by 50 per cent its contribution to most of the local charities.

Despite this reduction in expenditure, the Council anticipated a small deficit in 1970.

The performance of the City Council was made difficult by the Central Government in other ways. In 1968, the Ministry for Local Government did not approve the estimates until the middle of October, and in 1969, until late in June, resulting in maintenance and other work being postponed. The inevitable delays in preparing and receiving tenders meant that some schemes could not be carried out before the end of the fiscal year and would, therefore, have to be abandoned unless special permission were given to carry forward the finance to the following year. The Government also continued to severely limit the Council's borrowing power (cutting by two-thirds the City's ability to raise revenue through floating bonds), without ever clarifying the nature of its long-term policy.

Much time was wasted, the City Treasurer (Mr. Jones) complained, in discussion and correspondence on matters of trivial importance.[99] In September, 1970, he pointed out that almost a year had passed since the Council had applied to increase about sixty license fees and miscellaneous charges, involving only £50,000 a year, but approval had not been forthcoming because of doubts in the Ministry on a few items. Meanwhile, the anticipated income from this source had to be abandoned. More serious was the refusal of the Minister for Local Government to allow a ten per cent rent-increase for Council housing which would have enabled it to raise £144,000 to wipe off the deficit in the housing account and to meet the growing demand for repair and maintenance. In 1971, the Council's maintenance expenditure was only sh. 63.60/- ($9.00) per unit, which amounted to about half of what was spent in 1966, obviously hastening the deterioration of its housing stock.[100] Moreover, the Treasury after 1969 prevented the Council from collecting rates in such peri-urban areas as Dagoretti, despite the Council's annual expenditure in these areas of over £100,000.[101]

The various measures of the Central Government limiting the City Council's income were imposed at a time when the responsibilities of the Council were increasing for a population expanding at more than seven per cent a year. Many of those using the city's services were coming in from outside the city's boundaries, amounting to an estimated fifty per cent of those using the health centers and clinics. This caused the Council's expenditure to rise by 35 per cent between 1964 and 1969. The Council was also obliged in July, 1970 to increase by ten per cent its number of employees under the new Tripartite Agreement to alleviate unemployment, adding approximately £250,000 to the city's annual wage bill and the burden of dealing with those without education, experience, or motivation.

What Mayor Lugonzo most resented was the Central Government's practice of making important decisions affecting local authorities with little prior consultation or warning. He pointed out, in 1969, for example, that the Government had taken over responsibility for health, education, and roads from county councils after only a month's notice.[102] The fact that many of the ministries had proven themselves to be inefficient raised doubts about this move. The fears expressed in 1968 by the Association of Local Government Authorities regarding the Kenya School Equipment Scheme, according to Lugonzo, were fully justified. Among the scheme's faults were "delay in conveying equipment to schools; poor quality of equipment received; wrong issues, including issue of items not ordered; and increased expenditure on school equipment." None of the City Council's primary schools had received the equipment ordered for 1969. Unless something drastic was done to improve the scheme, Lugonzo concluded, it should be abolished, and those local authorities still responsible for primary education should go back to the old system. In regard to Nairobi, Lugonzo felt that the City Council could handle secondary education better than could the Ministry of Education which, because of its failure to build more secondary schools in the city, provided educational opportunity for only about thirty per cent of those in Nairobi completing the Kenya Preliminary Examination.

## Conclusion

Margaret Kenyatta, upon becoming Acting Mayor in February, 1970, was expected to be in a better position than Lugonzo to protect the interests of the Council by virtue of being the daughter of the President. Indeed, this appeared to be so. In August, 1971,

Mayor Kenyatta announced that the City Council would no longer
have to remit fifty per cent of its G.P.T. revenue to the Central
Government. In addition, the Council derived an extra £300,000 in
revenue from rates in 1971 as a result of its revaluation of land in
the city. That year, the Ministry of Local Government approved
without much hesitation the Council's proposed budget and, except
in such controversial matters as rent increases in city markets and
housing estates, allowed the City Council to carry on without interference.[103] Likewise, the legislation introduced the previous year
to give the District Commissioner veto power over local government expenditure was never implemented in Nairobi. In 1971
Councillors received a 25 per cent pay increase (raising their annual
allowances to £600). And in 1972, Council employees received
pay increases which brought them closer to the Central Government's salary schedule.

While the City Council gained considerable power to manage its
own affairs under Mayor Kenyatta, the integrity of the Council remained endangered by all the weaknesses discussed in the previous
chapter. The resulting inelasticity of control within the City Council, as was then pointed out, would continue to adversely affect
inter-governmental relations. The relationship between inelasticity
of control within the City Council and that between the City Council and the Central Government was most apparent in the area of
public housing, which will be the subject of the next chapter.

## NOTES

1. *"Mr. President, Distinguished Guests. . . ."* Selected Speeches &
   Messages, 1962-63 by Ald. Charles W. Rubia, Mayor of Nairobi.
   (Nairobi: Mayor's Parlour, City Hall, 1963), p. 25.
2. Cf. Peter MacDonald, "The Plight of the Poor," *East African
   Standard* (E.A.S.), February 5, 1965.
3. *Kenya Education Commission Report,* Part I (Nairobi: Govern-
   ment Printer, 1964), p. 51; Joint Working Party of the Youth
   Department of the Christian Council of Kenya and the Christian

Churches' Education Association, *After School What?* (Nairobi: Christian Council of Kenya, March, 1966), p. 11.

4. E.A.S., November 25, 1966.

5. *Annual Report,* 1965, p. 1.

6. Cf. Andrew Hake, "Planning a New Nairobi," *Venture,* Vol. XVI, No. 3 (March, 1964), p. 16.

7. E.A.S., July 8, 1966. Under pressure, Mr. Otiende was forced to retract this allegation.

8. E.A.S., September 29, 1966. Nevertheless, Nairobi with 4.53 hospital beds per 1,000 inhabitants was far better off than the rest of the country with only 1.12 per 1,000. Cf. Ministry of Economic Planning and Development, *Development Plan for the Period 1965/66 to 1969/70* (Revised Development Plan) (Nairobi: Government Printer, 1966), p. 316.

9. The legal position of Nairobi is unique under the 1963 Constitution in that for some purposes it is treated as a region; for others, as a local authority.

10. Cf. John Nottingham, "The Development of Local Government in Kenya" (an unpublished article), pp. 20-21.

11. P. 2 of Hearings, July 19, 1966.

12. Cf. Resolution of the General Purposes Committee, *Minutes of Proceedings,* Vol. XXXI, No. 9 (March, 1964), pp. 1456-57.

13. E.A.S., September 30, 1966.

14. (Nairobi: Republic of Kenya, 1966), p. 52.

15. *Ibid.,* p. 26.

16. P. 1 of Hearings, July 19, 1966.

17. *Ibid.*

18. (Nairobi: City Hall, 1966), p. 7.

19. P. 4 of Hearings, July 19, 1966.

20. *Ibid.,* p. 2.

21. *Ibid.,* p. 13.

22. E.A.S., September 30, 1966.

23. E.A.S., April 5, 1967.

24. E.A.S., April 12, 1967.

25. E.A.S., November 19, 1965.

26. "The Government and the Constitution in Kenya Politics," *East African Journal,* Vol. IV, No. 8 (December, 1967), p. 13.

27. *Not Yet Uhuru* (London: Heinemann, 1967), p. 276.

28. *The Anatomy of Uhuru* (Manchester: The Manchester U. Press, 1966), p. 85.
29. E.A.S., August 9, 1967.
30. E.A.S., May 6, 1965.
31. E.A.S., June 3, 1965. Earlier in the year (February, 1964) a loan to Nairobi from A.I.D. of £125,000 for a slum-clearance and housing project went through without much trouble because of the comparative absence of "strings" on the part of A.I.D. and because of the popularity of the project.
32. Finance Committee, *Minutes of Proceedings,* Vol. XXXI, No. 10 (April, 1964), p. 2007.
33. The Treasurer here attempted to elaborate on an explanation in defiance of the Mayor's wishes.
34. *Minutes of Proceedings,* March, 1965, pp. 1679, 1839.
35. Finance Committee, *Minutes of Proceedings,* Vol. XXXI, No. 12 (June, 1964), p. 2007.
36. *Ibid.,* p. 2008.
37. *Ibid.,* p. 2037 (at the Council's Ordinary Monthly Meeting).
38. *Daily Nation* (referred to hereafter by the initials D.N.), September 15, 1964.
39. *Memorandum of Evidence to the Local Government Commission of Inquiry* (Nairobi: City Hall, May, 1966), pp. 14-15.
40. E.A.S., September 15, 1964.
41. E.A.S., September 22, 1964.
42. *Sunday Post,* September 20, 1964.
43. D.N., September 24, 1964.
44. D.N., September 15, 1964.
45. E.A.S., October 8, 1964.
46. E.A.S., November 4, 1964.
47. D.N., November 5, 1964.
48. *Minutes of Proceedings,* April, 1966, p. 1863.
49. E.A.S., October 30, 1963.
50. E.A.S., July 28, 1965.
51. E.A.S., January 13, 1965.
52. E.A.S., November 5, 1964.
53. E.A.S., January 13, 1967.
54. E.A.S., January 14, 1965.
55. E.A.S., January 13, 1965.
56. *Minutes of Proceedings,* February, 1965, pp. 166-67.

57. E.A.S., April 8, 1965.
58. Waiyaki later became a leading member of the opposition party, the K.P.U.
59. Cf. chap. 5 above.
60. (Nairobi: Ministry of Local Government, 1965), p. 11.
61. E.A.S., January 4, 1966. Also cf. chap. 5 above, section on Africanization.
62. E.A.S., January 4, 1966.
63. E.A.S., February 3, 1966.
64. E.A.S., May 7, 1965.
65. E.A.S., January 27, 1966.
66. E.A.S., February 3, 1966.
67. D.N., February 3, 1966.
68. E.A.S., February 9, 1966.
69. E.A.S., February 4 and 5, 1966.
70. E.A.S., February 9, 1966.
71. E.A.S., February 11, 1966.
72. D.N., February 10, 1966.
73. E.A.S., February 4, 1966.
74. E.A.S., February 14, 1966.
75. E.A.S., February 11, 1966.
76. *Minutes of Proceedings,* March, 1966, p. 1747.
77. E.A.S., July 2, 1966.
78. *Minutes of Proceedings,* July, 1966, p. 67.
79. Cf. the statements quoted in E.A.S., November 24, 1966 and August 9, 1967.
80. E.A.S., March 15, 1966
81. *City Council of Nairc_ Annual Report for 1965* (Nairobi: City Hall, March, 1966), p. 8.
82. E.A.S., November 4 and November 25, 1966.
83. E.A.S., August 9, 1967.
84. Early in 1968 Rubia became chairman of the Nairobi branch of KANU in a contested election. Cf. E.A.S., January 29, 1968.
85. Lugonzo formally remained in the Council as mayor until August 1970, but he took a leave-of-absence after being nominated to Parliament.
86. E.A.S., November 3, 1969.
87. "Summarised Accounts and Balance Sheets for the Year 1969," Nairobi City Council, September 7, 1970, p. 3.

88. Medical Officer of Health, *Annual Report, 1969* (Nairobi: City Hall, 1969), p. 1.

89. Frederick T. Temple, "Planning and Budgetting for Urban Growth in Nairobi," Nairobi Urban Studies Group, February, 1972, pp. 17-19; D. N. Ndegwa, Chairman, *Report of the Commission of Inquiry* (Nairobi: Government Printer, May 1971), pp. 33-34.

90. E. L. Jones, *Review of the City's Financial Position, September, 1970; City Treasurer's Memorandum* (Nairobi: City Hall, 18 September, 1970), p. 5.

91. E.A.S., July 27, 1970.

92. Temple, *op. cit.*, p. 19; C. Gupta, "Summary of Findings and Recommendations," Nairobi Urban Studies Group, 31 July, 1971.

93. Mark Manyonyi, *Organisation and Methods Report on Unauthorised Absences — Cleansing Section of the Public Health Department* (Nairobi: O & M Dept., March, 1972), p. 5; Nairobi City Council, *Minutes*, Vol. XXXVII, Public Health Committee, 9.6. 70, p. 2091.

94. Vol. XXXVII, p. 1229.

95. Cf. Julius Kinothia, "The Risks Nairobi's Councillors Are Running," E.A.S., April 27, 1971.

96. J. P. Mbogua (Nairobi: City Hall, November, 1970), pp. 33-34.

97. E.A.S., March 13, 1969.

98. Cf. Jones, *Review of he City's Financial Position, op. cit., passim.*

99. *Ibid.*, p. 14.

100. International Bank for Reconstruction and Development (I.B. R.D.), *Economic Development in East Africa*, Vol. II — Kenya (Washington, D.C.: I.B.R.D., July 30, 1971), p. 19.

101. J. R. Yost, "Development Recommendations: Eastern Dagoretti," Nairobi Urban Studies Group, 22 December, 1971, pp. 19-20.

102. E.A.S., November 22, 1969.

103. Temple, *op. cit.*, pp. 12-14.

# 7 THE POLITICS OF HOUSING

## Introduction

Of all the problems facing the City Council in dealing with Nairobi's rapid population growth during the 1960s, housing was perhaps the most intractable. Though the City Council made available about 20 per cent of its budget for housing during this period, an estimated 15,000 still needed housing in 1966. And during the next three years, another 15,000 names were added to the waiting-list.[1]

The lack of housing was partly responsible for the existence in 1965 of between 5,000 and 10,000 illegal squatters. These people often combined "illegal hawking" with their "illegal squatting," setting up what one newspaper described as "cardboard and packing case shacks" on centrally placed vacant land. In one such area, "whole families, including young babies, were found to be living inside the warren of shacks which made up the illegal market."[2] The Nairobi City Council periodically attempted to clear-up some of the worst squatting-hawking places; but these "shanty towns" rose up as quickly as they were torn down.

The inadequate availability of housing also drove up the rents charged for private housing, even, it was claimed, in disregard of existing rent-control legislation.[3] At the same time, the majority of the standard single-roomed dwellings provided for Africans by the government had to be shared by three or more.[4] In addition, an estimated 7,000 Africans had to commute each day into Nairobi from outlying areas, often traveling as much as seven miles by bicycle.

What was considered imperative was a much faster rate of building. "It will be necessary to build a minimum of 6,000 new units of housing every year for the next five years to cope with the needs of new Nairobi," insisted Nairobi's Deputy Director of Social Services and Housing in 1964.[5] Recognition of the problem, however, did not forestall the widening of the gap between housing needs and accomplishments. Frederick Temple noted in 1972 that the rate of housing construction in relationship to population growth was more than three times slower after independence than previously.[6] Between 1964 and 1970, 4,647 units of housing were added to the Council's housing stock. Considering that the population of the city had nearly doubled during this period (rising from 275,800 in 1963 to 545,100), this was only one unit per 58.0 people. Before independence, 13,187 units had been constructed within the boundaries of the old city, representing one unit of Council housing for every 20.9 people. This meant an increasing shortage of houses within Nairobi. While some 33,000 housing units were estimated to have been required between 1962 and 1970, only 7,355 were actually built (1,390 by the National Housing Corporation, 4,859 by the Nairobi City Council, and 1,106 by the private sector).[7] The supply of approved housing, in other words, was increasing at only about one-sixth the pace of population increase. By 1972, the shortfall between the requirements for housing in Nairobi and the availability of housing was over 60,000 units.[8]

Lack of housing, however, was only one aspect of the problem. Because of the unemployment situation, many could not pay the rent, even when housing was available. An economic rent in 1964 for an adequate, though modest, dwelling unit (two rooms, separate kitchen, toilet and shower) came to 85 shillings ($12) a month, which was more than most Africans claimed they could pay.[9]

Even at 30 shillings ($4.20) a month, according to a 1965 report by Lawrence N. Bloomberg and Charles Abrams, the rent could not be afforded by over one-half of the households in Nairobi and Mombasa.[10]

Because of the increasing seriousness of Nairobi's housing crisis, it was, according to Tony Hurrell (an architect employed by the Council), "surveyed, analysed, discussed and pontificated upon 'ad nauseam'. . . . No subject is more likely to generate stronger social and political opinions."[11] The leading Councillors and officers were unable to develop consistent policies in regard to housing, preventing them from properly guiding their subordinates. At the same time, the Central Government tended to impose impossible goals upon the Council, while denying it the finances and leadership necessary to fulfill these goals. David Cook, a City Planner with the Nairobi City Council, observed in 1970 that "in government there would appear to be above 50 people with powers of delay and approximately half this number with powers of veto. Forget anyone and you get into trouble."[12] These people could more effectively frustrate than facilitate the formulation and implementation of policies. In any case, few seemed able to help significantly the Council in the performance of its activities.

## The Housing Waiting List

The waiting-list for the existing 106,000 Nairobi City Council housing units exceeded 50,000 by 1972. Such a long waiting-list had by then become meaningless inasmuch as it contained names compiled over a twenty year period, some of which were no longer living or in need of public housing. For this reason, the list was abandoned in October, 1972 by the City Council — an action considered unfair by the editor of the *Daily Nation* "to the thousands of people who have been in seasonal correspondence with the council for so many years, nourishing the hope that they will some day be housed or 'bed-spaced'."[13]

The new waiting list, however, like the old, would undoubtedly consist of people who were not homeless but anxious for cheaper, better housing, inasmuch as rent levels in the private sector had increased by more than 200 per cent since 1965, while remaining stationary for Council housing.[14] Because Council housing was considered so desirable, it tended to go to those with influence over the allocation process. As always, the least influential were also the least affluent. Since persons in middle and upper income brackets benefitted most from this housing, the system failed to assist the socially deserving and to maximize revenue from those who were subsidized by the scheme. It also discouraged the private sector from increasing its housing output, which only amounted to 250 a year during the 1960's.

Many politicians and administrators, it was claimed, were able to rent or purchase under their own names or those of relatives a number of Council houses which they could then sublet for several times the monthly rent or installments they were paying, regardless of the limits set by the Rent Restriction Department. In the spring of 1972, a spokesman for the City Council disclosed that between 80 and 90 per cent of the houses on one of the city's estates were being sublet illegally.[15] The effectiveness of the periodic inspections, it was pointed out, were hampered by the inability of the staff to determine the relationship of the resident women and children to the lawfully authorized tenants or purchasers.

The fact that administrators and politicians possessed Council housing made it politically difficult for the Council to increase housing rents even to cover maintenance costs. So adamant were the ministers, according to C. N. W. Siganga, the Director of Social Services and Housing, in his 1970 Annual Report, that one of them revealed his determination to veto any rent increases agreed to by the Minister for Local Government.[16] Because housing allocation became such a politically sensitive issue, the appointment of a new housing manager (who happened to be Kikuyu) was seen by the Luo, Abaluyhia, and Kamba Councillors (numbering 11 as against 28 Kikuyu/Embu/Meru Councillors) as being tribally motivated, undermining the position of the Council's only non-Kikuyu chief officer. This controversy dragged on for several years. When Mr. B. N. Gituiku was finally appointed Housing Manager in March, 1972, he declared his intention of ending the practice whereby privileged individuals obtained council houses in order to sublet them at exorbitant rates. "One man, one house," he claimed, irrespective of one's position, was to be the rule.[17] But it remains to be seen how successful he will be in this regard.

## The High Cost of Council Housing

The housing shortage was greatest for the lowest income categories (those earning under £600 a year).[18] These individuals generally lacked the political influence to obtain the older Council houses, and they found most of the newer Council houses too expensive. Whereas prior to 1964, 70.8 per cent of the Council's houses rented below 20/– ($2.80) a month, only 29.2 per cent of those built between 1967 and 1971 did so. Almost all (96.4 per cent) of the expensive housing (the units renting for over 500/– per month) was built after 1967. On the other hand, 99.2 per cent of the cheap housing (the units renting for under 85/– per month) was built before 1964. Whereas 92 per cent of the pre-independence housing was suitable for the 51.5 per cent of the African households earning less than £302 per annum, only 44 per cent of the post-independence housing was appropriate for this income group. With the destruction of 1,200 one-room rental units (the cheapest form of housing) to make way for the Kariokor Development Project, there were fewer Council-owned one-room rental units available in 1971 than in 1961.

After independence, the Nairobi City Council became increasingly interested in building units for tenant-purchase rather than rental. While all Council housing before independence was intended to be rented, only 55.1 per cent of the units after independence (as of 1972) were so designated. After 1967, the Council ceased entirely, apart from a few small schemes, to construct any rental housing. This was seen as "a step in the right direction in that it encourages and promotes the ownership of property in the City among the low and middle income wage earners who form the bulk of the population."[19]

It was estimated, however, that at least 70 per cent of the families inhabiting Nairobi in 1971 could not afford the cheapest conventional two-room structure that could then be built, costing about £850.[20] This meant, in the case of the New Pumwani Urban

Renewal Project, that only a small number of the original Old Pumwani homeowners could afford the new units that were intended for them. In 1969, it was reported that there were 224 "unsaleable" units here.[21] These were put forward for rent; but, since few of the Old Pumwani residents could afford the rents being charged under the Development Plan for Pumwani Location (being from three to six times the amount originally designated as maximum), most of these units had eventually to be turned over to wealthier people from outside Pumwani. "No amount of lamentations or gnashing of their collective teeth," wrote Dorothy Haldane, an employee of the National Christian Council of Kenya, "could alter the economic fact that either a subsidy was required to lower rents to a level Pumwani people could afford, or Council would have to back out of its promise to provide alternative housing to the victims of the renewal."[22]

The high cost of Council housing was due to a variety of factors: the lack of skilled craftsmen, the inadequate supervision of unreliable labor, the high cost of imported items (amounting to between 15 and 35 per cent of the total cost of a house), the rigidity of the housing code, etc.[23] Neither the City Council nor the Central Government made good use of the available professional experts to set proper guidelines for costing. African contractors, it was hoped, could be used to undertake much of the low-cost housing, but they were often required to redo inferior work, causing them to go bankrupt. While the Council continued to depend upon its 800-1,000 construction workers who could not be dismissed, however inefficient they were, it increasingly suffered from the absence of the Asian artisans and supervisors who had been replaced by Africans with less skill, experience, or motivation. Although a variety of experiments were undertaken to keep down housing costs (using precast concrete forms, timber, paint sprayguns, glass panels, black-cotton bricks, papyrus grass, sisal, etc.), construction generally was 50 per cent more costly in 1968 than in 1964. Consequently, the cost per unit in one of the Council's housing estates rose from £600 initially anticipated to more than £1,000.

Despite the obvious need to keep down the cost of housing, the

Councillors often insisted upon expensive housing: detached or multi-storied, with carports and even servants' quarters. "What the engineers considered to be good designs based on sensitive planning and reasonable financial disciplines," Siganga complained, "was often questioned, deferred in committees, and otherwise delayed."[24] "As representatives of the people," he rationalized, "they must be satisfied that what they are offering to the public is what is wanted." The Councillors, it was argued, despite all their weaknesses, did speak the language of the *wananchi* (the common people) in desiring high housing standards. However, as the Minister for Housing (P. J. Ngei) pointed out in 1967: "The ideal house, in which we would all like to live or to build for the people of this country, will tend usually to be much more expensive than we or they can actually afford."[25] Yet, the Councillors' naiveté regarding economics was apparently shared by certain top officials who insisted that the big cities of Kenya were wealthy enough to afford the "skyscraper" residential buildings being constructed in Singapore. Thus, it was necessary for a high-level team of Kenyan officials to travel to Singapore in the summer of 1971 to reach the conclusion that the experience of Singapore, with its lack of land and extreme density of population, was completely irrelevant to a city such as Nairobi, in which an estimated one-fourth of the land was then vacant.

Inasmuch as fifty per cent of Nairobi's families could not afford to pay more than shs. 50/− per month for their housing (based on an average annual income of around £150), the City Engineer's Department concluded that, given available resources and technology, the most that could be provided was a single-room tenement with provisions for shared services.[26] If given two rooms, the householders would ordinarily sublet one of them. After all, more than one-third of the city's population lived in single-room tenements, with some developments containing households of ten persons or more in one room.[27] But the Grade II by-laws permitting this sort of development was seen as a carryover from the colonial days and, as such, "not in accordance with African dignity."[28] Instead, the politicians and administrators were determined that Nairobi would be, in the words of Hunter Morrison (a Peace Corps volunteer working with the City Council), "the proud administrative center with tall buildings, clean industries, and wealthy citizens. . . :

> Expatriates coming to this city with a vision based upon other places run smack into this powerful notion of the Beautiful City. Predictions of fast-approaching urban chaos and admonitions to act with dispatch fall upon deaf ears. Our advice is not what most people want to hear. In giving it, we often appear less as neutral experts than as latter-day manifestations of the colonial administrator who built cheap and ugly urban housing claiming that this alone was what the African wanted and could afford. In advocating the continued construction of cheap housing, we appear to be backward-looking and not at all progressive.[29]

Morrison might have cited in this regard the 1971 admonition of Mr. Ngei, the Minister of Housing, against the planting of maize, onions, or vegetables in urban housing estates instead of "beautiful flowers, grass and trees."[30] Yet, as one letter to the editor of the *Daily Nation* pointed out, for whom was Nairobi to look beautiful?[31] What could be a haven for tourists could be a hell for many inhabitants. Too often, it was forgotten, according to Alek Rozental (an economist working for the City Council), that "Nairobi cannot expect to continue to function as a colonial enclave designed for the comfort of a narrow and privileged class."[32]

*Site and Service Schemes*

Even if the City Council's housing units could be reduced in cost, they would continue to be beyond the economic reach of the two-thirds of the City's families with incomes barely above subsistence level, including twenty per cent of Nairobi's labor force estimated to be unemployed in 1972. The only realistic alternative for these people was the so-called "site and service scheme," providing rudimentary services (water, sanitation facilities, roads, public transportation, schools, etc.) together with opportunity or encouragement for self-help construction. Indeed, a number of experts associated with the City Council argued that people be allowed to build the "cheapest form of shelter at minimum standards of acceptability," i.e., mud and wattle huts.[33] "Such dwellings may be ramshackle," Rozental noted, "their mud and wattle appearance may be jarring to many eyes, but they will be the best that a significant proportion of households will be able to afford."[34]

The most persistent supporters of site-service schemes were the members of the Nairobi Urban Studies Group, formed early in 1971 to undertake long-range planning for Nairobi's future. The Urban Studies Group, however, consisted mostly of expatriates, funded largely by international or foreign organizations and foundations. Often their reports seemed to be more directed to those funding them than to the City Council, ending up in files that were unread or unnoticed by the Councillors and chief officers. Consequently, they were seldom able to generate much political support for site-service schemes, even with the encouragement of the 1970-74 Development Plan, A.I.D., and the World Bank. While it was hoped that these schemes would provide for the housing needs of fifty per cent of the urban population, only 750 units in Nairobi resulted between 1964 and 1970, representing 16.1 per cent of the City's post-independence housing. "Development plan writers and other expatriates speak one language," Morrison concluded, "politicians and administrators another. The gulf between the two is immense."[35]

Those objecting to site-service schemes viewed them as inappropriate for a city such as Nairobi, being more suited to rural than to urban conditions. These schemes, it was feared, would inevitably lead to slums, spoiling the beauty of the city and bringing crime or disease. Many agreed with President Kenyatta's denunciation of ministers who advocated permitting "native houses" for Africans in the urban areas, recalling that these were the sort of houses that Africans had to live in during the colonial days.[36] Such ministers would be sacked, he warned. Moreover, according to the President, site-service schemes would inevitably encourage the influx of people from the rural areas who had been misled into believing "that their salvation lay in residing in towns or the City of Nairobi."[37] Thus, it was the Government's responsibility, not to facilitate the urbanization of these people, but to repatriate them to their home areas.

The practical problems of site-service schemes were also

emphasized by those opposing them. Indeed, the schemes attempted in Nairobi had never worked out as planned. Eighty per cent of those allotted plots in the Kariobangi Site-Service Scheme had by 1968 either sold their plots or were no longer living on them.[38] The regulations prohibiting the sale of these plots and absentee ownership proved unenforceable. Many of these plots were acquired by people interested in nothing more than quick profits.

## The Squatter Villages

Lacking a consistent, realistic approach to the housing problem, the City Council could not cope with a vast burgeoning of shanties and other forms of unauthorized construction. By 1971, it was estimated that one-third of Nairobi's population lived in unauthorized housing.[39] Many others lived in poorly serviced, overcrowded, and deteriorating dwellings. At least one-fourth of Nairobi's houses were unapproved, and that percentage was rapidly increasing, largely as a result of the activity of African land-buying societies, co-operatives, companies, or partnerships, sometimes collectively referred to as local resident associations (LRA's).[40] These LRA's were very effective in mobilizing local reserves of private capital to create inexpensive housing, ranging from shs. 40/- to shs. 150/- per month per room. Using large tracts of cheap land available for purchase, they managed to construct an estimated 5,000 dwelling rooms annually, from which they could recover their initial construction capital within less than a year, thereafter making as much as 120 per cent annual return on their original investment. "Such success has led to quick popularity among those with ready cash in Nairobi," Haldane writes, "and the company rosters (if they could be found) would show an intriguing web extending throughout both private business and public service sectors."[41]

Because these LRA's were viewed officially, in the words of the City Engineer's Department, as "the inefficient by-products of rapid urbanization," they were neither recognized or assisted in any way, nor supervised or controlled.[42] As a result, a large number of squatter villages emerged, usually without a water supply or a means of waste disposal, thereby greatly alarming the officers of the City Council. One place near the center of the city — Kaburini — was, according to the Medical Officer of Health, "so crowded with shanty dwellings that passages barely allowed anyone to pass through. A visit to Kaburini filled one with horror."[43]

The City Council periodically attempted to destroy the squatter villages, despite the 1970-74 Development Plan's admonition against doing so until the housing shortage could be reduced. In November, 1970, 49 shanty settlements, containing about 7,000 dwelling units worth an estimated $300,000 and accommodating perhaps 40,000 people, were pulled down or burned by the Council's askaris.[44] To prevent rapid rebuilding, some of the corrugated iron sheets and timber from the demolished shanties were confiscated.

The Council's 1970 demolition effort did not receive as much public approval as was hoped. Indeed, to quote Siganga, "the public outcry that followed this very innocent action was completely out of proportion with realities."[45] However, the realities included the need to take care of those left homeless by the demolition. Where could the Council find homes for shs. 40/– per month, such as was charged for some of the shanties?, Dr. L. M. Waiyaki, the member for Mathari, asked in Parliament.[46] Mayor Lugonzo admitted that the City Council did not have the £19 million necessary to provide housing for Nairobi's estimated 100,000 illegal squatters.[47] Even providing tents and food for one of the demolished shanty settlements proved too costly to continue for more than five days.

According to Mayor Lugonzo, the Council's struggle to prevent or discourage unauthorized structures was undermined by certain leading politicians who "would like to see slums and unsanitary surroundings mushroom in the city and then turn around to blame them on the City Council."[48] Most upsetting to the Council were the public comments of Dr. Kiano (the Minister for Local Government), expressing "horror" at what he called the wholesale burning of people's homes.[49] Dr. Kiano had personally approved the clearing of shanty towns, Lugonzo insisted, adding: "We do not wish to take issue with the Minister, but if he now feels we should stop our operation, then he must order us to do so." Yet, the Council's efforts to demolish shanties continued to have the firm support of President Kenyatta, who told the Councillors that they should ignore Parliamentary or public opposition, as they had a higher responsibility, that of governing the city effectively.[50]

What the City Council failed to recognize was the futility of destroying squatter villages without dealing with their causes. Almost as quickly as the shanties were demolished, they could be rebuilt. "It really boils down to who gets tired first," the editor of the *East African Standard* noted, "and it is sad to say that the shanty builders seem to be the more enduring."[51] Insofar as the Council succeeded in permanently destroying the shanties, it actually decreased the available housing stock. This, in the words of Haldane, "led to vastly swelling the demand, decreasing supply, and allowing greater exploitation to exist in those few areas which somehow escaped destruction through political intervention or other means."[52] In the process, the initiative of what the 1972 International Labor Organization study of Kenya refers to as the "informal sector" became discouraged.[53] This impoverished and economically deprived modern sub-sector, even when pursuing similar economic activities to those in the formal sector, was required to operate illegally on the periphery of the formal sector. The squatter villages, after all, were the reception centers for predominately unskilled and illiterate villagers, providing not only cheap housing, but also employment opportunities in marketing or family and cottage industries, education in productive and entrepreneurial skills, social support facilitating the search for wage-earning jobs, and close proximity to places of work.[54] Consequently, this destruction not only undermined the people's capacity for self-help, but also decreased the City's available goods and services.

The potential of squatter villages for self-improvement was evident in the case of Kitui Village, one of those uprooted in 1970 by the City Council's askaris. An official investigation of the village, following a letter describing its plight to the Chairman of the Council's Housing and Social Services Committee, revealed that it had been a well-organized community of about 800, squatting on an area of less than two acres.[55] The village had been administered by a council of elders, led by a powerful chairwoman. The church/school, which had been located amid the mud and wattle houses, also served as the social center of the village. Here a nursery school handling fifty children had functioned each morning. In the afternoons, it had been used for adult literacy classes regularly attended by about twenty people, and occasionally for health classes. With the help of a Danish woman, a Maendeleo Club (an organization for women) had been making traditional Wakamba jewelry, handicrafts, and basket work, earning profits averaging almost $300 per month. The village had also provided traditional dances on Sunday afternoons for visitors and friends. Obviously, these villagers did not fit into the shiftless, lazy, criminal stereotype of squatters held by many officials.

The destruction of Kitui Village left the community in despair, apathetic and hopeless. Why invest more money and effort into a place that was likely to be destroyed again? Meanwhile, however, there was no other place for these people to go. Most of those who remained after the destruction of the village survived in cardboard hovels with hardly any food, clothing, or blankets. There was no water or method of disposing of waste materials. "Conditions can be described as squalid, to put it mildly," the official investigation concluded, adding: "When faced with extremely adverse circumstances, these people, through their persistence and strength not only as individuals, but also as a group, have shown that they deserve, as much as anyone, a chance to make a decent life for themselves and for their children." But while a few charities provided limited assistance for Kitui Village, no official help was forthcoming, not even a reply to the village's application for site and service facilities.[56] Instead, the police again destroyed Kitui Village in September, 1972, arresting 292 people (mostly women and children) as vagrants — an action described by Mr. Maina Wanjigi, an Assistant Minister for Agriculture, as "punitive, badly motivated, and unacceptable in a free Kenya." The Nairobi Provincial Commissioner, Mr. Mburu, however, defended this new "clean up" as necessary because many unauthorized houses were being used as hideouts by gangsters who slept during the day but robbed people at night.

Many experts agreed with Mr. Wanjigi's argument that Nairobi's primary concern should be not so much the quality of housing within squatter villages as the quality of their physical and

social environment.[57] Insofar as the government could rid the existing squatter settlements of their uncollected human wastes, pesti-
lential open drains and ponds, inadequate and polluted water supply, litter and filth, and dark unlit lanes, it would not have to worry
about their visual appearance. In support of this position, a 1971
study of the University of Nairobi's Housing Research and Development Unit was cited. It showed that while sixty per cent of those
living in site-service schemes complained about communal toilets,
road lighting, dirt and rubbish, roads, water supply, etc., only four
per cent complained about the quality of their dwellings.[58] With
security of tenure and a system of positive incentives, people would
improve their housing as their income permitted. Even the local
resident associations, which were accused of "exploiting the poor,"
would not have to be feared because, as their number increased,
competition would force them to reduce their rent while offering
a better product.

To facilitate the functional development of squatter villages, a
number of suggestions were offered.[59] Only the most rudimentary
services, such as common water points and pit latrines, need be initially provided. Otherwise, there would be too much expense and
delay involved, considering the shortage of funds and the desperate
need for housing. But the organization of the housing areas would
have to be carefully planned, so that roads, public utilities, schools,
clinics, etc. could be later introduced without unduly disturbing the
settlements. The initial plots might be no more than 1/16th of an
acre, or the minimum possible under public health requirements.
Those acquiring the plots would be subject to a lease arrangement
that would encourage the improvement of property. For example,
a two-year lease might be initially given, extended another five years
for a timber house, and an additional twenty years for a stone
dwelling. This flexible lease arrangement could also be used to
maintain some control over the plots that were sold or rented by
the original allottees. While the allottees were expected to expand
their dwellings as their funds or space allowed, renting out those
rooms not needed for their families, they would be subject to conditions whereby the Council, at some specified or unspecified future
date, could provide certain services, for which they would have to

pay. In this way, the settlements could be improved without unduly burdening the City Council. Indeed, it was expected that the inhabitants would want more and better public services as their ability to afford them increased. Moreover, as it shifted the responsibility for management and rent collection to the private sector through these settlements, the City Council would have more funds for the provision of needed services.

## Mathare Valley

There was hope that the City Council might follow some of these suggestions in the case of Mathare Valley, the largest area within Nairobi of uncontrolled settlement, having, as of June, 1972, an estimated 80,000 people "living in shanties in unhygienic conditions."[60] Mathare Valley had long been used by Kikuyu squatters, being less than five miles from the central business district and the industrial area of Nairobi and yet somewhat hidden by the nature of the terrain along the southern banks of the Mathare and Gitathuru rivers.[61] During the Emergency of the 1950's, most of the squatters, then numbering about 5,000, were expelled; but they gradually returned during the early 1960's, including many ex-detainees, who had enough political influence to repulse a 1963 demolition threat. Thereafter, squatters who were expelled from other areas of Nairobi tended to go to Mathare Valley. This population influx was encouraged during the late 1960's by the activity of the local resident associations which, by November, 1970, had built, according to a Council survey, 1,220 houses containing 7,628 dwelling rooms. The residents were by then apparently well-organized, with village committees, officers, courts, and policemen functioning with varying effectiveness.

The impetus for the first Pilot Improvement Scheme for Mathare Valley came from President Kenyatta in 1969 for reasons that were never explained. "Some said the President passed the area almost daily and was concerned that the blight should be removed from the city. Others said that he owed a debt, personal and political, to the freedom fighters."[62] The coming parliamentary and local elections might have also figured in his thinking. In any case, the President's word is generally enough to get things started in Kenya.

The Minister of Housing, Mr. Ngei, appeared in the Valley with the District Commissioner, the Commissioner for Squatters, and the Mayor of Nairobi, announcing that all the people of Mathare would get free plots and building materials, £100,000 having been allocated for this purpose.

The 30,000 people estimated to be living in Mathare Valley in 1969 eventually discovered that the 100,000 pounds promised by the Minister was non-existent. Even if this money had been forthcoming, it was insufficient to rehouse more than 300 families in very low-cost housing or to prepare more than 600 site-service plots, exclusive of the promised free building materials and a major sewer needed for the proposed resettlement area. As it turned out, the government proved unwilling even to finance a pilot scheme of six experimental houses for the purpose of assessing the costs and benefits of heretofore untested low-cost housing techniques. The extent to which priorities were then askewed is indicated by the City Council's 1970 proposal to spend £75,000 for a ceremonial drive to be used for "state occasions," while willing to provide only £50,000 for a project affecting the residents of Mathare Valley.[63]

In 1971, however, the Nairobi City Council, with the approval of the Central Government, unexpectedly allocated £1,800,000 for a two-year program to provide 900 new houses and 1,650 site-service plots on a 115 acre section of the Valley.[64] Additional funds for this project were expected from A.I.D. and the World Bank. The houses and plots were to be carefully located on a grid, facilitating the gradual introduction of permanent access roads, street lighting, sewerage schemes, and latrines, replacing the temporary facilities that were to be provided. Roads, piped water, and trunk sewers were also to service the eight existing Mathare villages, which by then accommodated an estimated 65,000 people. The houses were planned as simple structures (each containing a bedroom, toilet, shower, and kitchen), built by "labor-only" African contractors, with space for an extra room to be added when the occupier could afford to do so. The site-service section was to be divided into plots having communal toilet and shower blocks and those complete with private facilities. The City Council also agreed to work together with the University of Nairobi and the National

Christian Council of Kenya to do the necessary survey work and planning for schools, clinics, shopping centers, open-air markets, and a cottage industrial area.

After nearly two million pounds had been put into the Mathare Valley project, with much of the infrastructure (roads, sewers, toilets, and street-lighting) installed in the western settlements of the Valley, it came as a shock to the City Council to be instructed in June, 1972 to cease further building of new houses, roads, and sewers in the Valley.[65] Just as the Central Government's initial enthusiasm for the redevelopment of Mathare Valley was never explained, its disenchantment (at least temporarily) with the project was also never elucidated. The reasons can only be surmised.

Administrative ineptitude blighted the project from the beginning. The necessary coordination of over thirty agencies spanning the Central Government, the City Council, and the private sector proved practically impossible to achieve. "A clear designation of leadership was never made," reports Haldane, "and no one was delegated the task of creating a common ground of factual information among participants."[66] Unexpected changes were frequently made in policy goals and client groups.[67] Because of the absence of a qualified resident engineer and of poor communication from City Hall to the site office-centers, there were frustrating or costly misunderstandings and mistakes. Likewise, communication often broke down between the City Council and the Central Government. For example, the Special Commissioner for Squatters, who was supposed to facilitate inter-governmental cooperation in dealing with squatters, severely criticized certain social welfare programs carried out in the Valley in 1970, apparently without realizing that these had been sanctioned by the District Commissioner for the Nairobi Area. This point was forcefully brought out in a letter from the D.C. to the Permanent Secretary, Ministry of Lands and Settlement, noting that "the Minister for Local Government is always consulted and authority sought before any funds are spent on any project in Nairobi." According to Morrison, however, the biggest problem for the resident staff of the City Council's Department of Social Services and Housing was the attitude of the Department's leadership, which "evidenced a singular disinterest in the project and throughout was politically less than courageous, preferring to avoid making controversial decisions whenever possible."[68]

The weakness of administration both resulted from and contributed to confusion over priorities for Mathare Valley: improving the existing squatter villages, providing permanent housing of good quality, introducing site and service schemes, or a number of variations in between. Anyone following the arguments too closely developed, in the words of Haldane, "a persistent nagging sense of vertigo."[69] There was constant political pressure from Councillors, officials, and potential clients to improve the houses and services that were initially planned: the unimaginative rows of undistinguished dwellings, the small rooms with insufficient ventilation, the unsightly pit latrines that were inconveniently located, the inadequate footpaths and roads, etc. While their complaints may have had some justification, they entailed the danger both of making the project too expensive for the government and of driving away those most in need of cheap housing, particularly the mud and wattle huts or the incomplete "self-aided" units which were considered undignified for a modern urban housing scheme. The muddled objectives of the decision-makers were perceived by many squatters as an indication of hostility. "They are simply chasing us," Dan Manyatta (a journalist) quotes one of them as saying: "They do not want us. We are an eye-sore. But where shall we go?"[70]

Indeed, the squatters of Mathare Valley were the object of official scorn. "From the beginning, Mathare Valley has had a terrible reputation as the home of criminals and ruthless people," one of the City Council's medical inspectors noted in 1971, adding: "They throw refuse everywhere and want our people to collect." Even this official, however, realized that the squatters might have been more sociable or cooperative were they not so insecure, neglected, and demoralized. The scholars working in the Valley were generally convinced that the people here were no more immoral, crime-oriented, or irresponsible than anywhere else.[71] Nearly two-thirds of the adult population were employed (though only twenty per cent were full-time wage earners), and most had resided in the city for over five years. As such, they were capable of a vigorous effort to organize themselves and to improve their standard of living.

Unfortunately, helping the squatter villages proved more difficult than anticipated, even when there was a genuine willingness to do so. The existing plot sizes were often too small or irregular, making impossible the proper installation of sewers, water, and roads. Actually, many villages were so densely populated that it was hardly feasible to demarcate individual plots so that charges might be assessed for services rendered. The land was usually owned by absentee landlords, many of whom refused to repay improvement costs. Since the land in the Valley had become highly inflated in price (rising from $392 per acre in 1960 to $6,020 per acre at an average by 1970), there were insufficient funds for the government to buy all of it at current prices. But the government's proposal to acquire the entire area by compulsory purchase at original prices was resisted by those politically powerful Africans who had bought this land from the former Asian landowners. What also complicated the situation was the difficulty of determining land ownership in certain parts of the Valley because of the inadequate records and survey, legal, and clerical services.

Many of the local resident associations (most of which took the form of limited liability companies, the simplest organizational form under Kenya's Business Names Act) tried to work with the City Council to get legal building approval. Some even paid employees of the Nairobi City Council to draw up plans, but this seldom facilitated negotiations with the Town Planning Department. Even using architects, surveyors, and lawyers, it can take between six months and one year to obtain the multiple approvals and permissions necessary to build a house, adding as much as $150 to the cost. Longer delays could be anticipated when exceptions to the regulations required the approval of the Ministry for Local Government. In any case, the standards for rental houses, formulated in colonial times when few Africans owned houses in Nairobi, were generally beyond the resources of the LRA's, prohibiting impermanent housing and more than five dwellings to an acre in unserviced areas.[72] LRA's would occasionally try to raise the funds necessary to fulfill Council requirements by expanding their membership, but this led to endless disputes over leadership, procedure, and contractual arrangements or stipulations, thereby undermining agreements worked out with the Council. Probably the biggest problem for the LRA's was the need to delay housing construction, pending the installation and payment of such required services as water, sewers, and roadworks (which could take as long as three years).

Being unable to meet the Council's financial, legal, and planning constraints and anxious to recoup investments, the LRA's eventually abandoned further negotiations with the government and proceeded with their plans, building nearly 8,000 rooms or family units in 1969 in Mathare Valley (over five times more than the City Council could annually build). While this housing was at least as good as much of the older public housing, it remained illegal. As mentioned earlier, however, many of those in positions of power were themselves investors in these companies. Although legalization would have made their investments more secure, they feared having to pay Council charges and taxes and being subject to governmental regulations and inspections. As such, they may have secretly supported or even initiated the government's abandonment of the Mathare Valley project. Consequently, incentives were eliminated for improving the living conditions in the Valley, under which 62 per cent of the children here examined in 1970 by the Nairobi City Council suffered from bilharzia, 81 per cent from roundworm, and 27 per cent from hookworm. Yet, the worse the living conditions became, the less likely it was that the building being done in the Valley could ever be officially approved.

The Mathare Valley project also involved the politically delicate problem of allocating plots and houses. Since the plots were originally supposed to be free to impecunious and worthy squatters, they were obviously in great demand. The Commissioner for Squatters feared that people would deliberately burn their houses throughout the city to be included in the allocation lists. Whatever was done for the squatters, he felt, would simply attract more into the city, thereby making it more difficult to expel the existing squatters back to the rural areas. As in the Kariobangi project, the Councillors were anxious to determine who would get plots, but the Land Commissioner (a European) was equally anxious to prevent this. This persistent conflict between the City Council and the Central Government over plot and housing allocation was seen as an obstacle to the continuation of the Mathare Valley project. Concern was also expressed about the previously mentioned problem of preventing the original allottees from selling their plots to those using them to build rental housing. While this was considered a gross misuse of the government's generosity, there appeared no way to prevent it.

So long as the Mathare Valley project seemed doubtful, many members of the City Council's professional staff, particularly in the Urban Studies Group, felt in a quandary. They needed to work closely, according to Morrison, with the small group of African politicians and administrators who shared both their concern about the rapid influx into the city of impoverished peasants and their affinity for site and service schemes.[73] But this was difficult to do without formal governmental support. "In other words," he wrote, "to proceed effectively, we simply need a turn-about in actual government policy." Meanwhile, the efforts that were being made to establish site-service schemes or to guide the development that was taking place in other parts of Nairobi, such as in Dagoretti, which was approaching Mathare Valley's level of unauthorized construction, had to be accomplished almost surreptitiously.[74]

Moreover, in the absence of meaningful policies for housing, the expensive master plan being prepared for the year 2000 was considered by a number of experts to be a waste of time and money. Such a plan also required basic decisions concerning transportation. A thousand additional vehicles a month were estimated to be entering the streets of Nairobi, necessitating more roads, traffic controls, and parking facilities which, while demanded by the elite, led to the congestion, noise, pollution, and inner-city decay faced by American cities. Instead of concerning themselves with "producing an architectonic design for a decade or two ahead," Michael Safier argues that planners in East Africa should be mobilizing the latent energies of the new urban settlers in order to channel them into productive activities.[75]

## Conclusion

One emerges from the study of Nairobi's politics of housing rather more depressed than one would from a similar study in a city such as Accra, Ghana. This feeling arises from Nairobi's greater potential for coping with its housing crisis and thus, the greater gap between possibilities and achievements. The Nairobi City Council's annual gross revenue is between three and four times that of the Accra-Tema City Council (taking into account the softness of Ghanaian currency).[76] In 1960, Accra managed to collect only £192,827 in rates from a population of 327,800, while Nairobi's rate income that year was £1,016,071 from its population then of 250,800. This indicates Nairobi's advantages over Accra in its ability to evaluate property, determine ownership, and enforce rate collection. Even to find and inspect property in Accra amid the often unmarked, intertwining alleys presents an overwhelming problem. The Nairobi City Council, on the other hand, according to Rozental, could collect a much higher percentage of the city's gross domestic product by shifting the incidence of revenue collections from the poor, the wage-earners, and the civil servants to the rich, the self-employed, and the professions.[77] In any case, despite the inadequacies of its manpower, the Nairobi City Council could afford to hire the quantity and quality of professional staff that Accra could hardly hope for.

Nairobi's advantages, however, are only apparent in the sections of the city seen by the tourists, the expatriates, and the elite. Here exist the parks and gardens, the tall public buildings and impressive hotels and theatres, the adequate sewage and drainage systems, the good water supply and other public services which are so lacking in Accra. Yet, as mentioned earlier, at least a third of Nairobi's population lives in areas which are considered an embarrassment to the City Council. "The City refused to recognize and service such areas, stating that they were only temporary and would be removed as soon as satisfactory alternatives were provided."[78] Nevertheless, the existing wealth differentials maintain the impoverished and economically deprived modern sub-sector (analyzed in the I.L.O.'s 1972 study of Kenya previously referred to), which has "only limited, fortuitous, and restricted access to the sources of income that generated the wealthy zone."[79] The people of this sub-sector, when not ignored, face the harassment of the powerful wealthy sections which benefit from the weaknesses of their unfortunate neighbors. Even shoeshine boys are hardly tolerated by the Nairobi City Council.

A similar segregation of sectors does not exist in Accra, despite obvious socio-economic differences within the population. This almost certainly makes life easier for the impoverished masses here, even amid the squalor they must endure. This may also partly explain the fact that Nairobi lacks the excitement or vibrancy of Accra or even Mombasa, Nairobi's sister city on the coast. "Beautiful downtown Nairobi," to quote a visiting journalist, "is about as dead as beautiful downtown Pennsylvania Avenue across from the new FBI building in Washington. Dead, that is, as regards *joie de vivre,* the easy laughter, even of the music that I had taken for granted was a part of the lifeblood of Africans wherever they are."[80] "Face it," admits a Kenyan journalist, "in this routine, rat-race city of leisure, life at night is often dull, mostly a bore."[81]

It may be significant that perhaps the most interesting and lively area, resulting from the oldest existing site-service scheme for Africans in Nairobi, was that part of Pumwani which had so far escaped redevelopment. With all its destitution, overpopulation, and crime, it is described by a survey group as being early in the evening "noisy and gay, one enormous nightclub."[82] Whereas the people of Pumwani regard themselves as a closely-knit community, "proud and independent in spirit, as can be seen among even the oldest residents who have constantly refused to join relatives living in other parts of Kenya," most of the population regard Nairobi more as a place to work temporarily than to live permanently.

One also emerges from the study of Nairobi's efforts to cope with its housing crisis convinced of the need to reexamine some recent propositions about bureaucracies in the Third World: that the more underdeveloped a political system is, the more likely the bureaucracy is to dominate the other political and governmental institutions; and that this political-administrative imbalance prevents the development of structures which could facilitate the interest articulation and interest aggregation necessary for political development.[83] A recent book, edited by Goran Hyden, Robert Jackson, and John Okumu, relates these propositions to Kenya.[84] According to the

authors, the organization of administration here is highly centralized, with an emphasis on maintaining control (law and order)
rather than on achieving real change or development. In the process, potential structures and devices for checking administration
(e.g., the legislature, the judiciary, the press, the functional associations, and the opposition parties) have been rendered relatively ineffective either by political discouragement or by socio-economic
circumstances. Consequently, the goals cherished by the leaders prevail over those sought by the masses. This means that the apparent
progress of Kenya (indicated by the rising gross national product)
benefits more the elite than the general public.

The argument presented in this chapter is that the Kenyan administration is powerful only in a limited sense. Those heading the
bureaucracy can certainly initiate or terminate programs, such as
the Mathare Valley project, without explanation to or consultation
with subordinates, representative institutions, or the general public.
But the ability to formulate comprehensive plans of great magni-
tude or innovation and to carry them out with the requisite efficiency
and effectiveness is beyond their capacity. Thus, in the case of the
squatters, the government could harass and even uproot them, but
it could not prevent or control them. And by denying the squatters
the means for improving their standard of living, the government
actually worsened the problems it faced.

The need to describe a powerful government that is also ineffective brings us again to the utility of the "elasticity of control" concept. This clearly emerges from this case-study of housing. The
leaders did not properly utilize the experts at their disposal, partly
because they did not understand these experts and partly because
they were unwilling to accept their advice. Consequently, their policies tended to be ambiguous and inconsistent. Without clear or
meaningful policies, the leaders themselves became confused as to
what they really wanted and lost much of their commitment to the
policies they had initially supported. Moreover, what was lacking
was the necessary coordination among and within ministries, agencies, and City Council departments, together with the necessary
competence, for successful implementation. Thus, the control sought

by the leaders could only be sporadically exercised, leading to endless "on and off," "stop and go" cycles.

Another reason for inelasticity of control was that policies were imposed without taking into account the needs and desires of the public. Insofar as the public exercised limited influence over the government, it ceased to respect the government, undermining its legitimacy. Because the government could not anticipate the willing cooperation of the citizenry, it had to rely upon the sort of coercive devices that tended to be very costly and of limited usefulness. This aspect of inelasticity of control, dealing with the relationship of the government with the public, will be the subject of the next chapter.

## NOTES

1. *East African Standard* (E.A.S.), March 13, 1969.
2. E.A.S., May 22, 1964.
3. E.A.S., editorial, August 18, 1966.
4. Cf. Lawrence N. Bloomberg and Charles Abrams, *United Nations Mission to Kenya on Housing* (Nairobi: Government Printer, 1964), pp. 5, 15, 27.
5. E. P. Wilkinson, "Nairobi's Population Growth and the Problem of Housing," Nairobi City Council, 1964, p. 3.
6. "Memorandum on Nairobi City Council Housing Stock," Nairobi Urban Studies Group, February 28, 1972.
7. City Engineer's Department (in association with the University of Nairobi, M.I.T., the Nairobi Urban Studies Group, and the National Christian Council of Kenya), "Interim Urbanization Projects: Preliminary Proposal," Nairobi City Council, 1972, p. 14.
8. Alek A. Rozental, "Nairobi Urban Study and the Housing Problem," Nairobi Urban Studies Group, August 3, 1972, p. 2.
9. Cf. E. T. Farnworth, "A Survey of the Problems of Re-developing Pumwani Estate," Nairobi City Council, 1964; Desmond Healey, "Housing: Nairobi's Biggest Problem," *Daily Nation*, April 14, 1964.
10. *Op. cit.,* p. 24.

11. "Low-Income Housing," Nairobi Urban Studies Group, May, 1972, p. 1.

12. "Nairobi: Some Solutions to Problems of Urban Growth," in Michael Safier, ed., *The Role of Urban and Regional Planning in National Development for East Africa* (Kampala: Milton Obote Foundation, 1970), p. 219.

13. October 6, 1972.

14. J. R. Harris, "A Housing Policy for Nairobi," in John Hutton, ed., *Urban Challenge in East Africa* (Nairobi: East African Publishing House, 1972), pp. 39-56; C. N. W. Siganga, *Annual Report for the Department of Social Services and Housing, 1970* (Nairobi: County Hall, July 1971), p. 3.

15. E.A.S., May 18 and 20, 1972.

16. (Nairobi: County Hall, July, 1971), p. 3. At the end of July, 1973, the Government did agree to rent increases ranging from 20 per cent to nearly 200 per cent, depending on the location, size, and attractiveness of the Council housing, despite the intense displeasure expressed by Councillors, labor union leaders, and MP.'s (E.A.S., July 28, 1973).

17. *Daily Nation* (D.N.), March 8, 1972.

18. Rozental, *op. cit.*, pp. 2-10; Temple, *Housing Memorandum, op. cit.*

19. J. Kabiru, *Annual Report of the Medical Officer of Health, 1969* (Nairobi: City Hall, 1970), p. 54; K. Njuguna, Chairman, "Annual Report of the Social Services and Housing Committee," Nairobi City Council, 31 July, 1970.

20. C. Gupta, "Summary of Findings and Recommendations," Nairobi Urban Studies Group, 31 July 1971; City Engineer's Department (in association with the U. of Nairobi, M.I.T., the Nairobi Urban Studies Group, and the National Christian Council of Kenya), *Interim Urbanization Projects: Preliminary Proposal* (Nairobi: City Hall, 1972), p. 10.

21. C. N. W. Siganga, *Annual Report of the Department of Social Services and Housing, 1969* (Nairobi: County Hall, July, 1970), pp. 11-12.

22. *Those Without. The Story of Three Years' Work in Mathare Valley and Other Settlements of Nairobi, Kenya* (Nairobi: National Christian Council of Kenya, 1971), p. 22.

23. Cf. Emil Rado and Judith Wells, "The Building Industry in Kenya," in Hutton, *op. cit.*, pp. 200-224.
24. *Annual Report, 1970, op. cit.*, p. 3.
25. Quoted, Hurrell, *op. cit.*, p. 1.
26. *Op. cit.*, p. 10.
27. Rozental, *op. cit.*, p. 1.
28. Cf. statement by the Minister for Housing, E.A.S., February 5, 1971.
29. Hunter Morrison, "The Site and Service Scheme: Problems General and Specific," Nairobi Urban Studies Group, July 30, 1971.
30. E.A.S., Feb. 5, 1971.
31. D.N., March 24, 1972.
32. "Long Term Framework for Nairobi's Development," Nairobi Urban Studies Group, Feb., 1972, p. 2.
33. John R. Yost, "Towards a Housing Policy for Nairobi," Nairobi Urban Studies Group, November, 1969. Yost's recommendations are based on an article by C. Rosser, "Housing and Planned Urban Growth: The Calcutta Experience," in Safier, ed., *op. cit.*, pp. 234-247.
34. "Long Term Framework . . .," *op. cit.*, p. 14.
35. *Op. cit.*
36. *Sunday Post* and *Sunday Nation,* July 23, 1972.
37. E.A.S., July 6, 1971.
38. Thomas S .Weisner, "One Family, Two Households: A Rural-Urban Network Model of Urbanism," University Social Sciences Council Conference, Nairobi, Dec., 1969, p. 4.
39. David Etherton, ed., *Mathare Valley: A Case Study of Uncontrolled Settlement in Nairobi* (Nairobi: Housing Research and Development Unit, U. of Nairobi, August, 1971), p. iv.
40. City Engineer's Department, *op. cit.*, p. 16.
41. D. Haldane, *Those Without* (Nairobi: National Christian Council of Kenya, 1971), p. 29.
42. City Engineer's Department, *op. cit.*, p. 16.
43. J. Kabiru, *Annual Report, 1969* (Nairobi: City Hall, 1969), p. 2.
44. International Bank for Reconstruction and Development, *Economic Development in East Africa,* Vol. II — Kenya (Washington, D.C.: I.B.R.D., July 30, 1971), p. 27.
45. *Annual Report, 1970, op. cit.*, p. 2.
46. E.A.S., November 20, 1970.

47. E.A.S., January 23, 1970.
48. E.A.S., October 17, 1969. The Mayor at this time may have been reacting to the suggestion of, among others, Dr. Mungai, Minister for Defence (E.A.S., August 27, 1969) that it was better to help people improve their housing than to demolish what they built.
49. E.A.S., January 23, 1970.
50. E.A.S., July 6, 1971.
51. June 5, 1972.
52. *Op. cit.,* p. 30.
53. Cf. "Informal Sector Development" (Technical Paper No. 22) in International Labor Organization, *Employment, Incomes and Equality: A Strategy for Increasing Productive Employment in Kenya* (Geneva: I.L.O., 1972), pp. 503-509.
54. Yost, "Towards a Housing Policy for Nairobi," *op. cit.,* p. 3.
55. "Kitui Village: A Cursory Glance," Nairobi Urban Studies Group, 1971.
56. E.A.S. and D.N., September 9, 1972.
57. Yost, "Towards a Housing Policy for Nairobi," *op. cit.,* p. 3.
58. Hurrell, *op. cit.,* p. 16.
59. Cf. T. Farnworth, "Report on the Nairobi Squatter Situation, Proposed Solutions," Nairobi City Council, June, 1970; Yost, "Development Recommendations: Eastern Dagoretti," *op. cit.*; Etherton, *op. cit.*; Haldane, *op. cit.*
60. E.A.S., June 3, 1972.
61. The history of Mathare Valley is discussed by H. Morrison, *Mathare Valley Report: A Case in Low Income Housing* (Nairobi: Urban Studies Group, May, 1972; Town Planning Section, *Mathare Valley Social and Economic Survey* (Nairobi: City Council, Sept., 1969); Etherton, *op. cit.*; Haldane, *op. cit.*
62. Town Planning Section, *op. cit.,* p. 9.
63. E.A.S., March 2, 1970.
64. Cf. article by Richard Derwent, E.A.S., June 30, 1971.
65. City Council of Nairobi, *Minutes,* Vol. XXXIX, No. 11 (June, 1972), p. 2390.
66. *Op. cit.,* pp. 16-17.
67. Morrison, "The Site and Service Scheme . . .," *op. cit.*
68. *Ibid.*
69. *Op. cit.,* p. 35; Morrison, *Mathare Valley Report . . ., op. cit.,* pp. 32-34, 72.

70. *Sunday Nation,* April 18, 1971.
71. Etherton, *op. cit.*; Morrison, *Mathare Valley Report . . ., op. cit.*
72. Town Planning Section, *op. cit.,* pp. 4-5.
73. "The Site and Service Scheme . . .," *op. cit.*
74. Yost, "Development Recommendations . . .," *op. cit.*
75. "Urban Problems, Planning Possibilities, and Housing Policies," in Hutton, *op. cit.,* pp. 27-37.
76. Comparable facts and figures are available from E. K. Akyea-Djamson, Chairman, *Interim and Final Reports of the Commission of Enquiry into the Accra-Tema City Council* (Accra-Tema: State Publishing Corp., 1969) and The City Council of Nairobi, *Memorandum of Evidence to the Local Government Commission of Inquiry* (Nairobi: City Hall, May, 1966).
77. "Long Term Framework . . .," *op. cit.,* p. 17.
78. Town Planning Section, *op. cit.,* pp. 4-5.
79. *Op. cit.,* pp. 503-509.
80. William Raspberry, "Impressions of Kenya," *Washington Post,* June 26, 1972.
81. "Fernandes on Sunday," *Sunday Nation,* February 20, 1972.
82. Enid de Silva, "Pumwani — The Slum Whose People Don't Want to Leave," E.A.S., September 18, 1970.
83. Cf. Lee Sigelman, "Do Modern Bureaucracies Dominate Under-Developed Polities? A Test of the Imbalance Thesis," *The American Political Science Review,* Vol. LXVI, No. 2 (June 1972), pp. 525-28.
84. *Development Administration: The Kenyan Experience* (Nairobi: Oxford U. P., 1970), *passim.* Also, cf. my review of this book in *The American Political Science Review,* Vol. LXVII, No. 1 (March 1973), pp. 253-55.

# 8 THE CITIZENS AND THE CITY COUNCIL

*Introduction*

Kenya's government, like that of most African states, has kept a tight lid on political competition. "A nationalist movement has no time for arguments about ideology, or for differences in economic and social programmes," Tom Mboya argued in his book, *Freedom and After.*[1] Parties, he pointed out, arise from class differences which are absent in Africa.

> Instead you have in newly independent states a government which derives its strength from the masses, and talks in terms of universal education, more hospitals, better food, more opportunities for a better standard of life for everybody. The areas of division are very limited — at least at the outset, until you have created new interests which may clash — and it is difficult to form genuine political parties. The divisions there might be would be those of tribe or individual ambition, but very rarely could there be genuine ideological or class differences. That is why the British are wrong in talking about democracy for us in terms of their own parliamentary institutions and political party set-up.

Mboya, however, did not agree with those who advocated a benevolent dictatorship for Kenya. "We leave our back-benchers free to get up in Parliament and speak their minds: we don't believe this destroys the strength and influence of the Government. On the contrary, we believe this adds to the strength of the Government."[2] In this regard, Mboya was supported by a statement from KANU headquarters in June 1966, that although the Party had the necessary majorities and national support to legislate for a one-party state, "we have not chosen to exercise our rights and powers in this way."[3]

According to Newell M. Stultz, "there has been little evidence in Kenya of any concerted attempt since independence to manipulate the character of the National Assembly so as to make it reflect the political objectives of the state."[4] Nevertheless, the limits of permissible debate were vague as well as narrow.

The members of Parliament who joined Odinga's Kenya People's Union (K.P.U.) were required to resign their seats and face new elections, and those who were reelected were never accorded the privileges of an "official opposition" within Parliament. Moreover, their ability to engage in political activity outside of Parliament was severely restricted. Based on legislation stemming from colonial days, half of Kenya's forty districts were regarded as "closed areas" where special permission was required for political activity. Such permission was seldom granted. Odinga was not even allowed to address the students of the University College in Nairobi when the students invited him to do so in January 1969.[5] Under an amendment to the Preservation of Public Security Act, the Government periodically arrested leading K.P.U. members or supporters, restricted political or trade union activity, and censored communications.[6] The threat of even more severe measures moved Odinga to accuse the Government of being more suppressive than the British in colonial days.[7]

Though the Kenya African National Union continued to be very popular throughout Kenya, particularly in Nairobi, its strength was derived from its association with Jomo Kenyatta and the national liberation struggle rather than from its organization and activity. Indeed, as John J. Okumu (a lecturer in government at the University College, Nairobi) pointed out, the charismatic nature of Kenyatta's power made the Party somewhat irrelevant because "by being the centre of attention he has managed to insert his own brand of leadership quite independent of the party he leads."[8]

Following the general elections in May, 1963, KANU increasingly lost its contact at the "grass-roots" level and its ability to arouse patriotism and enthusiasm among the masses — a fact admitted by Mboya in his capacity as KANU's general secretary, in a June 1964 speech which stressed the need for party revival.[9] After independence, according to Odinga in his 1967 autobiography, "no meetings were called of the national executive of the Governing Council." And he went on to note:

> Branches in most parts of the country were allowed to die; or at most were used at election time as election machines or to hang out the flags, usher the crowds and cheer an M.P. or Cabinet Minister at a public rally. Membership was not recruited, membership dues were not collected. Headquarters and branch rents, post office box rentals and telephone accounts were unpaid, and telephones were disconnected. As an arm of the government for popularizing development programmes, for encouraging the discussion of policy, for keeping the government alive to the needs of the people, the party was paralyzed.[10]

Only 500 people joined KANU in Nairobi in 1965, despite many appeals by the City's KANU branch for more members. "This is a very small number for a city the size of Nairobi," admitted the Nairobi branch treasurer, Mr. K. P. Shah, adding that people could not praise the leadership of Mr. Kenyatta and at the same time ignore his call to strengthen KANU by becoming members.[11] So apathetic were people in Nairobi in 1965 that the branch elections had to be postponed for the district's women's wing and youth wing because only three sub-branches had submitted names of their delegates.

"The Party means nothing," exclaimed one of the City Councillors in a 1964 interview, "manipulated as it is by a small group of Party leaders." One of the officials of the Nairobi branch was even more outspoken in his criticism of KANU. "The people of the country are unhappy because they have no work, and they are losing faith in the promises of the Government," he remarked, adding: "I spend most of my time trying to get jobs for people, but I am seldom successful. Why should the people care much about a party which cannot help them get jobs?" Significantly enough, KANU headquarters in Nairobi atrophied so badly in 1964 that this Party official had to take a job with the Nairobi City Council to support himself.

## KANU and the City Council, 1963-67

Though KANU continued to be organizationally weak, it retained the affiliation of the Nairobi City Council members. However, the significance of this affiliation was by no means clear.

As a result of the September, 1963 municipal elections which gave Africans control of the City Council, all but three of Nairobi's councillors gained their positions through the support of KANU. Indirectly, the same was true of the ten aldermen and the two nominated members. Soon thereafter, two of the successful independents announced their support of KANU, and the two defeated KANU candidates were installed as aldermen. This led a correspondent of the *Kenya Weekly News* to write:

> One cannot help but view with misgiving such complete party political domination of a local authority. Almost to a man the new councillors and aldermen are inexperienced in City Council affairs. The aldermanic bench will be filled with people, who unless they can prove otherwise, will be political cyphers as distinct from men who in the past have traditionally achieved the position by age, wisdom and experience of the city and its affairs.[12]

Yet, contrary to what might have been expected, the influence of KANU headquarters on decision-making in the Council did not seem obvious or persistent during the period being reviewed. Only occasionally did it make itself felt.

"We are a KANU Council," the remark was often heard, "and we must act in accord with the Party." However, while they acknowledged their indebtedness to KANU, the Council members were unsure of the extent and manner in which Party pressure was manifested. "The Party has had little impact on the City Council," one of them declared in a 1964 interview. "Tom Mboya, the top man in the Party, pays little attention these days to what is going on in the City Council, and the Minister for Local Government is not a strong party politician." But another (an Asian) maintained: "KANU does really control the City Council, despite the resistance of the Councillors to any intrusion on their authority." He went on to add: "Since the Central Government seems generally content with the administration of Nairobi, it doesn't meddle much in our affairs." This last remark was also the opinion of an official of KANU. "We make suggestions to the City Council," he noted, "but there is no need to interfere in the work of the Council."

The indication was that only during times of crisis would party pressure of some sort be noticeable. Thus, in October, 1963, Sammy Maina, the organizing secretary of KANU's Nairobi branch, publicly threatened to expel from the Party any Council member supporting an imminent revolt backed by certain non-Kikuyu Council members against the decision of the KANU leaders to keep Charles Rubia as Mayor.[13] Maina went on to say that while neither the Party Headquarters nor the Nairobi Branch intended to dictate, discipline and integrity must be maintained among the Party members.

Without KANU support, it was difficult to win or retain a City Council seat. For example, in the Nairobi municipal elections of June, 1964, only five persons were courageous enough to oppose the eleven official KANU candidates who were campaigning. The one Council member who lost KANU backing (an Asian) did not bother to compaign. The independent candidates (including the two who eventually won) were clearly motivated by personal or tribal considerations rather than ideological or policy matters. Their desire to maintain a KANU affiliation was indicated in a letter from one of them to the *East African Standard* stating that "if I will win the election, I will join KANU councillors in the City Hall. I will not stay as an Independent Councillor."[14]

Those campaigning in defiance of KANU (even when they wanted to maintain their association with the Party) were nevertheless warned of the consequences of displeasing those in power, such as loss of job opportunities. This sort of intimidation must have been behind the statement of the independent candidate in Jericho Ward in November 1964, indicating that he had withdrawn from the contest to prevent his career from being ruined.[15] Indeed, when the African ward of Shauri Moyo did elect a K.P.U. member to the City Council in 1966, it was punished by not being given the lighting and electrical facilities extended to other locations. This K.P.U. Councillor was often shabbily treated — for example, being excluded from a ceremony in which the City Council presented a £1,000 check to President Kenyatta for a charitable purpose.[16] He protested at this time that "State House is not KANU property and the money we were taking to the President has been contributed by taxpayers, including Shauri Moyo Ward which I represent," but it was to no avail.

Following the challenge of K.P.U. in 1966, KANU headquarters in Nairobi indicated that greater discipline would be exercised over local authorities. It asserted that "the party organization must be regarded as an essential unifying force binding the local authorities and the Government" and, as such, "all councillors elected on the KANU ticket must adhere to party decisions and discipline and promote the KANU government policies. Like the Parliamentary Group, they must have political leadership."[17] This proclamation went on to insist that "it is not enough for local authority candidates to expect party support in the elections and then think that they can run the councils without party supervision until the next election." It was noted that since most local authorities as well as the Central Government were controlled by KANU members, "there is no place for conflict between institutions deriving their mandate from one and the same party."

Following the 1966 assertion of KANU headquarters that "the election of mayors and county chairmen would from now on be the subject of party decision and not just the choice of a council caucus, as it was in the colonial days," it was expected that the choice of a successor to Rubia would be a party rather than a Council decision. There was evidence that this was the case inasmuch as Isaac Lugonzo, who was promoted to the Mayoralty from the position of Deputy Mayor in 1967, had not been popular enough the previous year to keep his aldermanic seat (to which one was elected by the Council members). However, in other decisions, such as the selection of committee chairmen and deputy chairmen, the influence of the Party was not apparent. "The Party can make suggestions," one of the City Councillors maintained, "but it can't dictate to us." The power of the Party in the City Council's decision-making was affected by the change in its role after independence.[18] Whereas prior to independence, KANU had been used to arouse and mobilize the masses to alter the status quo, it was subsequently used to maintain quiescence. The President derived a charismatic position (from the continued ritualistic respect for KANU), enabling him to be the ultimate arbitrator of disputes. For example, during the crisis over the decision of the City Council to purchase a Rolls-Royce, the officials of the Nairobi branch of KANU met and issued an appeal to the citizens "to remain calm," adding that, as the matter was in the hands of the President, it was useless for politicians to continue exploiting the issue.[19] While this appeal did not end the controversy, the decision of the Branch at this time to support the mediation of the President legitimized this procedure for the resolution of serious conflict.

### The Choice of KANU Candidates for the City Council

Since KANU members controlled the City Council, the question needs to be asked, on what basis did KANU initially support a candidate? The answer, as given in an interview in 1964 by a leading officer of the Nairobi branch of KANU, was that the final choices rested with the Branch Executive of the District Governing Council, consisting of seven men. "There were usually four or five candidates to choose from," he pointed out, "and the most important factors were education, popularity, and party loyalty." Excluded, he insisted, were tribal and racial considerations. It was also suggested that a great deal of attention was paid to the choices of the sub-branches in the various constituencies. In only a few cases were these rejected in the 1963 elections: once because of the inadequate education of the candidate and, in another case, because of a possible conflict between the candidate's position with the Kenya Local Government Workers' Union and that of councillor. However, other factors, including the viewpoint of the Mayor, may also have been taken into account.

The assertion that tribal and racial factors were excluded in choosing candidates for the 1963 elections would appear odd in view of the fact that, as it turned out, representation in the City Council was somewhat in accord with the racial and tribal composition of the City.[20] Actually, as a former employee of KANU made clear, tribal and racial considerations were not ignored. In this regard, certain members of the Cabinet had a considerable amount of influence in nominating KANU candidates for the City Council. It was as a result of a legislative arrangement worked out by the Central Government that several veteran European Council members were retained as aldermen (to the consternation of some of the African Councillors).

The importance of some of the political notables in the nominating process was stressed by an Asian Council member in a 1964 interview, suggesting that, if it had not been for the support of the top men in the Party, he would never have become a councillor because of his failure to "buy the support" of the Africans in his ward. "Mboya and some other Cabinet members wanted me because of my influence with the Asian community which, after all, pays most of the City's taxes," he contended. "Therefore, they put pressure on the Governing Council of the Branch and the leaders in my ward to put forward my name."[21] However, this councillor may have exaggerated his standing with the "top men in the Party" because he failed to be renominated when he came up again for election.

Following the September, 1963 elections which gave Africans control of the City Council, the KANU leaders had to face the problem of more carefully balancing the need for popular candidates with the need for capable ones. One difficulty was the apparent lack of interest in municipal government on the part of the educated elite. "There is no money in it," remarked a leading African member of the City Council, "and educated people don't want to take the trouble to appeal to the masses." Though City Council members received a stipend which seemed good to an ordinary worker in Nairobi, it was not enough to bring into local politics the most desirable sort of person. There was, of course, no African leisure class for this occupation. Moreover, some of the most qualified

Africans no longer lived where they could be in constant contact with the African masses. For all these reasons, the remark of one of Nairobi's political leaders that "intellectuals complain but don't participate" was somewhat justified.

In 1966, the Nairobi City Council recommended to the Local Government Commission of Inquiry that literacy in English be a requirement for candidacy to the City Council.[22] The absence of this qualification had earlier been criticized by the 1964 Nairobi Standing Committee Report of the Senate. Actually, literacy in English might have been required under the 1963 local government regulations, but it was not enforced. "The ordinary person does not see the importance of English," a leading African member of the City Council pointed out in a 1964 interview. One need not know English to be educated, he noted, adding: "A Frenchman or Russian, even if he doesn't speak English, can be qualified." The impracticality as well as unpopularity of a literacy requirement were apparently the reasons for the Government's rejection of the Commission's recommendation that the literacy qualification for Members of Parliament be extended to members of municipal councils.[23]

Since the choice of candidates was partly determined by the sub-branches, the improper way in which these sub-branches were organized and conducted was a source of concern to the leaders of Kenya. Very ominous was the recurrence of tribal meetings in connection with Party branch elections.[24] An effort was made to reform the procedure for nominating candidates at the KANU Reorganization Conference of March, 1966, but it was apparently unsuccessful. Rivalries between KANU supporters seeking the Party's nominations for parliamentary and local authority seats were demoralizing the Party, Tom Mboya warned in April 1967, adding: "It is also true that constant suspicion among Party members regarding future elections has resulted in weakening committee work and has sometimes led to deliberate packing of committees to ensure the candidacy of particular persons."[25]

The extent to which KANU leaders could influence the choice of candidates made by sub-branches was uncertain. In May 1966, when the Nairobi branch of KANU attempted to impose a candidate upon one of the Nairobi East sub-branches for a forthcoming by-election to the House of Representatives, it was quickly rebuffed. At that time, the KANU organizing secretary, Mr. Sammy Maina, was forced to agree that KANU officials would supervise but not participate in the selection of KANU candidates.

The struggle to control the sub-branches was intensified following a 1968 constitutional amendment requiring all candidates for Parliament and for local government posts to be nominated by a recognized political party. Independent candidates were disallowed because, it was said, they would only confuse the public. At the time of the 1968 local government elections, 500 women were reported to have marched through Nairobi complaining that the nomination of KANU candidates had been undemocratically carried out.[26] "We never had a chance to pick the candidates," the women yelled to Mwai Kibaki, the governing party's vice president for Nairobi. "We were never given a say in the nominations!" Brawls, demonstrations, and protest marches were then widespread, including the manhandling of a cabinet minister when he tried to present to the voters a slate of candidates that had been hand-picked in a backroom.

The concern over the nomination of KANU candidates finally caused the Government to introduce open primaries. It hoped in this way to reduce the growing restlessness of party branches and frustrated politicians. Following the defeat of a KANU candidate for election to the House of Representatives in Nyanza Province in 1969, President Kenyatta announced that new measures were to be introduced to prevent any intrigue aimed at giving seats to men of wealth or to relatives of party officials.[27] This, he hoped, would discourage M.P.'s from staying comfortably in Nairobi "looking for prostitutes" instead of going to their constituencies to explain Government policies to their people. How the introduction of open primaries would affect municipal politics in Nairobi remained to be seen.

### Municipal Elections

Because of the nature of the one-party system existing in the 1960's, there was a considerable amount of public apathy regarding the City Council elections. In the by-election of November, 1964, only thirty-eight voters in one particular ward bothered to vote out of a total of over 5,000 registered voters.[28] In the Ngara-West Ward by-election of January, 1966, where approximately 3,500 were registered, the incumbent candidate won by 159 to 4. In the 1965 City elections, only 11 per cent of those registered actually voted in the three wards where there were opposing candidates. Since the seven other Councillors up for re-election were unopposed, the people in these wards had no opportunity to vote. The next year, when K.P.U. entered into city politics, five of the Councillors faced opposition, but still only 16.5 per cent of the registered voters participated in the elections.

In addition to the functioning of the party system, other factors may have been responsible for the low turn-out at the municipal elections. One of these, according to Mayor Rubia, was that too little publicity was given to local government.[29] But it is difficult to determine the validity of this assertion. It must be kept in mind that, according to the 1962 Census, 41.6 per cent of African males and 57.8 per cent of African females in Nairobi aged 15 years and over indicated no formal education at all and that less than one-third of this population claimed more than four years of education. Also significant was the relatively low daily circulation of the English and Swahili press (less than 30,000 in 1964 for a population of over 300,000). Yet, it is remarkable how rapidly news seemed to spread about particular events, superficially indicated by the speed with which crowds gathered to cheer or demonstrate, attesting to the efficacy of radio and informal means of communication.

The confusion associated with the city elections, more than anything else, may have been responsible for the existing political apathy. In discussing the September, 1963 municipal elections for the Nairobi City Council, one well-informed European officer of the City Council related:

> Sixty per cent of those eligible turned out at the last municipal elections, but they did so amid great confusion. The geographical subdivisions for municipal elections are different from those for the national elections — 32 constituencies for the municipal elections

as against 22 units for the national elections. This meant that we had to combine some and divide others to get the elections carried out. This work was done by the District Commissioner's Office which, in turn, left it up to the chiefs, who were very careless for the most part. In some locations, such as Pumwani, there are no street names or, if there are, they may be different from the ones used by the people, and in many cases the numbering system is very unclear. The result has been a great many mistakes — for example, the striking off from the rolls of more than 600 tobacco workers in an area where the candidate was an employee of a tobacco company.

According to this same officer, £35,000 ($98,000) was needed to put Nairobi's voting rolls into satisfactory condition (covering the cost of the necessary registrars, typists, and equipment needed for the work), and this was an amount the City was then unwilling to pay for this purpose.

Prior to the municipal elections of June, 1964 (in which one-third of Nairobi's councillors were up for reelection), there existed a ban on public meetings stemming from the demonstrations of unemployed and other signs of political unrest that had occurred during the previous six months. The problem that this presented for the City Council was discussed by one of the officers in the Town-Clerk's Department in an interview at the time of this election:

> The Government finally agreed to candidates holding public meetings but only 3½ weeks before the elections, and it then insisted that the candidates go through a highly complicated procedure for getting this permission: a letter from the candidate to the Government Agent (the local representative of the Ministry for Home Affairs) which was then to be sent to the Ministry of Local Government for approval and finally to the Prime Minister's Office. We pointed out in vain that each stage of this process would take almost a week. Nevertheless, the candidates started to follow this procedure; but just when the bureaucratic wheels began to turn, the procedure was changed. A letter direct to the Prime Minister's office was required, which was what we had first suggested. Consequently, the candidates had to start all over again in seeking permission. Finally, just before the elections, the restrictions on

public meetings were lifted entirely, ending the great confusion and waste of time. But no wonder Africans say, "Why bother?"

In the summer of 1966, there was again great confusion surrounding the holding of municipal elections. "First, the Government wanted us to revise our voting rolls in accord with parliamentary rolls," related one of the City Council's legal advisors:

> Then they decided that this was too complicated. So we agreed to postpone the municipal elections until the rolls could be revised. But finally the Government decided to go ahead with the elections in June in fear of KPU — mind you, without consulting any of us. Of course, we had to use the old rolls for the election.

This election was so badly conducted that even the Mayor could not vote. "After always casting his vote at Makadara, he was told— on his *Third* visit to the polling station — that his vote had been transferred to Doonholm," observed a reporter, adding: "How and why the transfer had taken place is still a mystery which Mr. Rubia is trying to solve."[30] However, the confusion engendered by this election could hardly be a mystery to the Mayor, considering that the voting rolls were five years out-of-date, that the boundaries of some of the wards had in the meanwhile been altered, and that non-citizens were suddenly disenfranchised several days prior to the election.

"This farce must not be repeated," declared the *Sunday Post* in an editorial on the 1966 City Council elections, explaining: "For slipshod arrangements and rank public relations, it takes some beating."[31] So embarrassed were the City officials about the election that, contrary to previous practice, the press was not allowed to witness the counting of ballots. Eventually the City Council was prevailed upon to postpone the elections that were to have taken place in 1967 until new voting rolls could be prepared.

While the voting rolls may have been improved for the 1968 City Council elections, the handling of these elections hardly enhanced public respect for the Council. First of all, the circumstances leading to the failure of 21 Council members to secure KANU nominations were highly controversial. What had happened, according to those rejected, was the "imposition of handpicked candidates by interested cults."[32] Secondly, the disqualification of 40 Kenya People's Union nominees by the Nairobi District Commissioner, claiming that they had filled in their nomination forms incorrectly, had the odor of gross political manipulation. As the KPU candidates pointed out, officials at City Hall had not complained about any mistakes in their nomination papers when accepting the monetary deposits required for the election.[33]

As mentioned in Chapter 6, the turnout for City Council elections continued to be small, despite the 1970 Local Government (Amendment) Bill encouraging the candidature of numerous politicians, regardless of their party affiliation.[34] While 79 candidates contested for the 11 vacancies in the by-elections of December, 1970, less than ten per cent of the electorate bothered to vote. With so many candidates and such a small turnout, a candidate needed only a small number of votes to win. For example, in the by-election for Nairobi's Pangani Ward in August, 1972, the victorious candidate got only 70 votes against 61 for his nearest rival.

Among the factors considered responsible for the low turnout were: the illiterate and transient nature of much of the population, the difficulty of registering to vote, the inept handling of many of the elections, and the apathy of party leaders. Because local authorities had little power, the KANU National Organizing Secretary pointed out in 1970, the candidates did little to stimulate polling excitement.[35] What also might have been mentioned was the failure to publicize the elections in the press or over the radio. Moreover, active campaigning may have been discouraged by the 1970 law prohibiting individuals and organizations from sponsoring candidates for councillorship and disallowing campaign expenditures of more than $280 (£100). While this law was supposedly written to prevent ethnic groups from becoming involved in local elections and the buying of votes, it also reflected the government's desire to minimize the attention given to elections.

## The Public Impact on the City Council

While public opinion may not have readily made itself felt through party decisions or elections, it did so in other ways. Public demonstrations were sometimes effective. An unusual example of this occurred in the summer of 1967 when the newly installed Mayor of Nairobi, Isaac Lugonzo, threatened to expel prostitutes from the City. A demonstration of fifty women quickly formed to protest their being called prostitutes, led by the KANU branch women's organizing secretary, who claimed the women were better supporters of the Party than men.[36] The next day, Mayor Lugonzo retreated, saying: "There is no question of this Council 'going it alone' because it has no powers to do so." Thus reassured, the women left the Mayor in peace.

More common than demonstrations was the effort of groups, unhappy with City Council decisions, to publicize their protests in the press and to gain the support of ministers, Parliament members, and trade union leaders. This was certainly effective in the Rolls-Royce affair discussed in Chapter 6. Letters to the editors of the local newspapers caused the City Council to reconsider its plans for altering Kenyatta Avenue (the city's most important thoroughfare). When the City Council proposed early in 1973 to greatly increase the rents charged for Council housing, the secretary-general of Kenya's Central Organization of Trade Unions (COTU) warned that his organization would demand wage increases ranging between 30 and 50 per cent. Such a threat could not be lightly dismissed. Likewise, the comments of M.P.'s were of considerable concern to Councillors.

The City Council was usually quick — indeed, too quick, according to some observers — to react to comments, editorials or letters to the editor appearing in the local press. On the other hand, the City's public relations department often failed to anticipate trouble. It might have done much more to prepare the public for such controversial undertakings as an expensive addition to the City Hall in 1966 at a time when public housing was so much in demand.

City Council members were sometimes accused of mobilizing support in the city whenever they had a problem in the Council.[37] In truth, their ability to stir up public opinion may have been better than their ability to assess it. In any case, Councillors found it extremely difficult to anticipate reactions of the public to what was done by the Council.

When asked how he determined public opinion in his location, one Councillor maintained that he talked with three educated Africans and two uneducated ones, "and then I check what they said with three or four others." Some Couuncil members claimed to meet on a regular basis with members of their local KANU sub-branches and other groups, but others admitted that such meetings were quite infrequent, at least on a formal basis. Nevertheless, the Councillors asserted that they were in constant contact with their constituents.

It was alleged that Africans approached Council members or officers with their problems at all hours of the day or night. "I don't have any life of my own," one Councillor complained, adding: "Still, we must realize that this is our job." This Councillor acknowledged that it would be a long time before his constituents accepted a system of "office hours." In a similar vein, Mr. C. N. W. Siganga, the then Acting Director of Social Services and Housing, wrote in the introduction to the 1965 *Annual Report of the Social Services and Housing Department*:

> A realisation among Nairobi Citizens that the Department was now under the control of "their own men" opened a new facet among them. All officers of the Department were flooded with visitors bringing a variety of complaints, queries and problems, ranging from housing to family matters. It is to the credit of all officers concerned that they rose to the occasion. Patience, tact and firmness carried them successfully to the end of the year.[38]

## The Case of the Hawkers

In Nairobi, African interest groups were for the most part poorly organized and incapable of a sustained and well-coordinated political campaign. They lacked the necessary income, personnel, and communication facilities for this purpose. The best organized groups continued to be largely European or Asian in composition. "In the old days," noted G. A. Tyson (a former European civil servant) in a letter to the *East African Standard*, "normal practice was for the Administration to refer the drafts of Bills or regulations to the Chambers of Commerce, certainly in Nairobi and Mombasa, so that consideration could be given to their possible effect on employment in this developing country."[39] This writer went on to complain that this practice had apparently ceased, at least as indicated in the case of the 1967 Immigration Act and the Traders' Licensing Regulation. Yet, interest groups could not altogether be ignored.

The African groups that most persistently attempted to influence the policies of the City Council consisted of hawkers or itinerant traders, referring here to those selling from temporary stalls or moveable carts. Hawkers are very common in developing countries such as Kenya, where few people have the capital and knowledge to carry on commerce in more sophisticated ways. However, as mentioned in a previous chapter, the laws enacted during the colonial period (designed as they were for the benefit of the European governing class) greatly discouraged hawking. Despite this, the hawkers were estimated to have numbered about 2,000 in 1941.[40]

Among the arguments used against the hawkers at various times was the accusation that they were a menace to public health, particularly those who sold cooked food. They were also thought to be unsightly and dirty and a nuisance to the European and Asian housewives who objected to being badgered. Moreover, the hawkers presented an economic threat to the more respectable shopkeepers who provided the City Council with a good source of income. Above all, it was felt, they stimulated crime and unrest in the city.

It was this last contention that most strongly moved the Government during the emergency period of the 1950's to take action against the hawkers, most of whom happened to be Kikuyu because of the proximity of their landholdings to Nairobi. In 1952, the number of licenses issued to African hawkers was reduced from 732 to 594, and the next year, hawking of charcoal and tea by Kikuyu, Embu, and Meru was completely forbidden.[41] In 1954, the only street trading permitted in the commercial and residential areas of Nairobi was the hawking of newspapers, and even the licenses for this were carefully restricted.[42]

The arguments used by City Council members in their opposition to hawking were frequently ambiguous or contradictory. "It was felt that certain African hawkers were a risk to security," according to Mayor Alderman Mrs. Needham-Clark in October, 1958, "and that if we did not allow Africans to hawk cloth, the only fair thing was to stop it for everyone."[43] But the next month the Town Clerk suggested that the security argument was only secondary to the argument of unfair competition.[44] In a modern urban community, he explained, where there were adequate means of transport between residential and shopping areas, there was little need of hawkers. These contradictory remarks reinforced the conviction of many Africans that the real reason for the City Council's opposition to hawking was to keep Africans economically subjugated.

What complicated the hawking situation was the competition between Asian and African traders for business within the African locations. The solution arrived at was to give Africans a monopoly of business within their locations, while prohibiting them from trading outside these locations.[45] The difficulty, however, was that Asians often employed Africans to hawk in the African areas. This practice provoked the established African traders into using their influence in the African Advisory Council (or later, the Ward Council) to keep to a minimum the issuance of hawking licenses. On the other hand, those Africans anxious to trade throughout the city welcomed the assistance of Asian businessmen in resisting the frequent efforts of City Council committees to eliminate hawking altogether. The willingness of the City Council to tolerate hawking by Asians made it difficult to disallow hawking by Africans. This sort of consideration induced the Council's General Purposes Committee in 1958 to reverse its previous recommendation that cloth-hawking be entirely prohibited.[46]

With the tremendous influx of Kikuyu into Nairobi in 1960, following the lifting of the Emergency restrictions, and with the growing insecurity of the European-dominated City Council after the Lancaster House Conference, it was no longer possible to eliminate hawking by legislative fiat. Finding no employment in the city, these Kikuyu, many of them ex-detainees, were left with no alternative but hawking. To completely disallow hawking, it was felt, would drive them into crime — a reversal, it might be noted, of the old argument that hawking contributes to crime. Consequently, the question became, not whether Africans should be allowed to hawk, but how they should be allowed to do so, and how many.

In 1960, the number of licenses issued to hawkers was quadrupled to over 400, but this had to be doubled the next year to take care of the growing demand. Still, it was not enough. However, accelerating the issuance of licenses actually raised more problems than it solved. First of all, it upset the established African traders. According to the Nairobi African Chamber of Commerce (claiming a membership of about 500), a "shocking state of affairs" existed in the African areas of the city with traders falling on top of one-another at all the places where Africans gathered, such as the bus-stops.[47] Under the circumstances, they could not pay the rents or fees required by the City Council.

At this time (1961-62) the police complained that there were too many licensed hawkers to supervise and that many hawkers were operating without any licenses whatsoever by taking advantage of the situation.[48] The inadequate enforcement of regulations regarding the sale of food and drink impelled Nairobi's Medical Officer of Health in 1961 to warn:

> The hygienic standards of many of these stalls are deplorable, and could cause serious illness to the people who buy food from them. People with shops nearby have complained that they attract filth and disease. They are also used as an excuse by loiterers, who hang about the stalls to steal from parked cars.[49]

Also, it was noted, the irresponsible issuing of hawking licenses did not solve the basic unemployment problem. It merely encouraged more Africans to come into Nairobi to eke out a living in this way.

In 1962, the police were prepared to get tough with the hawkers; but, by then, KANU was preparing to take power, and the hawkers were politically useful, supposedly performing roles as "political middlemen" analogous to barbers and bartenders in the old-style American political machines. Thus, the then newly elected African mayor of Nairobi, Charles Rubia, went to the defense of hawkers when the Government, supported by the City Council, refused to increase the number of hawking licenses from 1,130 to

1,500.[50] Declaring his readiness to resign on this issue, Rubia reportedly pounded on the mayoral desk and shouted: "If the police and the administration are going to dictate to the Council what the Council should do, I am going to take this matter to the higher authorities who control the police and the office of the administration." Later, in defending his position, Rubia commented at a luncheon for members of the press:

> Off the record, I would like you to know that I have personally been very much torn on this question. On the one side, there has been the demand for rigorous control, and a reduction of licenses. I was supported by the appropriate committee on a compromise figure, and lost their support in open Council. My personal position was this — that we cannot ignore the hunger and misery caused by an over-crowded city, by clamping down as if it were five years ago. On the other hand, we must retain some control — because if we let it go altogether it would be difficult, and probably impossible to win it back when conditions improve.[51]

Rubia's intervention on behalf of the hawkers gained him the popularity that he sought, but at the same time it paralyzed any effort to deal effectively with the hawkers. So exasperated were the police with the attitude of City Hall, according to one informant, that they ceased to be concerned with the hawkers, particularly when the City Council, in response to the protest of hawkers, withdrew the requirement that photographs be attached to hawking licenses. Without these photographs, it was difficult to prevent those with licenses from renting or lending them to others, thereby frustrating all means of control. This meant that for all practical purposes at this time there was a *laissez-faire* policy towards hawkers, justified, according to a City Council spokesman, by the prevailing socio-economic conditions:

> If there is little the Council can do to remove the large number of unemployed and destitute from the city, we have to live with the problem until there is work and provision for them outside the urban areas.
>
> What we try to do is strike a humane balance between demands of established traders who regard widespread hawking as

a threat to their livelihood, and the claims of hungry people who seek to earn some food through petty trading.[52]

This *laissez-faire* policy towards hawkers, however, could not continue indefinitely. By October, 1963, there were estimated to be at least 2,000 illegal hawkers (i.e., those without licenses), often selling under appallingly unhygienic conditions.[53] In one market area, 600 rats were caught by employees of the City Council within one week; and the scavenger work caused by illegal hawking was considered beyond the City Council's resources. Yet, to increase rentals to take care of this service, it was contended, would drive the legitimate stallholders out of business, pressed as they were to compete with illegal hawkers.

Thus it was that Mayor Rubia was finally forced to support measures that would curb illegal hawking. "Representations have been made by many citizens and organisations . . . concerning the deterioration in the control of hawking in the centre of Nairobi — including the appearance of the direct sale of foodstuffs from barrows in the highway, which is something that the City Council has never allowed for public health reasons," he declared in October, 1963, adding: "Resentment is also felt by hawkers who have taken up and paid for proper licenses, existing traders, and, of course, municipal stallholders and ratepaying shopkeepers."[54]

The hawkers immediately felt threatened by the Mayor's remarks. "We understand that African shopkeepers and hotel owners are the spearhead of the movement against hawkers and have made strong representations to the City Council and the Government seeking our removal and extinction," protested Mr. Macharia Kibicho, the chairman of the Nairobi Hawkers' and Traders' Association, in a statement to the press. Kibicho admitted that hawkers were an "eye-sore" and made the city dirty, but he ventured to ask: "What use is a clean city if 90 per cent of its population is starving, jobless, and forgotten?"[55] This rather apologetic position was coupled with the argument that hawking was an alternative to crime and was "healthy competition to big businessmen."

A little later (December, 1963), Mr. R. Warigi, who had by then replaced Mr. Kibicho as the spokesman for the Nairobi Hawkers' and Traders' Association, rejected the apologetic tone of the displaced chairman, in exclaiming:

> Hawkers are not a public nuisance. They are pursuing legitimate and honest means of obtaining subsistence at this critical period of economic depression and unemployment.... The medical and health reasons that hawking is dangerous to city health cannot be justified now.[56]

Warigi went on to add that it was "absolute nonsense" to claim that uncontrolled hawking had led to Nairobi's becoming an "eyesore." With this militant stance, he prepared to lead the hawkers, who periodically gathered at Akamba Hall in Nairobi, in their struggle against the regulations of the City Council deemed to be "oppressive."

Towards the end of November, 1963, the Hawkers Sub-Committee reached agreement on a number of resolutions: (1) to build four new open-air markets and to extend one other; (2) to prohibit unlicensed hawking outside these open-air markets; and (3) to confine the sale of tea and food to the thirty kiosks to be constructed within the open-air markets, unless sold under license in conformity with the prescribed health regulations.[57] Several months later, a prohibition on the hawking of charcoal (the cooking fuel most commonly used by Africans) was added to the earlier resolutions of the Hawkers Sub-Committee.[58]

The hawkers quickly reacted to these resolutions. The *harambee* spirit, exclaimed Mr. Kibicho (then the Chairman of the Kenya Street Traders' Society) at a meeting in Akamba Hall, included the poor as well as the rich; and it was the poor, "not the rich, fat, and well-dressed," who were the customers of the hawkers in Nairobi.[59] The hawkers had basically three objections to the markets being set up for them by the City Council: (1) they were inconveniently located for both hawkers and customers; (2) the space allotted to each hawker was insufficient (particularly for such bulky items as charcoal); and (3) there were inadequate opportunities and facilities for the sale of cooked food. It was also claimed that the hawkers of food and tea outside the official markets could not afford the £50 ($140) carts required to meet the health regulations and would thus be forced out of business to the detriment of the poor workers who depended upon them.

The charcoal hawkers were most alarmed by the proposed regulations. They claimed in an *Open Letter* that the decision to cancel their licenses had been reached as a result of the pressure of those with sufficient income to operate large charcoal stores and dumps. "There is a very great number of hawkers selling charcoal in Nairobi," they pointed out:

> If their present activities are stopped they will only contribute to another increase in work-seekers and unemployed persons. . . . Much as we would like to co-operate and assist the Council in framing suitable policies for all Nairobi citizens, it would be impossible for our charcoal members to understand why charcoal hawking could not be continued as before in view of the fact that it has been going on for some time.[60]

Copies of this letter were sent by this group of hawkers to all ministers and to all the members of the National Assembly representing Nairobi, in addition to all City Council members. This indicated their awareness of the sensitivity of the City Council to criticism stemming from the Central Government and legislature, which they hoped to provoke.

Finally, the City Council prompted by its Chief Medical Officer's warning of the possibility of plague, decided in May 1964, to clear forcefully one of the worst of the areas used by squatters and hawkers.[61] It did so with the help of 140 KANU Youth-Wingers, who had had a month's training with the City Council under the unemployment relief scheme. This campaign, "Operation Clean-up," was the result of close co-operation with the Central Government which followed an appeal by the General Purposes Committee of the City Council to the Kenya Government for a joint-policy on hawking.[62]

"Operation Clean-up" was an indication of what could be undertaken by a government that had confidence in its political strength. The willingness of the Councillors to go along with this quite vigorous coercion of the hawkers was attributed to party pressure by a European member of the City Council:

KANU plays an important role, not in little but in big things —
in the matter of hawkers and squatters, for example. Though
many Councillors may want to protect hawkers and squatters, the
Ministers and other Africans of influence are determined to get
rid of them. Since those who want to remain councillors or aldermen must have the support of the Party, they must go along with
what the Party wants. An independent, even if he is a Kikuyu
and personally liked, doesn't have a chance.

However, the Council may not have needed the spur of party
pressure to "crack down" on the hawkers. Many of the Council
members had come to share a common outlook with the rising
African bourgeoisie — one that viewed hawkers as "unprogressive"
and "bothersome." This was indicated by the increasing need of
Council members to "declare their interest" when contracts or use
of property came up for official discussion. In other words, a large
number of the Council members were now well-established businessmen. They were also anxious to maintain Nairobi's reputation
as a "civilized, modern place," and what was considered "civilized"
and "modern" was surprisingly close to the opinion of the previous
European rulers. For example, the selling of cooked meat by African butchers, though admittedly a traditional practice, was disallowed. Likewise, hawkers were not allowed to construct stalls because they then ceased to be viewed as proper hawkers. "Hawking
means hawking," explained Mr. F. Hinawy, the Nairobi City Council Public Relations Officer. "There is nothing more to it. The
trouble comes when the word hawking is enlarged to suit the
convenience of many hawkers."[63]

Yet, the problem of the hawkers did not end with "Operation
Clean-up." During 1966, over 3,000 in Nairobi were charged with
hawking without a license or with misusing their licenses, and in
1967 it was reported in the press that hawking had reached the
stage of crisis.[64] "Shoeshine boys, newspaper vendors and curio
sellers spread their goods over public pavements in such a manner
as to cause obstruction to pedestrians when intending purchasers
stopped to view," complained one of the members of the City
Council.[65] A similar complaint came from traders in the Council
markets who contended that their businesses were being under-

mined by those who were illegally selling near these markets. The Town Clerk admitted in 1969 that many people were trading without licenses and that the Council had virtually no control over such activities as cycle and shoe repairing, but what was most disturbing was the improper sale of food (particularly meat) and beverages.[66]

Since neither the opening of new markets nor the occasional campaign against illegal hawkers seemed to overcome the hawking problem, the City Council members were understandably discouraged. In desperation, the Sub-Committee on Hawkers and Licensing Policy proposed in April, 1967 (what Africans had scorned when broached during the colonial period) that "an approach be made to the Government to assist the Council in controlling the influx of people into Nairobi, as, in the opinion of this sub-committee, the problem of hawking cannot be dealt with effectively if people continue migrating into Nairobi."[67]

Dealing with hawkers might have been easier, had they been reasonably united and certain of what they wanted. As it was, they were divided into many organizations, the number and importance of which were constantly changing. Of the four important ones representing the hawkers in 1962 (the Kenya African National Traders' and Farmers' Union; the Nairobi Vegetable and Fruit Traders' Association; the Kenya Auctioneers', Hawkers', Marketers' and Traders' Union; and the Federation of Nairobi Traders' Association), only two were apparently in existence a year later. "The hawkers refuse to work together because of poor leadership," explained a well-informed African City Councillor in a 1964 interview. For example, the Nairobi Hawkers' and Traders' Association, it was pointed out, originally agreed to support the City Council's plan for dealing with hawkers. Its leadership was then apparently overthrown or disregarded by its secretary who, on behalf of the charcoal hawkers (numbering about 150), "wrote a very rude letter to the Council."

So confusing was the testimony of one group of hawkers before the General Purposes Committee that the African Councillor translating from Kikuyu to English had to request their return when their case was clarified and in conformity with what they had originally proposed.[68] The poor organization of the hawkers meant, according to a European officer of the City Council, that African Councillors were beginning to think that the various hawking groups were "generally one-man operations, fronting as important associations of some sort to gain concessions." Consequently, the representatives of hawkers occasionally complained of being treated with disrespect or ignored by City Hall.

Despite their inadequate organization, the hawkers did not hesitate to present their grievances in quite extravagant ways. For example, in 1964 the Acting Secretary of the Nairobi Hawkers' and Traders' Association threatened to stage a sit-down demonstration at the office of the Commissioner of Police where they would stay and expect the Government to feed them until all members of their association got their hawking licenses.[69] The next year, the chairman of the Kenya Street Traders' Society announced that each member of his association would take his family to the home of the councillor in his ward for feeding, school fees, tax and housing unless the Council changed its policy with regard to open-air markets.[70] "We wished to be told by the Council," he exclaimed, "whether small traders are banned in a country where independence has been gained."

These forms of protest were similar to those used by relatively unsophisticated people lacking powerful political leverage in other parts of the world. Their relative effectiveness in Nairobi may relate to the fact that most City Council members here, unlike cities in North America or Western Europe, lived with the poor and could therefore not easily escape the importunity of the hawkers. There was also the possibility of violence. "On several occasions in the past, city inspectors who have attempted to arrest hawkers and street traders have been beaten and stoned," wrote Michael Harris in the *Sunday Nation* of October 13, 1963. "The minute officialdom attempts to carry out its responsibilities, the word spreads like wildfire and soon the unfortunate inspector is faced with a crowd of several hundred."[71]

Like politicians everywhere, the Nairobi City Council members reacted to the conflicting pressures and perplexing circumstances with inconsistency in their speeches and actions. This inconsistency

exasperated the officers of the City Council who were convinced
that a "strong arm approach" was needed. "It is essential that once
the people in authority take a decision of policy, that decision is
supported and pursued to its ultimate end," wrote one of the African officers in his report to the Social Services and Housing Committee, adding: "There is nothing worse to the public than to appear undetermined, changing and even irresolute, as those who do
not agree with such a policy mainly paralyse the actions of those
who make the policy and those who are required to execute such
a policy."[72] This officer elaborated in a way that is worth quoting
at length:

> On the question of hawkers in general, one sees a lot of this
> irresolution and lack of determination. If I may, I would hasten
> to add that this is not an accusation levelled against councillors
> alone, but the officers too are at times at fault. A good instance
> of this is the question of the selling of meat in the Open-Air
> Market where a matter which appeared relatively simple took
> over a year to decide, with endless references back in the council
> as well as waste of valuable time in discussion. There has also
> been other examples where the Council has resolved to clear hawk-
> ers in one or other parts of the City, only to find that the matter
> is discussed backwards and forwards without any decision made
> over a period of up to six months or more. In the meantime, the
> problem increases as those charged with the execution of policy
> are not able to take firm action. Whenever they attempt to do so
> they come under criticism. The normal question is: "When did
> we approve this action and where is the Minute?" If, on the other
> hand, no action is taken, there is constant criticism as soon as the
> problem starts getting out of hand. For example, when discussions
> started over the tea sellers in Mincing-Lane Market, there were
> only three or four hawkers then. Now there are over ten and the
> problem continues to grow.

The case of the hawkers illustrates the weakness of the Nairobi
City Council, despite the support and discipline of a government-
supported national party. To eliminate illegal hawking required
the sort of highly efficient and determined administration as had
existed during the 1950's but which the post-colonial regime had

yet to develop. The administration was, of course, undermined by the disunity and uncertainty of political leaders who had to contend with very difficult socio-economic conditions.

The illegal hawkers were saved by the fact that they performed a useful service. The situation was such that hawking was the cheapest and easiest way for Africans to sell and buy what they needed. On the other hand, some Africans were gaining more sophisticated commercial skills and abilities, and they hoped to challenge the commercial domination of Asians and Europeans in Kenya. These people were opposed to hawking, but, important as they were politically, they could not alter the situation which gave rise to hawking.

"Until unemployment is considerably reduced," an African officer of the City Council acknowledged, "we will only be able to keep the worst aspects of hawking under control, but we can't eliminate them by any means." It was merely hoped that the City Council would get a certain grudging respect from the hawkers, following the periodic display of overt power. However, while the hawkers themselves were too poorly organized to offer constructive advice to the Council, they were also too poorly organized to cooperate with the decisions that were reached. In any case, all indications were that disciplinary action taken against the hawkers would continue to be of a cautious, piecemeal nature, ever conscious of their potential for troublemaking.

## The Politics of the Informal Sector

The 1972 International Labor Organization study of Kenya referred to in the previous chapter necessitates a reassessment of the role of hawkers in an underdeveloped country.[73] It is argued by I.L.O. that the gap between the growth of population (3.3 per cent annually) and wage-earning employment (1.9 per cent between 1964 and 1967) makes growing unemployment in Kenya inevitable, particularly in the major towns where the African population expanded during the 1960's at over ten per cent a year. To try to stem urban migration or to expel non-wage earners from the towns was not only futile but also counter-productive. Likewise, the government could never provide enough jobs for the unemployed, however hard it tried, just as it could not provide enough housing. Therefore, instead of jobs, the government should be primarily concerned with increasing employment opportunity.

The self-employed in Nairobi, according to the I.L.O., earned about $240 annually (£90) and provided real services for the low-income segment of the population — selling, exchanging, repairing, transporting, and even making or assembling much of what was needed by those unable to afford the amenities enjoyed by the elite. Thus, to view the self-employed as constituting nothing more than a health, fire, or political hazard was a mistake. Since nearly a third of the African urban population were working in this "informal sector," to uproot them was impossible. At the same time, the scarcity of good agricultural land in Kenya (less than ten per cent of the land area) made the alternative of agricultural employment also impractical. Yet, the government continued to treat the informal sector with contempt, thereby hurting the poor who patronized this sector, increasing unemployment, diminishing national output, and frustrating those anxious to succeed in the urban environment. "The informal sector, particularly in Nairobi but to varying degrees in all areas, has been operating under extremely debilitating restrictions as a consequence of a pejorative view of its nature. Thus there exists an imminent danger that this view could become a self-fulfilling prophecy."[74]

In addition to increasing unemployment and decreasing income, the harassment of the informal sector had other dysfunctional consequences. It caused the country to rely heavily on large, sophisticated, foreign-owned or managed firms, using capital-intensive technology and foreign acquired or expatriate skills, necessitating protected markets and the loss of foreign exchange. The informal sector, on the other hand, operating on a small scale with inexpensive and labor-intensive technology and with skills acquired outside the formal school system, could manage with a minimum of foreign exchange and without the regulations (tariffs, quotas, and trade licenses) that undermined competition and raised prices. "In 1967 there were scarcely 200 African businesses in Kenya larger than a country store or a craftsman's workshop, and even these few were mostly still small affairs."[75] Inasmuch as Africans generally lacked the skills, education, contacts, capital, and experience to compete with the well-established firms, they would have to remain within the informal sector. However, with the proper encouragement (including investments, help in developing labor-intensive techniques, purchasing arrangements, and marketing facilities), links could be established between the formal and informal sectors facilitating the transfer of income and skills. Otherwise, the Africanization of businesses would be retarded and resources would continue to be spent for the benefit of the affluent rather than for the majority of the population.

Among the suggestions made by the I.L.O. was a major reform of existing trade and commercial licensing practices, removing unnecessary licenses, substituting health and safety inspection for licensing, and issuing licenses to any applicant able to pay the license fee. Such a reform would eliminate the existing black-market in licenses of all types, particularly in transport, while lowering the prices that stemmed from the monopolistic profits of license-holders. For example, public transportation in Nairobi could have been facilitated by the small African owner-operators of the estimated 400 "pirate taxis" (those without licenses) in 1971, had they been given the same police protection, hire-purchase terms, and fuel-tax concessions as those sanctioned by officialdom.

In 1971 the City Council derived only about one per cent of its revenue from licenses for hawking, trading, and other commercial purposes in Nairobi. At the same time, police action against unlicensed businessmen was very costly. Since only eight of the thirty-five types of licenses listed in the hawkers and street-traders regulations for Nairobi could be defined as involving potential health hazards, this expensive and largely futile police operation was unnecessary. The I.L.O.'s suggested reform would decrease this expense while increasing the revenue required to adequately impose health regulations upon those within the informal sector (estimated to be 25 per cent) handling food. Hawkers then could generally be provided the security needed to maximize employment and income.

Whatever the merit of the I.L.O.'s analysis, it was unlikely to have much effect on the City Council's policies. The Council took no official notice of the I.L.O. report (which was published in the fall of 1972 but which was available to the leading politicians and administrators before then). The Council's 1972 proposals were along the lines that had proved unsuccessful in the past: (1) to construct permanent stalls for renting to street traders; (2) to provide plots for small industries (furniture making, bicycle repairing, tailoring, fabrication of metal goods, etc.); (3) to eliminate licenses to businessmen who did not operate from established Council stalls or plots; and (4) to rid the City of all unlicensed entrepreneurs.[76]

At the same time as the Council attempted to eliminate unlicensed businessmen, it proposed to raise the rents for market stalls and business premises by as much as 100 per cent in some cases.[77] "Traders have for some time been charged uneconomic rent," it argued, and unless rents were raised, a deficit of more than £20,000 could be expected in 1973. However justified, such an increase was particularly disturbing for those having difficulty paying rent in markets where business had declined because of the departure of Europeans and Asians, parking problems, the inadequacy of water and other facilities to maintain efficient and hygienic operations, the lack of room for the handling of goods and the movement of pedestrians, the need in some cases for larger stalls or more assistants than allowed, and the insufficiency of police protection. The City Council's insistence that all businessmen work within approved market stalls or plots was unrealistic inasmuch as it failed to take into account the nature of the informal sector. Those within this sector often need places of business near their residences and customers, necessitating movable rather than fixed locations. Moreover, the City Council avoided recognizing the expense and difficulty of providing sufficient land for small industries and enough well-constructed and properly serviced stalls for traders. In any case, it tended to favor the politically influential rather than the more needy or deserving.

The City Council's highly publicized 1972 clash with the open-air barbers might have been avoided, had it taken cognizance of the I.L.O. report. In 1971 the Council considered the possibility of erecting barbers' kiosks in suitable areas away from eating stalls, but never did so. Nevertheless, it went ahead in February 1972 to enforce the by-laws prohibiting open-air hair cutting, arresting a number of barbers. The barbers then formed an association (the Outdoor Barbers' Union), claiming a membership of 350, and approached Mr. Maina Wanjigi, an Assistant Minister of Agriculture, known to be sympathetic to hawkers and squatters. Mr. Wanjigi arranged a meeting of the barbers with President Kenyatta at his Gatundu home, from which a letter was supposedly written to the Council allowing the barbers to carry on their occupation, pending an investigation of their licenses applications and the building of kiosks for them. Unfortunately for the barbers, the magistrate hearing their case accepted Mayor Kenyatta's statement in court, denying that the Council had received instructions from either the Government or President Kenyatta to suspend any of the City Council's by-laws.[78]

Despite this judgment against them, the barbers continued their occupation, having no alternative. One of the barbers was quoted as saying:

> We are law-abiding citizens. All we want is for the City Council to allow us to build our own kiosks at a given place where we can carry out our business and pay the hawking licenses, which of course should be reasonable. This would end our problem with the City Council and we could live a happy and satisfied life.[79]

Whatever the Council eventually decided to do about the open-air barbers, it would have to act quickly. Otherwise, as Joe Kadhi, a columnist for the *Sunday Nation,* pointed out, the barbers would be forced either to break the law or "swell the number of unemployed and further complicate the national problem of joblessness."[80] Considering the Council's performance on behalf of the hawkers and squatters generally, the barbers could not be very hopeful.

The plight of Nairobi's outdoor barbers illustrates the limitations of the "pluralist model" for understanding the City Council's decision-making. The assumptions of the pluralist model include:

(1) that there are numerous groups attempting to influence government; (2) that the political marketplace is not characterized either by monopoly or by oligopoly — i.e., no group or combination of groups is so powerful as to exclude others from exercising power; and (3) that the government respects and encourages group conflict — i.e., that it does not prevent the political activity of groups or neutralize their political influence.[81] Most American political scientists accept and utilize the pluralist model in explaining American urban politics because of the diversity and complexity of the American elite, the common culture of Americans, the necessity and difficulty of winning elections, the meaningfulness of constitutional limitations, and the independence and assertiveness of the press. The nature of American culture, economy, and politics has stimulated the development of a great many powerful interest groups with sufficient financial, legal, and communication resources to make their influence felt.

Even in America, however, there are those who are disadvantaged politically within the prevailing liberal pluralistic system, just as there are those who are disadvantaged economically within the existing free enterprise system.[82] While the wealthy may not themselves occupy official positions, they can to a large extent determine the content and administration of policies, insofar as the community leaders are dependent upon them for jobs, loans, taxes, campaign contributions, favorable publicity, and the financial support of public programs and charities. The poor, on the other hand, have great difficulty in making their influence felt, being usually less educated, less informed, and less active in political or organizational work and having limited contacts with businessmen, journalists, publishers, lawyers, officials, and politicians. While the poor are generally politically handicapped, certain American minorties suffering from current or previous racial or ethnic discrimination (i.e., the Blacks, Puerto Ricans, Chicanos, and Indians) are particularly so, having been denied access to schools, jobs, craft union membership, social and professional organizations, business opportunities, and legal and communication resources available to other groups.

In Kenya, as has been indicated, the pluralist model is far less meaningful than in the United States. The existing African associations lack the leadership, organization, and funds to influence the government and to force administrators to provide better services.[83] While elections are not meaningless in Nairobi, they are not taken seriously enough for existing groups to hold accountable those in power. Likewise, although groups may have more leeway in Kenya than in many African countries to utilize the press and to take advantage of intra-governmental divisions, they cannot legally or politically challenge or require the elite to take their interests into account.

The affluent minority in Kenya has always exercised far more influence over decision-making than the impoverished majority. Prior to independence, governmental policies were largely determined by and beneficial to the European elite. The domination of an elite was supposed to end with the coming to power of an African government. The public is told, Marc Ross writes, that colonial vestiges are being removed from Kenya, "but what they are not told is that the expatriate elite is now being replaced by an African bourgeoisie virtually as uninterested in abolishing economic inequalities as the previous regime."[84] Consequently, the I.L.O. suggested parallels with Latin American experience, "in which inequality becomes deeply locked into the structure of the country and only the most drastic remedies can change the situation."[85] This makes it very unlikely that the government will significantly help the informal sector at the expense of Africans who increasingly benefit from the existing formal sector.

Insofar as groups are denied political opportunity to influence governmental decisions, they are likely in various ways to weaken or undermine the legitimacy of the political system. Inelasticity of control thereby results. In other words, as the control exercised by the public over the government becomes inelastic, the control of the government over the public becomes similarly inelastic. "It is disappointing to record the almost total indifference of most of the public to the problem of illegal hawking and shanties," Nairobi's Medical Officer of Health noted in his 1969 *Annual Report*. However, the real truth was that so long as the informal sector is insufficiently taken into account in decision-making, the Nairobi City Council cannot expect much cooperation from the public.

Kenya, after all, must be regarded, to use Gunnar Myrdal's phrase, as a "soft state"— one in which public obligations are not only minimal but also inadequately enforced.[86] The people are obviously aware of the weaknesses of the government, and they know how to take advantage of them. "The enforcement of the by-laws on trade premises was handicapped by the outcry from the general public when prosecutions and heavy fines are imposed by the City Council Magistrate," wrote S. J. Getonga, the City Council's Acting Town Clerk in his 1970 *Annual Report,* noting that this outcry caused the City Council to postpone for a period of four months action against butchers who illegally roasted meat in their butcheries. So far, the informal sector has managed to ignore or escape many of the policies directed against it. But the greater the government's effort to enforce these policies, the more likely the public is to turn to demonstrations, strikes, disruptions of administration, and even violence. Such actions, however, hardly facilitate solutions to the basic urban problems confronting the Nairobi City Council.

## NOTES

1. (London: Andre Deutsch Ltd., 1963), pp. 88-89.
2. *East African Standard* (referred to hereafter by the initials E.A.S.), November 30, 1963.
3. E.A.S., June 24, 1966.
4. "Parliament in a Tutelary Democracy...," *The Journal of Politics,* Vol. XXXI, No. 1 (February, 1969), p. 1031. Also cf. C. J. Gertzel, "The Constitutional Position of the Opposition in Kenya: Appeal for Efficiency," *East Africa Journal,* Vol. IV, No. 6 (October, 1967), pp. 9-11 and Yash P. Ghai, "The Government and the Constitution in Kenya Politics," *East Africa Journal,* Vol. IV, No. 8 (December, 1967), pp. 9-14.
5. Cf. Henry Bienen, "Kenya and Uganda: When Does Dissent Become Sedition," *Africa Report,* March/April, 1969, pp. 10-14.

6. Cf. "Kenya Refuses to Free 8 Opposition Leaders," *The New York Times,* Sunday, October 9, 1966.

7. Laurence Fellows, "Kenya Votes Ban on Odinga Allies," *New York Times,* April 29, 1966.

8. "Charisma and Politics in Kenya," *East Africa Journal,* Vol. V, No. 2 (February, 1968), p. 16.

9. E.A.S., June 15, 1964.

10. *Not Yet Uhuru* (London: Heinemann, 1967), pp. 271-72.

11. E.A.S., January 4, 1966.

12. "Standing on the Corner with Jack Ensoll," October 4, 1963.

13. E.A.S., October 1, 1963.

14. E.A.S., June 1, 1964.

15. E.A.S., November 17, 1964.

16. E.A.S., February 8, 1968.

17. E.A.S., June 24, 1966.

18. Cf. Marc Howard Ross, "Class and Ethnic Bases of Political Mobilization in African Cities," American Political Science Association, 1972 Annual Meeting, pp. 23-24.

19. E.A.S., February 9, 1966.

20. Thus of the 41 Council members in October, 1963, there were 17 Kikuyus, 10 Asians, 6 Luos, 3 Europeans, 3 Luyias, and 2 Kambas.

21. Other Councillors also mentioned having to pay as much as £100 ($280) to people in their wards, usually Youth Wingers, to campaign for them. The payment was generally in the form of beer and food.

22. *Memorandum of Evidence to the Local Government Commission of Inquiry* (Nairobi: City Hall, May, 1966), p. 3.

23. *Sessional Paper No. 12 of 1967,* pp. 3-4.

24. E.A.S., February 5, 1965. Note the warning here given by Sammy Maina, KANU Nairobi Branch Organising Secretary.

25. E.A.S., April 6, 1967.

26. Cf. Lawrence Fellows, "Kenyans Display Growth of Democratic Spirit," *New York Times,* July 26, 1968.

27. E.A.S., June 2, 1969.

28. E.A.S., December 1, 1964.

29. E.A.S., January 5, 1965.

30. *The Sunday Post,* July 3, 1966.

31. *Ibid.*

32. E.A.S., August 2, 1968.

33. E.A.S., August 9, 1968.

34. E.A.S., July 17, 1970.

35. E.A.S., December 16, 1970.

36. E.A.S., August 23, 1967.

37. Cf. statement of Coun. Yusuf Ali in the Council monthly meeting, *Daily Nation,* April 6, 1966.

38. (Nairobi: City Hall, March, 1966), p. 1.

39. E.A.S., February 3, 1968.

40. Cf. Mary Parker, *Political and Social Aspects of the Development of Municipal Government in Kenya with Special Reference to Nairobi* (London: Colonial Office, 1948?), p. 19.

41. *Annual Report of the African Affairs Department,* 1953, p. 6.

42. Statement of the Town Clerk, E.A.S., April 16, 1954.

43. E.A.S., October 8, 1958.

44. E.A.S., November 1, 1958.

45. E.A.S., June 28, 1951.

46. E.A.S., March 6, August 14, October 8, 15, and 22, 1958.

47. E.A.S., August 29, 1960.

48. *Minutes,* General Purposes Committee, Vol. XXX, No. 2 (August, 1962), pp. 158-59.

49. E.A.S., February 20, 1961.

50. E.A.S., August 1, 2, 1962.

51. *"Mr. President, Distinguished Guests . . .,"* Selected Speeches, 1962-63 by Ald. Charles W. Rubia, Mayor of Nairobi (Nairobi, Kenya: City Hall, 1963). Speech of November 23, 1962, p. 58.

52. E.A.S., September 17, 1962.

53. Cf. E.A.S., November 5, 1963; Michael Harris, "The Hawking Problem," *Sunday Nation,* October 13, 1963.

54. E.A.S., October 18, 1963.

55. E.A.S., November 13, 1963.

56. E.A.S., December 19, 1963.

57. *Minutes,* Vol. XXXI, No. 6 (December, 1963), pp. 926-27.

58. *Minutes,* Vol. XXXI, No. 8 (February, 1964), pp. 1282-84.

59. E.A.S., January 13, 1964.

60. From the Nairobi Hawkers' and Traders' Association, February 27, 1964.

61. *Minutes,* Vol. XXXI, No. 11 (May, 1964), pp. 1847-48.

62. E.A.S., May 22, 1964; *Minutes,* Vol. XXXI, No. 9 (March, 1964), p. 1464.

63. Quoted, Karim Hudani, "Hawking: What is the Solution?" *Daily Nation,* April 11, 1967.

64. *Ibid.*

65. *Minutes,* May, 1967, p. 1976; E.A.S., August 24, 1966.

66. Cf. Report of Mr. J. P. Mbogua, E.A.S., July 1, 1969.

67. *Minutes,* April, 1967, p. 1766.

68. Cf. *Minutes,* Vol. XXIX, No. 11 (May, 1962), pp. 1390-91.

69. *Sunday Nation,* January 12, 1964.

70. E.A.S., April 28, 1965.

71. Harris, *op. cit.*

72. *Item No. 5* (a), Social Services and Housing Committee, February 7, 1966, pp. 10-11.

73. *Employment, Incomes and Equality: A Strategy for Increasing Productive Employment in Kenya* (Geneva: I.L.O., 1972), pp. 5-29, 90-101, 209-210, 224-232, 493.

74. *Ibid.,* pp. 5-6.

75. Peter Marris and Anthony Somerset, *African Businessmen: A Study of Entrepreneurship and Development in Kenya* (Nairobi: East African Publishing House, 1971), p. 1.

76. City Council of Nairobi, *Minutes of Proceedings,* Vol. XXXIX, No. 11 (June, 1972), p. 2393; E.A.S., March 10, 1972.

77. E.A.S., February 8, 1973.

78. *Daily Nation,* November 20, 1972.

79. *The Sunday Post,* November 26, 1972.

80. November 26, 1972.

81. Cf. Nelson W. Polsby, *Community Power & Political Theory* (New Haven: Yale U. Press, 1963); Murray S. Stedman, Jr., *Urban Politics* (Cambridge: Winston Publishers, 1972), pp. 84-95.

82. Cf. Edward C. Hayes, *Power Structure and Urban Policy* (New York: McGraw-Hill, 1972).

83. Cf. Robert H. Jackson, "Administration and Development in Kenya: A Review of Problems Outstanding," in Goran Hyden, Robert Jackson and John Okumu, eds., *Development Administration: The Kenyan Experience* (Nairobi: Oxford University Press, 1970), pp. 332-33.

84. *Op. cit.,* p. 32.

85. *Op. cit.,* p. 101.

86. *Asian Drama,* Vol. I (New York: Pantheon, 1968), p. 66.

# 9 THE STRUGGLE FOR PROGRESS

*Introduction*

In November, 1972, reports were issued by the Kenya National Assembly's Public Accounts Committee and by the Controller and Auditor-General indicating that almost all the county and municipal councils were guilty of "deplorable mismanagement."[1] Receipt books, store ledgers, inventories, financial documents and records were all poorly kept; procedures for financial control and internal supervision were inadequate; and public funds were being improperly spent. Corruption was evident in all aspects of local administration, including the handling of tenders, the payment of allowances and salaries, the operation of tenant-purchase schemes, the allocation of plots and houses, and the hiring of staff. "Councillors in our various local governments should all resign and give way to more energetic people who are prepared to run various local governments in a satisfactory manner," insisted Joe Kadhi, the *Sunday Nation* columnist.[2]

In its defence, the Association of Local Government Authorities in Kenya (A.L.G.A.K.) pointed out "the grave situation of lack of a sound financial base in the local authorities, particularly county councils, emanating from lack of a clear policy on the financing of local development."[3] Inasmuch as local authorities shared the same administrative problems as did the Central Government, they resented the harsh criticism by those in the Central Government. After all, the Ministries had overspent more than £2,600,000 during the 1970-71 financial year, according to a 1972 report of the Controller and Auditor-General. The Ndegwa Commission Report (1971), which is one of the best official studies of African public administration during the post-colonial period, enumerates all the shortcomings discussed in the previous chapters:

> little or no delegation of operating responsibility from the senior officers down to their juniors; consequent overburdening of these senior officers with minor, routine work decisions at the expense of their concentrating on major matters of policy and programmes; misunderstanding by some junior officials of their job purpose and, more important, of their role in the organization especially in relation to their fellow officials; over-centralization of authority in Nairobi; poor communication, both within the Ministries and Departments themselves and between these separate organizations; consequent lack of programme co-ordination, both at headquarters and in the field; poor employee-management relations, reflecting misunderstanding, fear and frustrations on the part of the junior civil servants and an apparent lack of concern for their problems by their seniors; weak and irregular discipline by management that engenders lack of commitment by the staff to meeting programme objectives within set time targets; and, overall, an operating situation that under-utilizes the human resources now in the Civil Service.[4]

Until these shortcomings can be overcome, the Ndegwa Commission report concludes, the Kenyan bureaucracy cannot be expected either to handle the routine administration of public business or to meet the new challenges of change, growth, and development. The question, of course, remains, how might this be done?

Within the City Council, there has been considerable interest in structural reforms — the reorganization of personnel or procedure in such a way as to increase efficiency. Following the job evaluation exercise carried out by Inbucon International Ltd. in 1972, Mr. J. P. Mbogua, the Town Clerk, advocated incorporating all the sections currently involved in personnel problems within a manpower planning unit. This unit was to be concerned with all aspects of personnel management, from setting guidelines for controlling the growth of the establishment to determining salary increments. However, since this manpower planning unit would have brought a shift of authority to the Town Clerk's Department, within which the Establishment Section was located, the other department heads resisted its creation, even after it had been agreed to in principle by the City Council. Likewise, they opposed the suggestion that the Town Planning Section of the City Engineer's Department be shifted to the Town Clerk's Department — a move that was intended to bring more forcefully to the attention of Councillors and officers the need for careful and comprehensive planning.[5] By the end of 1972, the Town Clerk still complained that the proper procedures for filling vacancies were not being followed and that the Council had not evolved a real training policy. "The present training structure lacked co-ordination and consequently there was duplication or fragmentation of effort."[6]

Following the 1972 report of the Controller and Auditor-General on County Councils and Municipal Councils, the Town Clerk was particularly concerned about the need to adhere strictly to the tender procedures laid down by the Local Authorities Regulations of 1963.[7] As matters stood at present, he pointed out, "officers and councillors were running the risk of being surcharged." He therefore insisted that no tenders would henceforth be submitted to any standing committee unless the chief auditor and chief attorney in charge of conveyancing indicated their satisfaction that legal requirements and financial regulations had been met.

What is likely to happen, regardless of the administrative reforms undertaken by the Nairobi City Council, is an increasing effort to shift power to the Central Government. The Ndegwa Commission report made a number of proposals which would have this effect.[8] It reiterated the recommendation of the 1966 Local Government Commission of Inquiry and the 1967 Sessional Paper No. 12 that a Local Government Service Commission be established which would deal with the appointment, promotion, and discipline of all officers earning over £700 a year. Even more significant was the proposal that future mayors and chairmen and their deputies be selected by the Minister of Local Government from a panel of names submitted by the elected councillors meeting under the supervision of the District Commissioner.

## Evaluating the Reform Proposals

The import of the elasticity of control analysis that has been presented is to cast doubt on solutions envisaging structural changes to increase or decrease control over local authorities. First, such solutions mistake the proper question, which is not "Should there be more centralization or decentralization?" but rather: "How can there be more centralization as well as decentralization at the same time?" It is not a contradiction to suggest that countries need both strong central and strong provincial governments, notes W. Arthur Lewis, "since governmental functions are now so numerous that there is plenty of room for both."[9] Moreover, where strong central government controls do not exist, local authorities invariably have very restricted functions.[10] In other words, the effectiveness of central governments depends upon the vitality of local governments, and vice-versa.

Second, these solutions assume that more or less centralization can be arranged simply by a shift of authority. Any transfer of authority, however, to be meaningful, must be legitimate. It must therefore be socially as well as legally sanctioned. Otherwise, it is likely to be ignored. The process of shifting authority necessitates informal as well as formal arrangements, involving many aspects of the political system.

Third, structural changes affecting the inter-governmental balance-of-power take for granted that central or local authorities could satisfactorily utilize any additional authority bestowed upon them. In the absence of considerable preparation, this assumption is dubious in most cases. Much trouble has been created in underdeveloped areas by attempts to give local authorities more responsibility than they can handle or by disregarding the willingness of local people to accept and discharge responsibility. Similarly, central governments have met with failure when they have tried to undertake measures beyond their capacity, because resources as well as authority must be commensurate with responsibility. In any case, the question so often asked as to the "proper role" of local authorities is meaningless without regard for the particular circumstances involved.

In regard to Kenya, there has been considerable doubt as to the capacity of the Ministry of Local Government to utilize effectively any additional authority given to it over the City Council. The Ndegwa Commission itself pointed out "that the Ministry of Local Government is understaffed at the professional level and has not been able to exercise much supervision in the field over the work of local authorities."[11] Because it was constantly falling behind in the auditing of local accounts, it had to pass much of this function on to the Controller and Auditor-General. The Nairobi Development Committee, which was supposed to coordinate the policies and activities of the Central Government and the City Council in implementing the National Development Plan, became as moribund as the earlier Nairobi Standing Committee of the Senate because the Local Government Ministry's Permanent Secretary did not have time to be bothered with it. Likewise, the failure of the Public Service Commission to eliminate ethnic and other non-professional considerations from affecting personnel administration within the Civil Service made it unlikely that the proposed Local Government Service Commission would be any more successful.

The achievement of elasticity of control requires the creation of ways to delegate authority and, at the same time, to supervise and guide those to whom this authority has been delegated. Both processes must go on simultaneously. "The methods of supervision and control," to quote the 1962 United Nations' report on decentralization prepared by the Technical Assistance Program, "must be consistent with the degree of authority delegated."[12] Only those capable of effectively and responsibly handling authority should be given authority. To be "responsible," the exercise of authority must be "responsive" to the source of this authority. Ultimately, this involves an educational process — the preparation of subordinates for the undertaking of an increasing amount of responsibility based upon norms of behavior that are thoroughly instilled. At the same time, the corrective instrumentalities (those agencies or devices by which criticism can be made and reform take place) must be invigorated.

What is here suggested would appear to be good administration at any level and of all types. Most successful managers and executives recognize the importance of training their staffs to undertake an increasing amount of the requisite work-load and decision-making, and also of improving their ability to oversee and check what goes on. American Telephone and Telegraph, for example, is thought to be successful because it operates on the principle of pushing down from the top as much responsibility as possible and then judging and rewarding subordinates on their ability to handle it.[13]

What is essential for elasticity of control is the selective granting or withholding of authority on the basis of trustworthiness. In its 1962 decentralization report previously quoted, the U. N. Technical Assistance Program emphasized that "local authorities differ in their capabilities and require different treatment by the central government."[14] How this might be done is suggested by Henry Maddick:

> The relationship between central government and local government will change as each matures. . . . If this developing relationship is accepted, then guidance of the local authority should be inversely proportional to its maturity. The detailed assistance of the first stage gives way to the more general help of the second and finally to the advice and consultation of the third — subject to the check on the legality of expenditure and the abuse of power.[15]

Unfortunately, few governments have attempted this sort of arrangement because it requires just the sort of administrative ingenuity and flexibility that is especially rare in underdeveloped countries where they are most needed. Instead, local authorities or subordinate units of government are all treated much the same way, regardless of their possibly varying capabilities. However, where selective decentralization has been tried, the results have been promising. This is reported to have been the case in Western Nigeria where the government granted "financial autonomy" to those councils which earned it by a good financial record over a period of years.[16] This meant that a local authority, after several years of good audit reports, was freed from having to seek the Ministry of Local Government's approval of its budget and having to submit to quarterly inspection. At the same time, it continued to be subject to annual audit review.

The achievement of elasticity of control is not to be expected easily or quickly, as the history of any Western nation indicates. The constant effort of French or Frankish monarchs during the Middle Ages to centralize their regimes by means of regular inspectors or agents, only to have the whole system eroded and feudalism reinforced, has been studied by Fesler, who concludes: "In this light the feudal system was a field administration system twisted awry."[17] In other premodern societies, according to S. N. Eisenstadt, the practice was for the members of the bureaucracy, once their positions were secure, to evolve their own traditions and values and to maximize their autonomy.[18]

Regarding American cities, the assertion of Edward C. Banfield and James Q. Wilson may be true "that machines, bosses, and boodlers are almost everywhere things of the past, that the mayors of the larger cities are apparently all honest and reasonable, and that the day-to-day management of city services is generally in the hands of professionals who are chosen for merit."[19] But this is a relatively recent development. During much of the nineteenth century, according to Scott Greer, "the big, wicked city was deemed incapable of governing itself. State legislatures responded with 'ripper legislation' aimed at destroying the powers of the city."[20] However, this sort of reaction seldom did much good; and the public, in frustration, turned to movements for direct legislation and for municipal home rule.[21] At the same time, constitutional restraints were imposed on the state legislatures; but by reducing the capacity of the state legislatures to coordinate independently elected administrative officers and legally autonomous boards and commissions, the reform of local government was made even more difficult.[22]

In Great Britain, as in the United States, the reform of local government has been a long, tiresome process. During the eighteenth and nineteenth centuries, local government in Great Britain was described by Sidney and Beatrice Webb, as "an orgy of corruption."[23] During much of this period, Gerald Caiden points out, autonomous local authorities were so firmly entrenched and the upper classes so apathetic that the public bureaucracy rarely functioned beyond London.[24] Under these circumstances, efforts at reform were persistently foiled.

Caiden, in summarizing the evolution of administrative reform in Europe following the French Revolution, notes the importance of population growth, the development of urbanization, the spread of education, the improvement of communication and transportation facilities, the expansion of trade and commerce, and the declining power of monarchs and religious authorities.[25] All these changes increased the functions of the state, thereby facilitating as well as necessitating the enhancement of administrative services. Consequently, public law was developed, to which the bureaucracy was subjected, with clear chains of command and accountability, supported by improved financial and judicial controls. What occurred in Great Britain, write Ronald Wraith and Edgar Simpkins, in explaining the gradual decline of corruption, was the spread of education to enlighten public opinion regarding malpractices, the growth of commerce and industry to encourage a middle class opposed to corruption, the rise of professional groups anxious to raise their status, and the improvement of inspection, auditing, and other supervisory procedures.[26]

## Conclusion

Insofar as leaders appreciate the desirability and implications of elasticity of control, it is to be hoped that they will take whatever opportunities that arise, however small, to implement it. Indeed, short strides rather than long leaps may be even preferable. For this purpose, they must attempt, first of all, to prepare subordinate units to undertake increasing responsibility; secondly, to delegate authority to those that are able and willing to accept additional responsibility; thirdly, to ensure that those with authority have the financial and administrative resources to properly exercise this authority; and, finally, to gain cooperation through ways that are influential or persuasive rather than coercive or demoralizing.

Ultimately, these improvements will depend upon societal reform: the reduction of corruption, primordial discrimination, ignorance, insecurity, and ideological rigidity. But dynamic leaders could take advantage of the advanced communication facilities now available to alter popular attitudes and practices more rapidly than the Western nations were able to do in modernizing their administrations. Otherwise, they are unlikely to escape stagnation and neocolonialism.

This leads us to conclude that ultimately the future of the Nairobi City Council depends on the economic and political health of Kenya as a whole. One can be optimistic or pessimistic, depending on how one balances the existing functional and dysfunctional developments: the increasing output of the school system, the strength of the economy, and the relative stability of the government; as against rising socio-economic inequality among Africans, continued inter-ethnic and inter-racial tension, and growing political and administrative corruption.

While education is expanding, there are still too few reaching the higher levels of qualification required by the country. At the same time, while the growth of the economy continues at a rate of more than six per cent a year in real terms (with the level of foreign exchange reserve holdings being bolstered by tourism), this may be undermined by a population expansion estimated to be 3.3 per cent annually. So long as per-capita rural income remains less than ten per cent that of urban income, the continued influx into Nairobi will depress the average earnings per head here and generally exacerbate urban problems. Even if the rate of employment can be expanded by more than four per cent per annum over thirty years, at least one-fourth of Nairobi's estimated labor force of over one million by the end of the century will be unlikely to find wage-earning jobs of any kind.[27] These problems could certainly endanger the existing political stability, already threatened by the attempted coups and presidential assassinations that have been reported.

In spite of all the difficulties mentioned, the controls affecting the governing of Nairobi could become more elastic. Indeed, Dr. Kiano promised in 1971 to give more responsibility and status to any municipality which showed by its record significant progress in financial management and in promoting the welfare of *wananchi.*[28] However, the embarrassing revelations of the 1972 Auditor-General's report necessitated, according to Dr. Kiano, an intense investigation, district by district, "to find out where the loopholes were and to make sure that there would not be a repetition of inefficiency, poor financial adminisration or any other form of misuse of public funds."[29] Because of favoritism in plot allocations, the Government decided to appoint Plot Allocation Committees under District Commissioners. Although the Local Government Service Commission Bill (taking away from local councils most of their power in personnel administration) had been rejected by the National Assembly, Dr. Kiano indicated that it would be reintroduced unless local staff committees could rid themselves of political and ethnic considerations.

Late in 1972 the Nairobi City Council was informed that it might lose £1,700,000 in 1973 from Graduated Personal Tax collections because of retentions by the Central Government and transmissions to other local authorities.[30] This, of course, seriously undermined the City Council's financial programs. However, its financial difficulties were supposed to be considered by a Nairobi development planning committee, composed of M.P.'s from the Nairobi area, four Permanent Secretaries, and top officers from the City Council, to be formed in 1973 to facilitate exchanges of views on all matters affecting the council and the Central Government.[31] Yet, the future of the City Council depends not on this or any other committee but on developing harmony among the races and tribes, a professional approach to administrative problems, and an enlightened public opinion. Hopefully, the communication of criticism necessary for the enactment of reform will not be stifled by political fears. The provisions for this need not be the same as those currently used in the Western democracies, but they must operate in such a way that progress, however defined, can take place.

## NOTES

1. *East African Standard* (E.A.S.), 1972; Joe Kadhi's commentary in the *Sunday Nation,* November 19, 1972.
2. *Ibid.*
3. E.A.S. editorial, December 8, 1972.
4. D. N. Ndegwa, Chairman, Report of the Commission of Inquiry (Nairobi: Government Printer, 1971), p. 85.
5. Frederick T. Temple, "Planning and Budgetting for Urban Growth in Nairobi," Nairobi Urban Studies Group, May, 1972, p. 26.
6. E.A.S., December 5, 1972.
7. E.A.S., February 10, 1973.
8. *Op. cit.,* pp. 226-28.
9. *Politics in West Africa* (Toronto and New York: Oxford U. Press, 1965), p. 55.
10. Cf. United Nations Technical Assistance Program, *Decentralization for National and Local Development,* ST/TAO/M19 (New York: United Nations Publication, 1962), p. 27.
11. *Op. cit.,* p. 218.
12. *Op. cit.,* p. 24.
13. Tom Wicker, "The Awesome Twosome," *The New York Times Magazine,* January 30, 1966, p. 64.
14. *Op. cit.,* p. 27.
15. *Democracy, Decentralization, and Development* (London: Asia Publishing House, 1963), p. 40.
16. Ronald Wraith, *Local Government in West Africa* (London: George Allen and Unwin, 1964), p. 27.
17. "French Field Administration: The Beginnings," *Comparative Studies in Society and History,* Vol. V, 1962-1963, p. 81.
18. *The Political System of Empires* (New York: Free Press, 1963), p. 159.
19. *City Politics* (Cambridge, Mass.: Harvard U. Press and M.I.T. Press, 1963), p. 148.
20. *Governing the Metropolis* (New York and London: John Wiley and Sons, 1962), p. 148.
21. Cf. Anwar Syed, *The Political Theory of American Local Government* (New York: Random House, 1966), pp. 77-100.

22. Cf. Herbert Kaufman, *Politics and Policies in State and Local Government* (Englewood Cliffs, New Jersey: Prentice-Hall, 1963), pp. 40-41.

23. *The Development of English Local Government* (London: Oxford U. Press, 1963), p. 116.

24. *Administrative Reform* (Chicago: Aldine, 1969), p. 94.

25. *Ibid.*, pp. 83-88.

26. *Corruption in Developing Countries* (London: Allen & Unwin, 1963), p. 208.

27. Alek A. Rozental, "Long Term Framework for Nairobi's Development," Nairobi Urban Studies Group, February, 1972, p. 8.

28. *Daily Nation,* February 12, 1971.

29. E.A.S., September 23, 1972.

30. E.A.S., December 5, 1972. In June of 1973, the Government decided to substitute a sales tax for G.P.T.; but, such a tax, at least in Nairobi, may prove to be more regressive and difficult to collect than the G.P.T. While the Government promised grants equal to the amount to be lost with the abolition of G.P.T. in 1974, the City Council was fearful of the financial implications of this tax change. It announced in August, 1973, that school fees would be raised and that work in the housing estates would be stopped (with the manual workers involved being dismissed). However, Mr. Mwai Kibaki, the Minister for Finance and Planning, remained unsympathetic with the City Council's situation. "The Council's problem," he said (cf. interview with Michael Kabugua and Adrian Grimwood, *Sunday Nation,* August 12, 1973), "is their development programme which is much bigger than the inflow of funds to finance them and this is exactly the same problem facing the Government on a national level. If they have a financial problem, it's like everybody else's problem and has nothing to do with the abolition of GPT."

31. E.A.S., March 8, 1973.

# SUBJECT INDEX

Administration (*see also* Nairobi City Council): conflict with politicians, 14-15; corruption, 288; Kenyan problems, 238, 288-89; miscellaneous African problems, 14-16, 19, 243-45

Africanization in Kenya (*see also* Nairobi City Council): definition of, 152-53; private sector, 106-10; public sector, 106, 152-55; slowness of, 46

Agriculture (*see also* economic development): colonial discrimination in Kenyan, 44; inefficiency of African, 8

American Agency for International Development (A.I.D.) (*see also* Nairobi City Council, Rubia): case of, 188-92; terms of, 188-90, 192

Asian settlers (*see also* Africanization, Nairobi City Council, racial discrimination): citizenship, 111; departure, 111; discrimination against, 109-12, 153-55; disunity, 43; fearfulness, 111; history of, 68; opposition to European control, 42-43, 68-69

Ayodo, S. O. (*see also* centralization, Nairobi City Council, Rubia): career of, 193-94

Centralization (*see also* decentralization, elasticity of control, Nairobi City Council): difficulties in Kenya, 183-85, 292; problems of, 18-21, 291-93

Colonial policies, Kenya: effect on African rural population, 44; "dual policy," 71; effect on Kenya, 81-82, 97-98; effect on Nairobi City Council, 81-82; neglect of African urban needs, 50, 52, 55-56, 74; "paramountcy of native interests," 71-72; pass system, 59-60; paternalism, 56-57; "racial partnership" ("multiracialism"), 72-73

Decentralization (*see also* centralization, elasticity of control, Nairobi City Council): arguments for, 9; effect of grants-in-aid, 10; failure of, 17-18; fears of, 10; idealization of, 9; meaninglessness of, 20-21; opposition to, 10-11, 17; requirements for, 31; unauthorized, 20

Economic development (*see also* unemployment): barriers to African, 8; dependence on non-Africans, 112-13; effect of non-

African departure, 113-14; effect of poverty, 127-28; future of Kenyan, 296; socialism in Kenya, 107, 121

Education (*see also* Nairobi City Council): achievements in Nairobi, 162-63; conflicts over control of, 176-77, 215; decisions affecting, 176-77; disadvantage of Kenyan Africans, 45, 105-06; disadvantage of Nairobi Africans, 51; racial integration of, 104-05

Elasticity / inelasticity of control (*see also* centralization, decentralization, Nairobi City Council): desirability of, 27-30; effect of corruption, 24-27, 29; implications of, 291-93; meaning of, 22-23, 25-26, 28, 30-31; requirements for, 23-24, 26, 28-30, 245, 292-93; situation in Kenya, 97, 127, 134, 244-45, 283, 296; situation in Kenya, 97, 127, 134, 244-45, 283, 296; situation in Nairobi City Council, 159, 162-63, 166-67, 170-71, 209, 210, 297; situation in Western democracies, 23-24, 30, 294-95; situation in underdeveloped countries, 23-24, 26, 293-94

Elections (*see also* Nairobi City Council): difficulties of African municipal, 11-12

Elite, Kenyan African (*see also* European settlers): development of, 98, 122-23; domination by, 242-43, 283-84; effect of, 123, 296

Ethnicity ("tribalism") (*see also* Nairobi City Council): description of Kenyan, 75-76; discrimination, 123, 155-56, 165-66;

effect of colonialism, 73-75, 123-25; inter-ethnic conflict, 81, 122-23, 125-26, 155-58, 194, 296; Kikuyu domination, 77-78, 125-27; Mboya's mediation, 126

European settlers (*see also* Asian settlers, colonial policies, racial discrimination): anti-Asian campaign, 70-71; domination of Nairobi politics, 41-43, 87-95; exodus of, 111; housing in Nairobi, 52-53; opposition to common roll, 69-70; political strategies of, 40-41; rural elite, 40-41

Hawkers (*see* interest groups, Rubia)

Housing (*see also* Nairobi City Council): administrative incapacity, 238; allocation of public, 224-25, 240-41; Asian, 53-54; discouragement of African owner-occupied, 57-58; effect of shortage of, 6, 230; European, 52-53; high cost of, 222-23, 225-28, 238; local resident associations (LRA's), 229, 239-40; Kitui Village, 232-33; Mathare Valley, 236-41; reasons for shortage of, 5-6, 222-23; shortage in Nairobi of, 220-21, 223-25; shortage in urban Africa of, 5; site-service, 58, 228-230, 233-35; squatters, 230-35, 238-39

Income (*see also* economic development, unemployment): causes of low *per-capita*, 7-8; effect of colonialism on rural African, 44-45; effect of increased, 6, 115; rural-urban gap, 6, 117-18; urban African, 6-7; urban Kenyan, 115

# INDEX OF AUTHORS